A Hunger Most Cruel

Ukrainian Short Fiction in English

A Hunger Most Cruel

Selected Prose Fiction

by

Anatoliy Dimarov

Yevhen Hutsalo

Olena Zvychayna

Translated by Roma Franko
Edited by Sonia Morris

Language Lanterns Publications
2002

Canadian Cataloguing in Publication Data

Main entry under title

Dimarov, Anatoly, 1922-
  A hunger most cruel

      (Ukrainian short fiction in English)
      ISBN 0-9683899-7-X

1.Ukraine--History--1921-1944--Fiction. 2.Famines--Ukraine--
History--20th century--Fiction. I. Hutsalo, Yevhen, 1937-1995.
II. Zvycha_ina, Olena. III. Franko, Roma Z. IV. Morris, Sonia V.
V. Title. VI. Series

PG3940.D55 2002   891.7'93   C2002-910815-2

Design and concept: © Roma Franko and Sonia Morris
Translations: © Roma Franko
Editorial Assistance: Paul Cipywnyk
Cover production and technical assistance: Mike Kaweski

© 2002 Language Lanterns Publications
Web site: www.languagelanterns.com

Printed and bound in Canada by
Hignell Printing Ltd., Winnipeg

Contents

**The words in the Glossary are underlined the
first time they appear in a story.*

Anatoliy Dimarov

Anatoliy Dimarov: Biographical Note

An avid student of human nature, Anatoliy Dimarov has used his talent as a writer to transform his insightful observations about urban and rural life in both the former Ukrainian S.S.R. and present-day Ukraine into absorbing, psychologically astute stories that are universal and timeless in their appeal. A journalist by profession, his keen eye, his knack for spotting a good story, his pithy style, his deep understanding of the psyche of the characters he is portraying, and his warm and witty sense of humour combine to make his works eminently interesting and readable.

Dimarov was born in 1922 in Myrhorod in the Poltava region of Ukraine. When the area was ravaged by the Terror-Famine of 1932-33, his father, Andronyk Harasyuta, was denonunced as a kurkul, and his sons from his first marriage had to flee to avoid persecution. To protect his second family, he persuaded his young wife—the daughter of a priest— to leave him, take a teaching position in a distant village, and raise their two sons under her maiden name, Dimarov.

After graduating from high school in 1940, Dimarov served in the Soviet Army until he was wounded in 1943. For the next few years, he worked as a journalist and took correspondence courses from the Institute of Literature in Moscow. A prolific author, he has written an impressive number of novels, several collections of short stories, narratives based on autobiographical material, and a two-volume autobiography. His works have also appeared regularly in anthologies, journals, and literary newspapers. The story "The Thirties," completed in 1966, appeared in the West in the literary journal *Suchasnist* in 1989.

Dimarov's stories are rooted in the everyday lives of ordinary people, and through the unexpected twists and turns in his plots he unfolds before his readers a vast panorama of life in Ukraine. Focussing on seemingly unremarkable characters, Dimarov explores turning points in their lives, and by doing so, uncovers moments of great joy and intense tragedy that, although peculiar to a particular character, are profoundly revealing of the human condition.

Widely respected as one of the foremost prose writers of his era, Dimarov was awarded the prestigious Taras Shevchenko Prize of the Ukrainian S.S.R. in 1981. Over two decades later, he continues to pursue his writing career in Kyiv.

The Thirties
(A Parable about Bread)

Having made the rounds of almost all the villages in his region and spoken with many people, Hryhoriy Ginzburg returned to Khorolivka. Too exhausted to stop in at the regional office, he hurriedly ate a bit of supper, went to bed, and fell asleep almost instantly.

When he awoke around midnight, he could not get back to sleep. His head ached, and terror gripped his heart. He once again mulled over Stalin's article, "A Year of Great Change," and recalled his conversations with the peasants who were in no great hurry to join the <u>kolhosps</u>. He also recalled the phone calls from the provincial office, the phone calls during which he had been rigorously grilled: "How do matters stand with the <u>serednyaks,</u> Comrade Ginzburg? They aren't joining? They're wavering? That's bad, really bad . . . Read Comrade Stalin's article. Read it and take it to heart—before it's too late."

It was this veiled threat that incensed Hryhoriy the most. You see, those who were higher up had already taken this article to heart—their hearts were always ready to do the bidding of those at the top—and now they were drawing from Comrade Stalin's words the conclusions expected of them. And later, those lower in the ranks would begin to take it all to heart as well, and then it would be impossible to make sense of anything, even if one had a century in which to do so.

So what are you going to do, Comrade Ginzburg? You—the Secretary of the Regional Committee, a communist who up to now considered yourself a faithful follower of Lenin. Are you also going to take Stalin's bidding to heart? Are you going to spit at the older peasants that you met with during these last few days? The ones who came to you with their agonizing worries and concerns?

As soon as he arrived at the office, Ginzburg leafed through the newspapers awaiting him there.

Almost every column in every paper loudly trumpeted the new offensive against the kurkuls—the beginning of an unprecedented mass movement to gather all the peasants into collectives. And every successive issue assumed an increasingly impatient tone with respect to those who were wavering, who still had doubts about the headlong rush to change the psychological nature of the serednyaks.

Hryhoriy reflected on those newspapers all through the day, and finally concluded that he could no longer remain silent. It was now or never.

And so he wrote a letter to Stalin, the man he was accustomed to trusting implicitly, the man he viewed as Lenin's heir.

"I am employed as the Secretary of the Regional Committee in Khorolivka in the province of Poltava, and therefore I am able to speak only about my region," Ginzburg wrote. "After reading your article, I decided to verify, one more time, my impressions of its impact by visiting almost all the villages in my region. I met with political activists and with peasants, and had lengthy conversations with them. And all that I saw and heard, all that I experienced, has prompted me to write you this letter.

"Dear Joseph Vissarionovych!" Ginzburg continued. "I am a communist first and foremost, and that is why I would not be true to myself if I did not voice the reservations that I have regarding the universal collectivization of the country as proclaimed in your article. I do believe that in many regions there has indeed been a transformation in the psychology of the serednyaks, and that, as a result, they have joined the collectives en masse. We ought to rejoice in this fact, welcome this movement, and build on it.

"But what are we to do where this transformation has not yet occurred? In a region, for example, like Khorolivka? If we proclaim an all-out effort to complete the process of collectivization within the next year or two—as is already being done by some hotheads—is such a step not a gross violation of the principle of voluntariness defended to the very end by Lenin, and also defended so vehemently by you in all your works? Are we to resort to leftist tactics and act like Trotsky, who called on his followers not to stand on ceremony, but to forge ahead and build socialism at the expense of the pitiless exploitation of the hardworking peasantry? Instead of a systematic campaign of education and persuasion, are we to take a stand that involves compulsion, brute force, and repression?

"Will this not be a blow to the union of the proletariat with the hard-working peasantry?

"Will this not ruin our rural economy?

"Will this not compromise the building of socialism in the eyes of the many upright people on whom we rely in our daily work, people who unconditionally trust the Soviet government?

"I would be very grateful, my dear Joseph Vissarionovych, if you would reply to my letter. I am convinced that I am not the only one who is troubled by the questions that I have raised.

"Hryhoriy Ginzburg, a member since 1913
of the All-Union Communist Party (Bolsheviks)"

Would Hryhoriy Ginzburg have written this letter if he had known how dearly he would pay for it? If he could have foreseen what would happen two months later?

Hryhoriy waited for a reply for exactly two months.

November rustled by in swirls of yellow withered leaves, and December's icy hooves resounded as they clattered by. And then January ushered in the year nineteen thirty with snow, frost, and blizzards.

The villages hunkered down amidst towering mounds and drifts of snow. And the cottages, buried in the snow, looked lower than they really were. It was as if, squatting, hiding, and benumbed by the cold, they had pulled white caps down over their eyes in the half-hearted hope that the New Year would pass by without noticing them.

Go away, get away from us! Why are you hovering over us? We did not summon you; we have not lived long enough with the Old Year as yet. Keep on moving; maybe you are awaited somewhere—but do not disturb us.

Do not disturb us, or our cattle chewing their cuds, ruminating in warm barns, pens, and stables. Cattle so accustomed to our hands that they will not accept even a fistful of hay or the tiniest bit of grain from a stranger.

And do not disturb our fields, these dear plots of land in which even the smallest lump of soil has been kneaded by our fingers and sprinkled with our sweat—sprinkled so generously that there is no need for rain.

And yet, this is the land you want me to renounce—to rip it out of my heart and give it away to strangers.

Do not interfere with my destiny—let me contend with it myself.

Go away! Get away from here! Vanish into regions unknown. Do you hear? Pass us by!

But January does not listen. It stops in every village, at every cottage. It knocks vigorously on every door, thumps impudently on every gate, and tugs at the hem of every benumbed farmer's cloak or sheepskin coat.

No matter how hard the peasant digs in his heels, no matter how much he resists—clinging to the door, the gate, or the last picket in his fence—nothing helps. It is in this manner, facing backwards, that he is dragged into the year nineteen thirty. And he realizes what has happened only when he finds himself in a kolhosp.

The New Year brought with it raging winds. They were especially fierce out in the steppes where they whipped up the powdery snow and yanked viciously at the telephone wires stretching like naked nerves from Khorolivka to the city of Poltava. And more than once a connection was lost, and words trickled down impotently from wires that coiled around the poles like ripped out veins.

"Khorolivka! Khorolivka! Put Ginzburg on the line! The Secretary of the Regional Office . . . Ginzburg? Comrade Ginzburg, this is the Provincial Committee . . . You must come at once to meet with the Provincial Committee! With the other members of your bureau! Immediately! By order of the First Secretary!"

"What did you write?"

This is the question that greets Hryhoriy when he drops in to see a close acquaintance—you could even say he was a friend—before going to meet with the First Secretary. The friend is sitting at his desk, rummaging among some papers, and when Hryhoriy walks in, he does not get up or extend his hand in greeting. Instead, in an ill-disguised judgemental tone, he asks: "What did you write?"

"Perhaps you might greet me first?" Hryhoriy responds softly. He stops in the doorway, and melted snowflakes tremble like dewdrops on his tousled, windswept hair.

"Forgive me," says the chairman of the Provincial Committee, the one who is a close acquaintance, the one who could almost be called a friend. "But, you see, I don't have time for that right now . . . Do you know why you've been summoned? Your letter was sent here from Moscow. From Stalin's office." The last sentence is uttered in a whisper. "With an order that it be looked into locally . . ."

"My letter?" Hryhoriy is stunned. "But what has it to do with the Provincial Committee? I sent it to Stalin . . . I sent it as a personal letter to Stalin!"

"I don't know anything about that," the chairman shrugs his shoulders. "This matter is not within my area of competency. I just want to warn you that you must prepare yourself for the worst. Your letter has been judged here as the vicious sally of a right-wing opportunist, a degenerate . . ."

"Who judged it?" Hryhoriy interrupts him angrily.

Just then the door opens, and a young woman pokes her head into the room: "Vasyl Trokhymovych, they're waiting for you!"

"I'm coming!" the chairman jumps to his feet, visibly relieved that this unpleasant conversation is being terminated. Hastily gathering together his papers, he glances at Ginzburg who, stunned by what he has just heard, is still standing by the door. "Forgive me . . . I have to run . . . the authorities!"

The First Secretary's reception room is crowded. Some people sit motionless, quietly carrying on subdued conversations; others rifle feverishly through papers and scribble hasty notes; still others pace nervously and, from the expressions on their faces, it is obvious that they do not see anything except the tall massive double door framed in black leather that leads to the office of the First Secretary.

Hryhoriy, tightly squeezing his hands into fists, finds an empty chair and sits down. He has suddenly begun to shiver, as if he had been chilled to the bone by the freezing cold and is only now beginning to warm up a little. Bowing his head to conceal the furious twitching of his right cheek, he grows perfectly still.

Even though Hryhoriy does not feel guilty, he cannot help but be alarmed. The chairman's warning to prepare for the worst, the urgent summons to appear along with the members of his bureau, and the daunting reputation of the First Secretary who, after being in Poltava for just a month, has already established himself as a cruel, ruthless man—all these things do little to give him any peace of mind.

Hryhoriy sits and anxiously recalls the contents of his letter to Comrade Stalin; he simply canot understand what there might be in it that could result in an accusation of right-wing opportunism.

What was in it that could possibly be construed as going against the politics of Lenin?

His entire letter was based on the words of Lenin. On a quotation taken from Lenin that everyone knew, and that he could recite from memory at this very moment.

Ginzburg sees clearly in his mind's eye the page with that particular passage marked with a red pencil—he had marked it himself—and the individual words that he had underlined in it:

"Transforming the petty landowner, reshaping his nature and attitudes, is a matter that *requires several generations*. And this transformation—restoring, so to say, the health of the petty landowner's psychological nature—can take place only if there is a solid material base: technology, tractors and machines to work the land *on a massive scale,* and electrification *on a massive scale.*"

That was what Lenin had said—several generations. Not one or two years, but entire generations. And, even then, only on the basis of mechanizing and electrifying the villages on a massive scale.

And one additional point made by Lenin. Something that related directly to what was currently happening: "In no circumstances is progress to outstrip the masses; it is necessary to wait until the desire to move forward grows out of the personal experiences of these masses, out of their own struggle." Moreover, this quotation was cited by Stalin as well, warning against forcing the peasants into kolhosps by administrative means, decrees, or coercion . . .

"Don't seek refuge behind Lenin! We know how to cite quotations without your help!"

"You'd do better to tell us instead: what is the percentage of collectivization in your district?"

"Why have you taken the kurkuls and the remnants of the White Guard under your wing?"

"How much did the kurkuls pay you to write this letter?"

And Hryhoriy Ginzburg who has done his utmost to retain his composure, finally breaks down and shouts: "I refuse to answer provocative questions!"

"Aha!"

Hryhoriy feels almost physically assaulted by the animosity of the people who have gathered in the First Secretary's boardroom to judge his case, an animosity that with every passing moment is growing in intensity. He can sense that the atmosphere, filled with their venomous exhalations, is becoming ever more strained. And the longer he stands at the end of the overly long table, the more difficult he finds it to speak, to collect his thoughts.

All the more so because he is continually being interrupted and bombarded with questions and accusations.

He craves a drink of water. But the glasses and the decanter of water are at the other end of the table, and no one thinks to offer him a drink.

"I've said everything that I have to say," Hryhoriy finally states. And that is when the First Secretary of the Provincial Committee finally speaks.

Up to now he has not opened his mouth, and it is difficult to surmise whether or not he condemns Ginzburg. His round, carefully shaved face is immobile, stony, and his grey eyes are indifferent, as if he sees neither Ginzburg nor his own comrades-in-arms and, if he does see them, he is not the least bit interested in them. It is only when Hryhoriy says that he has finished speaking, that he raises his head, shaved to a steely blue, and addresses him, just as he was about to sit down.

"Wait, Ginzburg. I have a question for you." He speaks softly, and his words scarcely rustle in the large boardroom. He seems confident that, no matter how softly he speaks, he will be heard.

Everyone falls silent, and Hryhoriy, turning to face the First Secretary, freezes.

The First Secretary continues sotto voce: "How is it that in neighbouring districts the serednyaks have joined the kolhosps en masse?"

"I don't know . . ."

"Because in those districts the kurkul network of spies and agitators was destroyed," the First Secretary explains patiently. "The authorities were able to convince the serednyaks of the superiority of the kolhosp order."

"And we were't able to," Hryhoriy says with bitter sarcasm.

"Weren't able to, or didn't want to?"

"Weren't able to."

"But perhaps you didn't want to?"

And when he does not receive the desired response, the First Secretary asks one more question: "Do the members of the District Committee share your views?"

"I am not in a position to answer for others," Hryhoriy responds dully.

"Who is present here from Khorolivka?"

Lyander and Putko jump to their feet. And still another man belatedly scrapes his chair as he also gets up, but Ginzburg does not even turn his head to see who it is.

"Are you in solidarity with your Regional Secretary?"

"I was always against him!"

It is Putko speaking.

"I've had more than one disagreement with Ginzburg about critically important political issues."

It is Lyander speaking.

"I categorically condemn Ginzburg's political line."

It is the head of the Regional Educational Committee speaking.

"Be seated, comrades . . . Who else wants to have a word in this matter?"

Immediately, several hands shoot up. Ginzburg sits down. Numb, he bows his head. Even after everyone who wished to speak has spoken, and the First Secretary has the floor again—even then Ginzburg does not raise his head.

The First Secretary opens his remarks with an overview of the state of affairs in the Khorolivka region.

The district is rife with White Guard elements and with kurkuls and their henchmen, and it is these people who have corrupted the entire party structure in that district. Yes, the entire structure! And these are the consequences: a malicious dismissal of the most pressing problems, a subversion of the Party's policies, a total disruption of the plan for universal collectivization, and a breach of trust with respect to the plans of the Central Committee to expand the kolhosp movement.

"Not a pretty picture, comrades."

"A disgraceful one!" a member of the bureau calls out.

The First Secretary furrows his brow in annoyance—he cannot tolerate interruptions when he is speaking.

"Now we move on to the case of Ginzburg . . ."

Hryhoriy does not move a muscle.

The First Secretary is now talking about muck: "You've immersed yourself, right up to your head, in right-wing opportunistic muck . . ."

About Ginzburg's hostile activities: "There is no other way of evaluating your letter except as a blatant attempt to besmirch the Central Committee of the All-Union Communist Party (Bolsheviks) that is adhering to Lenin's principles, and to compromise Lenin's policies about the universal collectivization of the working peasantry . . ."

About a hostile inner circle: "It has to be said that members of the Regional Committee of Khorolivka have been politically blind, for they did not make a timely examination of your inner circle of White Guards and kurkuls . . ."

About Ginzburg's conduct here, today, at the meeting of the Provincial Committee: "You did not understand anything; you did not learn anything; even now you are continuing to affirm your right-wing opportunistic inventions that the serednyak has not matured enough to join the kolhosp, and that, in the province of Poltava there can be no mass movement of the peasants towards universal collectivization in the near future. And, therefore, you are speaking as a political bourgeois who has lost faith in the policies of our party . . ."

"He's an enemy, not a bourgeois!" a member of the bureau calls out.

"It's one and the same thing . . . And please, do not interrupt me. So, we must arrive at the only possible conclusion: that you, Ginzburg, are morally corrupt and politically bankrupt; you are no longer a communist; you have turned into an active assistant of the White Guards and kurkul elements and become their spy and provocateur in the ranks of the All-Union Communist Party (Bolsheviks)."

After finishing his statement, the First Secretary is silent for a few moments. Then he turns to the members of the bureau: "What do you propose, comrades?"

"Remove him from his post!"

"Expel him from the Party."

"Put him on trial!"

"Reconstitute the entire bureau in the Khorolivka region!"

The last proposal evokes much scraping of chairs where the members of the bureau are seated.

"Dissolve the party organization of the Khorolivka region on the basis that it is corrupt and has disintegrated!"

The First Secretary approves all the proposals. Except for the last one. "I think, comrades, that there is no need to dissolve the entire party organization. The party structure, on the whole, is healthy, and the communists of Khorolivka will honourably manage their historically important assignment with respect to universal collectivization . . . What say you, members from Khorolivka?"

"We will! We will!"

"That's good . . . I will now put to a vote the means that have been proposed to rejuvenate the party organization in the Khorolivka district."

The members of the bureau, unanimously, and with an almost jealous eagerness, show their approval by raising their hands; however, depending on their rank, they raise them quite differently. The members sitting closest to the First Secretary raise their hands in a perfunctory manner, with their elbows remaining on the table. During the course of the day, they wave those right hands of theirs like flails so often that they probably do not have the strength left to raise them. But those seated farther back fling their arms out towards the First Secretary like school-children, ostentatiously lifting them as high as they can until their very joints crack, as if to say: "Look at me! At me! Just look and see how devotedly I'm voting."

But perhaps all this has not really happened? Perhaps Hryhoriy has just imagined all of it? And, after all, what does he have to do with any of it?

"Ginzburg! Lay down your party membership card!"

There it is—the most terrible thing that could happen! It is all over for him now!

Hryhoriy rises to his feet; not a muscle moves on his stony face.

He walks up to the table covered in red felt—a table as large as a gallows. He is walking towards his death, even though neither the First Secretary nor those sitting near him suspect anything as yet. Only Hryhoriy knows what he is about to do.

He stops a couple of steps away from the table and raises his hand to a side pocket of his tunic. Not the pocket in which he keeps his party card, but the one in which he has his pistol, the Browning that he brought home from the Civil War.

The button, sewn on the pocket by his father, rebuffs his attempt to undo it. Twisting its metal head in despair, it stands firm and refuses to go through the buttonhole. Finally Hryhoriy rips the flap off the pocket, and the button, torn off with it, lands on the table.

Seizing the pistol, he shouts at the First Secretary: "I won't give up my party card as long as I'm alive. Take it from my corpse!"

He raises the gun to his temple . . .

The meeting of the bureau of the Provincial Committee comes to an abrupt end. Shocked and pale, everyone vacates the large boardroom.

Hryhoriy is carried out; his pistol and party card lie on the table. The smell of gunpowder lingers in the air, and the rug on which Hryhoriy toppled headfirst is marked by a large, dark stain. The rug, of course, will be changed, the room will be aired, and the pistol and party card will be removed—and there will be nothing left to remind anyone about the Regional Secretary who lost his class-consciousness, sank into the muck of right-wing opportunism, and became a degenerate, a kurkul sympathizer.

That is why we will not place him in a coffin draped in red bunting, nor will we send him to Khorolivka so that the villagers can pay him their last respects with music, a funeral assembly, and a party salute. He does not deserve it!

We will give orders to have him taken to a morgue where indifferent doctors, after performing an autopsy on his skull, will write an official report that the bullet entered the right temple, damaged such and such a membrane, and caused his death—as if all this is of some importance, as if someone is actually going to study the record book at some future date.

And so we will ship Ginzburg to the morgue, and there, after the autopsy, they will place whatever is left of him in a makeshift coffin, haul him off to the cemetery, and hurriedly dump him into the ground—why fuss over someone like that! They will not place either a marker on his flat shallow grave, or the five-cornered red star that shone for Hryhoriy while he was alive. They will not place anything on it.

And it will be in vain that old Isaak, insane with grief, will search for the grave of his only son; it will be in vain that he will press money into the hands of the caretakers in the hope that they will tell him where his dear Hryhoriy lies buried . . . It all will be in vain . . .

Because the caretakers do not know where Hryhoriy is buried.

But finally, one of the caretakers, overcome with pity for the old man, will lead him to a fresh grave and tell him that his son lies buried there. He will not take any money, even though Isaak tries to slip him a few crumpled bills.

"What are you doing, old man! Do you think we have no conscience left at all?"

And, angrily shrugging his shoulders, he will walk away.

And then, when he glances back, he will see Isaak's stooped figure leaning over the fresh mound drifted over by snow. The old man will stand there without stirring, as if he no longer were a living person, but a mournful monument, alienated from everything that is alive. And it will cross the caretaker's mind that perhaps the old man no longer has any need of the money . . .

No one ever saw Isaak in Khorolivka again. No one knows if he returned from Poltava, or if he stayed there. Perhaps he dropped in at home for a moment, gathered up a few of his wretched belongings, and went back to see his son's grave again. But perhaps he never did leave the stranger's grave; perhaps he froze in grief over it and became petrified as thick layers of snow settled on his stooped back and bowed head. And the occasional visitor who happens to come to this godforsaken spot will halt in amazement, impressed by the incredible monument of grief and despair, the creation of a gifted sculptor . . .

Perhaps that is what happened.

But we will not go into that cemetery, for fear that we too will be accused of sympathizing with right-wing deviationists, or be called degenerates, abettors of class enemies, or even covert White

Guards—although we may not have even been born when the White Guards were operating. So we will not search out the unknown grave of Hryhoriy Ginzburg—we cannot be of any assistance to him in any event; instead, we will head back to Khorolivka where a comrade, who was sent to strengthen the party organization in the Khorolivka region, is now the Regional First Secretary.

This new secretary, Ivan Ivanovych Suslov, treats the peasantry as a reactionary petty bourgeois element that, if given half the chance, would devour and absorb all the gains made by the proletarian revolution, sucking them in like quicksand. And that is why, even if he does not come out openly against the policies of the New Economic Policy—as a Bolshevik, he feels that it is his duty, first and foremost, to adhere strictly to the party line— nevertheless, in his heart he does not accept this new policy, viewing it as a tragic error that will impede the progress of the country for at least ten years

Finally, the Central Committee of the Communist Party comes to its senses and corrects its error.

After reading Stalin's article "A Year of Great Change," Ivan Ivanovych is not able to contain his delight. He slams his fist on the table and strides excitedly about the room, whistling his favourite song about a locomotive, a commune, and a rifle.

Ivan Ivanovych arrived in Khorolivka with views on the peasantry that he had held for a long time; they were well-developed, like a creed carved in stone.

Credo Number One.

Every peasant is a potential bourgeois. There is no essential difference between the richest and the poorest peasants; there are only those who have already become kurkuls, and those who are still aspiring to that status.

When it comes to profiteers and kurkul henchmen, the matter is clear: they are to be rooted out completely, to their very last paltry fingernail. And as for the rest of the villagers, the foundation has to be knocked out from under their feet—the foundation that gave birth to, gives birth to, and will continue giving birth to petty bourgeois tendencies. And the sooner the petty bourgeois base is destroyed, the more quickly the peasant will be forged into a builder of socialism, a faithful partner of the proletariat.

Credo Number Two.

The peasant does not know what he wants. Given his age-old backwardness, he has always opposed, opposes now, and will continue to oppose anything new, anything progressive, even if it holds out to him the promise of a prosperous life in the foreseeable future. And so, we cannot wait for decades until the village begins to move forward and voluntarily turns its face towards socialism. With a firm, proletarian hand, we have to seize it and turn it—be it willing or unwilling—one hundred and eighty degrees towards socialism.

Credo Number Three.

The social restructuring of a village, like a revolution, cannot be undertaken with white kid gloves. Only ineffectual, yellow-bellied intellectuals keep prattling about it not being necessary to apply any pressure on the serednyak during the period of universal collectivization.

The Party has placed before its members a task of universal-historical importance: to complete the process of collectivization by the spring of nineteen thirty-two.

We must respond to this challenge as true Bolsheviks: we will greet the upcoming spring of nineteen thirty-two with universally established kolhosps. In this way we will deal a decisive blow not only to the kurkul elements that are sabotaging the delivery of grain, but also to the right-wing opportunists—the friends of kurkuls, who, during the elections to the village Soviets, attempted to nullify the agreement about universal collectivization by adding to it the words: "insofar as it is possible," and "on a voluntary basis." And there were even those who shouted forthrightly: "We don't want any of it! Cross it out!"

"Comrades! We have listened to First Secretary Comrade Suslov. Who wishes to speak now?"

Putko casts a severe look around the hall in which the district communists have gathered.

"Speak up, comrades!"

"May I speak?"

A hand goes up at the back of the hall, and a commotion erupts. Chairs thump, and the communists rise to make way for a tall man with a heavy-set handsome face and a black moustache. Looking curiously at the man making his way ponderously towards the stage, the secretary asks: "Who is that?"

"It's Hanzha from Tarasivka. He and Ginzburg were two of a kind."

Ivan Ivanovych's eyes instantly narrow.

Hanzha walks onto the stage and takes his place at the podium. It is only now, when the light falls directly on him, that everyone can see how emaciated he has become. He casts an intense look around the hall and steps forward.

"Fellow Communists! We have lost a Comrade—a Bolshevik . . . a revolutionary . . . a follower of Lenin . . ."

"Who is he talking about?" Suslov asks Putko.

But before Putko can reply, Hanzha edges forward even farther and, in a voice ringing with tension, says: "Please rise and, with a minute of silence, honour the memory of our dear Comrade Ginzburg."

There is a deathly silence in the hall.

"Step down! Right now!" Putko shouts at Hanzha.

"No, that's fine, let him continue," Ivan Ivanovych contradicts him. "We should know what our enemies are thinking."

Putko turns to Hanzha again and sternly orders him: "Speak to the matter at hand! Without any provocations!"

"Well, I can do that as well," Hanzha agrees. Turning heavily to face the presidium, he speaks directly to Suslov: "It's all rather strange, Comrade First Secretary . . ."

"His name is Ivan Ivanovych Suslov!" Putko prompts him loudly. "You should remember it by now."

"Thank you for reminding me. I forgot; I'm growing old . . . It's all rather strange, Comrade Suslov. You haven't been here very long, you haven't met with anyone, and you haven't spoken with the people; the first thing that you do is call a meeting of the communists—and pronounce a prescription for all our ills . . ."

"Listen, Hanzha—speak, but speak to the point."

It is Putko who says this. Oh, that Mytrofan Onysymovych Putko is no simpleton.

"That's fine, let him talk."

Not a muscle twitches on Ivan Ivanovych's face. But his eyes grow brighter and mercilessly clearer.

"You're calling on us to squeeze the well-to-do peasant pitilessly, to force him into the kolhosp. But have you ever considered what the net result of this will be? The peasants are not cattle that can be lassoed and placed in a yoke . . ."

"So, the kolhosp is a yoke?" Lyander cannot restrain himself. "We'll remember your words, Comrade Hanzha! Oh, yes, we'll reme-e-e-mber!"

"Don't try to intimidate me, for I'm already intimidated. Maybe I didn't express myself all that well, but I am firmly convinced that it's too early to speak about universal collectivization. It's just too early!"

"If that's the case, Comrade Hanzha, then how are we to assess the January resolution of the Central Committee of the Communist Party?"

It is Ivan Ivanovych who is speaking. He puts the question calmly, almost amiably.

"What resolution?" Hanzha does not understand.

"About the tempo of the collectivization. Where it is written, black on white, that Ukraine has to complete its collectivization by the spring of nineteen thirty-two. What is your view of this resolution?"

Hanzha turns pale, but his voice is firm: "I view it as an erroneous directive from above."

This time it takes Mytrofan Onysymovych quite a while to bring the meeting to order.

"What's he doing? What's he doing?" Hanzha's wife Olha groans, nervously twisting a red kerchief in her hands.

And Volodya looks around with a confused expression on his face as if to ask: "What did Uncle Vasyl say? Did I not hear correctly, or did I imagine it? He must be out of his mind to be saying things like that!"

"Well, it's all clear now," Ivan Ivanovych says, rising to his feet. "You may sit down. We'll consider your case later."

They consider Hanzha's case the very same day, at the meeting of the Regional Committee.

Before the meeting, Olha does not let her husband out of her sight; she follows him around, pleading with him.

"Just say that you were wrong! That's all!"

Her words are a groan filled with pain and despair. The despair of a woman who still loves her husband and who wants to save him, to keep him at her side.

And the pain of a Communist who is losing a Comrade.

"We've quarrelled. In the last while we've quarrelled a lot, but I'm promising now that I won't be so uncompromising, I'll be more understanding, and I won't annoy you. Just come to your senses, think it over, and admit your mistake! Tell them that you did not understand that resolution properly. Don't be so stubborn! Do you hear me? Tell them!

"I've never cried. I've never, ever cried. Even when I buried my first two husbands, the Comrades never saw my tears. They were proud of me, proud of my stoicism, and they called me an iron woman. But look at my eyes now—they're filled with tears. I'm ashamed of them, but I can't help it . . .

"Tell them! Do you hear me? Tell them!"

Hanzha carefully frees his hand from Olha's grasp and looks at his wife, his eyes scalded with pain.

"Do you know what is most sacred to me?"

"What?"

"The truth . . . I would be the first to damn myself if I departed from the truth."

He does not depart from the truth.

He stands before the members of the bureau, and he has no intention of recanting.

He has dug the hole into which he now must fall.

"Do you still think that the policy set out by the Central Committee on universal collectivization is erroneous?"

"Yes, I do."

"What is your opinion regarding the well-known position of Comrade Stalin about the development of the kolhosp movement, as laid down by him in the world-renowned articles "A Year of Great Change" and "Concerning Questions of Agrarian Policy in the USSR"?

"My opinion is that they contravene the policies of Lenin."

This unheard-of audacity sends shivers up the spines of some members of the bureau.

They vote as a body, in anger, to expel Hanzha from the Party. They also vote as a body to have him sent to trial as a right-wing opportunist, a degenerate kurkul, an agent of the White Guards, and a vicious slanderer of the Policies of the Central Committee and of the General Secretary, Comrade Stalin.

And there was a trial, and the incensed prosecutor thundered his class-motivated speech, and the judges looked severely and mercilessly at Hanzha who, during one of the most difficult moments of the class struggle, had revealed himself as a deserter, a political turncoat, a traitor to the proletariat of the world. All this was clear to these righteous judges. Not a single doubt entered their class-pure hearts; they had convicted him even before the trial was held.

So all rise—the court has reconvened from its five-minute consultation and is prepared to read its righteous verdict into the record.

Rise, Comrade Olha. There is no need for you to avoid the eyes of the judges! You found the strength within you to conquer your love for this incorrigible man and to reveal the truth about him. Even though every word of yours was a nail in the coffin that is the verdict.

You are a courageous woman, a true fighter, Comrade Olha!

And you, Volodymyr Tverdokhlib, young Communist and passionate soldier of the revolution, also rise to your feet. It was not easy for you to testify against your Uncle Vasyl, against your godfather who—do you remember, dear Volodya?—put his wise hand on your impatient shoulder and said with great sufferance: "Oh, Volodya, Volodya, it is not that simple, Volodya!" And even though your soft bass register quavered, and your voice was breaking, you also condemned the former communist Hanzha as a class enemy.

The court is reconvening. All rise!

But why are you not hurrying to stand up, you—the man who has turned grey overnight? Why is your head lowered, and why are your powerful shoulders sagging? What burden has fallen on you, crushed you so mercilessly that it seems you will never again straighten up?

Hanzha grits his teeth, clenches his hands with their missing fingers—and rises to his feet.

Three years of imprisonment, followed by a three-year suspension of his legal rights. The sentence would have been even harsher, but his humble origins work in his favour.

Not a muscle stirs on Hanzha's face. Walking out under escort, he does not even glance at Volodya, or at Olha. He has ripped both of them out of his heart.

Because it is not enemies who are terrifying—it is traitorous friends.

It is not the sword aimed at one's breast that is terrifying—it is the knife that is treacherously plunged in one's back.

No matter what noble intentions honed that knife . . .

And so there was the trial, and there was a prison cell, and the first night in that cell—the most difficult night for a prisoner. And there were thoughts that do not beset a person anywhere the way they beset him behind prison bars. When he is left all alone, not for just an hour or two, but for many long years.

We will not bother him on this first night—things are difficult enough for him as it is. Let us move away from the prison bars, because the guard has turned his head in our direction. He is listening and watching—God forbid that he should see us! He will take aim according to the statutes, fire—and your soul will fly right out of you!

Let us flee as fast as we can to our homes, and let us thank God that, as yet, the windows are not barred, and there are no prison locks on the door. My house stands apart, all by itself, and I know nothing at all about what has happened.

I do not know anything. I did not see anything. I did not hear anything.

And as for that man who has just been sent to prison—I do not know him; I just found out about him from you, and until this moment, I had never even met him.

I did not walk through the village with him; I did not hold long soul-searching conversations with him; I did not seek his advice— how to live, whom to believe, on whom to rely. And even if I did meet up with him by chance, I sensed from the very first glance that there was something not quite right about him. He did not, you know, smell quite right . . . There was something about him that instantly put me on guard.

An enemy, you say? With the kurkuls, you say? Up to his ears in muck? My, my, my! Who would have thought it?

Although, if one stops to think about it, things did seem to be heading in that direction. There was that Ginzburg . . . And then— Marta . . . And Prykhodko, as well . . . No, not Ivan, Mykola.

So you say they gave him three years? Well, he must have earned it, because they don't sentence a person without reason. That's how it is: you meet a person, talk with him, even invite him into your home, and then—there you have it! Oh, there are people like that in this world! They won't warn you: it's like this, you see, don't come near me, because I'm sinking into the mire. And if you aren't careful, I'll pull you down with me . . .

It's Hanzha I have in mind, of course . . .

And, after all this, just try to be friends with people! Just try to figure out who they really are!

Both Olha and Volodymyr Tverdokhlib paid the price for not "figuring out" who Hanzha really was. Immediately after the trial they went to the meeting of the Regional Committee. The status of collectivization in the region, especially in Tarasivka, was being examined. It was being examined rigorously, with a highly principled frankness. And there was no denying that a disgraceful picture was emerging. The percentage of land that had been collectivized was unacceptably low, the Village Soviets were infested with class enemies, and the kurkuls in the villages were violently resisting the policies of the Party.

Someone tries to suggest that there really are no kurkuls left, that all of them were shipped out beyond the boundaries of the province a year ago.

But Ivan Ivanovych, who is chairing the meeting, decisively condemns this attempt to cover up the class struggle in the village: "There still are kurkuls among us! Yes, there are!"

And he slams his fist on a sheet of paper lying on the table.

"Comrade Tverdokhlib, how many profiteers were unmasked as kurkuls in your village?"

"Two!" Volodya leaps to his feet like a schoolboy.

"And how many households are there in Tarasivka?"

"More than three hundred."

"There you have it, comrades. More than three hundred households, and only two kurkuls were found. And do you expect me to believe this fairy tale? Where was the vigilance of the Tarasivka communists?"

No one speaks. They all bow their heads under the merciless stare of the First Secretary.

It is only Comrade Putko who does not bow his head. Not wishing to be confused with the "masses," he has taken a seat at the end of the table next to Comrade Suslov. And when Ivan Ivanovych angrily asks: "Where?" and slams his hand down on the paper, Mytrofan Onysymovych also thumps his hand down on the table and casts an accusing look at the gathering, as if he too is asking: "Where? Where was your class vigilance that so many kurkuls were overlooked? And if there were no kurkuls, why didn't you come and borrow a few from me? You were cozying up to Ginzburg, were you? So, take your lumps now, and don't try to implicate me, Mytrofan Onysymovych, in your actions."

"Comrade Suslov," he says aloud, "I think we must punish the communists of Tarasivka, make an example of them. So that others are not tempted to emulate them."

The secretary raises his hand and does not even blink when Olha shouts angrily: "And where were you?"

"Huh!" he thinks. "She's asking where we were! It's no use asking us now where we were then. Now, as you can see, we're the ones at the presidium table! And if that's the case, then you don't ask us—it's we who ask you! And if that's the case, then accept a severe reprimand for relaxing your class vigilance and bear it in good health! Phew! What a brazen woman, asking us where we were!"

Tverdokhlib received just a warning.

They took into consideration his youthfulness, the brief time that he had been a Party member, and the fact that he had realized the importance of the matter at hand and had testified at the trial in an exemplary manner.

The prosecutor even praised him at a meeting of the bureau— if only there were more communists like this one!

And so it turned out that the bureau did not so much punish Volodya at that meeting as encourage him.

After the meeting, Ivan Ivanovych came up to him and Comrade Olha, shook hands with both of them, and said: "Take care, Comrades! Don't betray us."

And then, speaking directly to Volodya, he added: "We'll recommend, Comrade Tverdokhlib, that you be made head of the kolhosp. Will you be able to handle it?"

Volodya gasped in delight. "Yes, I will, Comrade. I'll handle it! Even if I'm threatened by torture or death, I'll never abandon the party line."

And it does not matter that the kolhosp Volodya is to head has not even been born yet, and that, in their dreams, almost all the householders in Tarasivka see their own fields, their own cattle, their own farms—all their own, not held in common. It does not matter. Volodya does not doubt for even a minute that he will force them to dream other dreams, that he will drum those pernicious dream-visions out of their heads.

There will be a kolhosp, Comrade Suslov! And there will be a plan—a plan that will be fulfilled one hundred per cent!

Volodya walks out of the district office in a state of exhilaration. His ears blaze like lanterns, his cheeks are flaming, and his lips settle into a smile. And everything would have been fine if he had not suddenly recalled Uncle Vasyl, and if it had not been for Comrade Olha: weary and gloomy, her face an ashen grey.

He gets into the sleigh and, inviting Comrade Olha to sit down beside him, tries to cheer her up: "Maybe they'll let him go."

Olha turns away and does not say a word.

They drive out into the fields on the well-packed winter road. All around there is snow, snow, and more snow. The boundaries are covered over, the fields blend together, and it is impossible to say where one field ends, and another begins. The winter has unified and collectivized the land without asking for the peasants' assent and, passing over it with a white plough, has sown it with snow.

But it is not snow that Volodya sees—it is dense fields of wheat; he does not see flocks of rooks—he sees happy people flocking to work in the kolhosp fields; and in his heart, a heart that belongs to the Party, he hears the sweetest music—the rumbling of tractors, the hissing of steam engines, the chugging of threshing machines, and the surging of the choicest grain as it pours in an unending stream into kolhosp bins.

And then—a caravan of carts, festooned with red flags, hauling the grain to the state's storage bins. The first carts in the entire region, and he, Tverdokhlib, is at the head of them . . .

Oh yes, that's where his path lies!

But in Tarasivka alarm bells are ringing; save yourself, whoever can—a great misfortune is approaching!

Who started the rumour? Who was the first to set the alarm bells ringing? It is impossible to get to the bottom of the matter, not even if you scour the entire village, leaving no stone unturned.

But, by the village office, the hunched figure of an old woman shows up darkly, like a calumny tolled by that terror-driven bell, like a hardened scrap of foam left behind by the wave of human slander. Up to now she huddled on her <u>oven bed</u>, forgotten by people and by God, but today something has moved her to come and sit by the regional office where she weeps bitterly and inconsolably, her face streaming with tremulous, senile tears.

"Why are you crying, granny?"

"How am I not to cry, my son, when people are saying that everyone will be slaughtered! If only they were just going to slaughter the officials, the ones at the top, but they're going to do away with all of us, one by one."

"Go home, granny, and stop crying. Don't be afraid; no one is going to lay a hand on an old woman like you . . ."

"Do you suppose they'll stop to figure out who's old and who's young? They're going to slaughter all of us, one by one . . ."

"But granny, who is going to do the slaughtering?"

"How am I supposed to know that, my son? If only they don't slaughter the children!"

"Do you see that?" Volodya turns to Comrade Olha. "We haven't even had time to get back home, and the kurkul is already hard at it! It's obvious that far too few kurkuls have been identified and dispossessed!"

Granddad Khlypavka—dressed in a sheepskin coat, felt boots, and a cap inherited from Granny Natalka's late husband—comes out of the village office. As he unhitches the filly, he informs them: "There's a lot of talk going on here, and lots of rumours are being spread."

"What kind of talk?" Volodya draws his eyebrows together in a stern thin line.

"All kinds of talk," the old man backs away from giving a direct response. But, at the same time, he cannot refrain from asking: "Volodya, is it true that they're going to turn our village into a commune? That everyone will be thrown together under one roof—both men and women—and that afterwards the children will be parcelled out like chicks among the households?"

"Who told you that?"

"Well . . . people are talking," the old man runs his fingers through his beard. "It seems that there was a man who drove through our village and said: 'Prepare yourselves for the Final Judgement. Eat as much as you can from your own bowls while you still can, because soon you'll all be slurping slops from a common cauldron.'"

"You'd do better to unhitch the filly more quickly, Granddad, instead of spreading these dangerous kurkul rumours!" Volodya abruptly ends the conversation. "And tell the executive to call the Party activists together."

"But where's Vasyl?" the old man wants to know. "Did he go home? Or did they detain him in the regional capital?"

"They detained him," Volodya replies, thoroughly out of sorts now. "But not in the capital—in prison!"

"What do you mean—in prison?" the old man's jaw drops in astonishment.

"Just what I said: they sentenced him to three years in prison for counterrevolutionary activities. Is that clear? And I don't have time to talk nonsense with you. Unhitch the horse and go get the executive members!"

Volodya goes off to the village office, but the old man stands dumbstruck in the middle of the yard, thinking: "Oh, Vasyl, Vasyl! Why didn't you protect yourself?"

"Granddad, how long are you going to stand there like a post?"

It is Volodya speaking.

Ugh! A fine fellow he's turned out to be!

Unhitching the horse with trembling fingers, the old man leads it into the stable.

And after he has taken it to its stall, he asks it bitterly, reproachfully: "So, you've lost your master, have you?"

The horse, sighing remorsefully, breathes heavily in his face.

And the old man, no longer able to restrain himself, breaks down and weeps. He wipes his eyes with his grimy sleeve, but the tears keep flowing—inconsolable, salty, bitter tears.

"So that's how things have turned out, my dear Vasyl . . . Who would have thought . . . And, to make matters even worse, that young whippersnapper is yelling at me . . ."

Throwing the horse some hay, he walks out of the barn. But instead of going to find the executive members, he goes home. He takes off his coat, paces the room like a lost soul, and then goes to the cupboard and pulls out a bottle of homebrew.

"This is for you, my dear Vasyl!"

The homebrew burns his palate and rushes into his stomach in a fiery stream. And the old man fills his tumbler again.

"May God keep you in His care!"

And Granddad Khlypavka drinks more than he has drunk in a long time. The liquor makes his head spin, propels his sluggish blood through his old, swollen veins, and fills his withered body with militant vigour. Seizing his heavy pear wood staff, he sets out to free Vasyl.

"I'll get you . . . you bastards! May your souls burn in hell!"

He rushes to the village office and heads for the post with the iron rail and heavy hammer that serve as a fire alarm. Seizing the hammer, he begins pounding the rail with all his might.

"Hey, my good people! Save Hanzha!"

In response to the intolerable clanging, the communist committee members dash outside, and Volodya tears the hammer out of the old man's hands.

"Lock him up in the cooler. Let him sleep it off until morning."

The old man instantly falls silent and meekly submits to being led off to jail. He lies down on the straw, turns his cheek this way and that way to settle in more snugly, and falls asleep.

Shaken and unhappy, the members of the local cell of the Communist Party—made up of Komsomol youth, teachers, and a committee of poor peasants—go back into the village office. The men, avoiding each other's eyes, grimly puff their home-grown tobacco and hide behind the smoke. The women teachers whisper softly among themselves, and Comrade Olha looks as if she has been taken down from a cross. You see, it isn't all that easy to forget a person . . . A person who has been the head of the village council. A communist. A person who, mind you, established Soviet rule before our very eyes. Who fought for the Soviet order without giving a thought to sparing either his strength or his life.

"So what are we to make of it? He was trusted by the authorities in the district and respected by the people, and now all of a sudden he's an enemy? How can things turn out that way?"

It is Petro Neshcheret speaking. Perplexed, he raises his thin brows and looks around in all directions with eyes that are clear, like those of a child.

The old men puff even more vigorously on their cigarettes, shrouding themselves in a still denser cloud of smoke. Even Volodya feels momentarily embarrassed, but he instantly controls himself and says as sternly as he can: "It's not up to us to judge these matters, Petro. They see things more clearly—who is a friend, and who is an enemy. And if they've sentenced him, then it means that there was a reason for it, and there's no point in all this demagoguery."

Well, what an interesting word he has come up with! The devil knows who could repeat it! The peasants lower their heads in alarm.

"That's true," Neshcheret agrees. "The authorities, of course, see things more clearly . . ."

"And you didn't know that until now, you poor fellow?" Ivan Prykhodko asks mockingly. "The eyes of the authorities are not at all like yours and mine; they can see through everything. For instance, you've tramped around this earth for forty years, and you still don't know who you are. But the authorities need to take only one look at you, and they can instantly tell you where you belong—in a prison, or in a collective . . ."

"Well, that's enough," Tverdokhlib interrupts irritably. "Just look at the corner you've talked yourself into—putting the collective on the same level as a prison! So shut your stupid face, Ivan, and be thankful that I don't have time to deal with you right now. (After his visit to the regional centre, Volodya feels a heady sense of power—he can get rid of any villagers that he wants to.) I don't want to have to deal with you, Ivan. Right now I have to deal with the collective that we are about to establish. So, this is how the matter stands . . . It has been proposed that our TOZ form a collective. And the Komsomols who are not yet members of TOZ should make a declaration today about their intention to join the kolhosp. Along with their parents. And the poor peasants as well . . ."

"Can we take some time to think about it?"

Volodya glances sharply at the man who asked the question: "You can think about it later! But right now—you either declare your intention to join, or you part company with TOZ. And with the village as well."

"Why with the village?" the shout comes from near the door.

"We're getting rid of all the kurkuls! We've handled them with kid gloves long enough."

The meeting breaks up long after midnight. The village slumbers under a white winter quilt, and the blue shadows of dreams creep from house to house. The mild frost crunches and squeaks underfoot. This year, praise God, the winter is not too fierce; it is, you could say, a winter made for farmers. It put down a covering of snow to prevent winterkill, and it did not allow the frost to indulge itself—to gobble up within a month the desiccated manure and straw stored as fuel in the autumn. If only every winter were like this one!

"But one winter does not erase the memory of another one," the peasants chat among themselves. "Remember the winter last year? It took less than a minute for your ears to freeze."

"Yes, but then the summer was as a summer should be. But with this kind of winter, the summer won't be hot—the old people won't even be able to warm their bones."

"Well, it's as the old women say—if it won't be like this, then it will be like that. It's all in God's hands."

"Oh, sure, God . . . Nowadays even God is so afraid that He can't see what's happening to us down here. You can yell and shout until you go hoarse, but it won't make any difference—He won't hear you."

"Uh-huh . . ."

But no one will say out loud what that "uh-huh" means. Even though every one understands what it means and why it was said.

And so, as they disperse, they talk about many things: about the weather, about the prospects for the new harvest. But they do not talk about the one thing that is most painful, most alarming. The topic that will keep many an eye from closing, that will make even the softest pillow seem like a stone. The topic that, until daybreak arrives, will make you twist and turn, as if you have a thorn in your side.

Because it is fine and dandy for you, Volodya, to shout about a kolhosp; you're getting paid by the regional centre to do just that. You get wages—wages for doing nothing. Every month you get a fresh <u>kopiyka</u> to live on. So, no matter what, you will survive.

Tractors . . . combines . . . They harvest and thresh . . . But will they not thresh me at the same time, thresh me so well that all you will hear is my bones being crunched?

And what's the big hurry? I, you see, have not even become accustomed to being a member of TOZ. But you, Volodya, are already dragging me into a kolhosp.

You say we're going to live well? Rivers of milk, banks of jellied pudding? Electricity? Press a button—and the ploughs till the soil by themselves; press another one, and mounds of flatbreads cover the table . . . You speak well, Volodya, very well . . . I could listen to you for ages: about your rivers of milk and a life like in paradise. But let's strike a deal—first, you get me those buttons, and then you can court me to join the collective.

That is what he would say if he did not fear Volodya. But, as it is, he pulls his cap down over his eyes and says: "Uh-huh."

As for Volodya, he's so angry that he's sizzling: only twelve of the thirty-seven activists agreed to join the collective. He has to get rid of the laggards, get rid of them so there won't be a trace of them left! Damn kurkul henchmen!

As for the Komsomol members who are trying to sidestep the issue, it will be easier to deal with them. Tomorrow morning there will be a Komsomol meeting, and the matter will be put to them clearly and directly—either join the kolhosp, or say goodbye to your Komsomol card. But what is to be done with people like Protasiy? He's as stubborn as an ox: "If you keep bothering me, I'll even withdraw from the TOZ."

Volodya cannot restrain himself. He bangs his fist on the table: "Stop all this counterrevolutionary talk!"

But Protasiy, leaping to his feet as if someone had poured hot coals down his back, bellows at Volodya like a bull: "Do we have freedom, or do we not? If you're so anxious to bang your fist, bang it at your wife!"

There you have it—an integrated collective! There you have it—one hundred per cent collectivization!

At the thought of Comrade Suslov, at the thought of the meeting that is coming up with the Secretary of the Regional Committee, Volodya feels hot all over.

What will he tell Suslov? How can he look him in the face?

Volodya does not sleep that night; he does not close his eyes until morning arrives. And when it does arrive, grey as weariness itself, it will glance out like a demon from under gloomy brows and hold out no promise of anything good. Except, perhaps, a meeting with Granddad Khlypavka.

"Did you have a good sleep?"

The old man does not speak or look at him. He is bloated from the homebrew. Enough straw has become entangled in his dishevelled beard to light a fire in a stove.

"Aren't you ashamed to get drunk like that?" Volodya asks more gently. "Do you even remember what you were up to yesterday?"

The old man's lips twitch, and his beard jerks.

"You alarmed the entire village, struck me in the face . . ."

It is only now that Granddad Khlypavka finally glances at Volodya. In his puffy red eyes there is the angry obstinacy of old age. "You deserved more than that, you son of a bitch. Phew!"

The old man spits on the floor and stalks out of the village office. And as he walks down the street, he cannot calm down. He recalls Hanzha once again, and his heart flames. Entering his house, he sits down on a bench near the threshold—as if it was not his own home—and lowers his head.

"What's wrong with you?" Granny Natalka asks him.

The old man raises his eyes—eyes that are clouded with a veil of sadness.

"Bake some turnovers, my dear Natalka . . . with potatoes and beans."

"O Lord," Granny Natalka thinks, faint with fear, "is he going to die?"

Because ever since they have lived together, he has never called her his dear Natalka. He has called her a devil. And an Egyptian Satan. And even a witch. But now it is "my dear Natalka."

"What's got into you, old man?"

"Bake the turnovers, my dear Natalka; boil some eggs, kill a chicken, and I'll get some salted pork fat . . . I'm going to take a parcel to Vasyl."

The oven blazes, and the turnovers are baked. The eggs are hard-boiled, and a speckled hen simmers on the stove. And villagers come to their cottage bringing with them whatever they can.

"How will you get it to him?" Granny Natalka asks with concern as she ties the heavy bundle.

"I'll get it to him. Good people will help me."

And help him they did. They drove him right up to the prison.

"Thank you, my good people! May God grant you good health," the old man says gratefully. And then he knocks with his staff on the huge gate framed in iron.

A tiny window opens, and a severe face looks through it: "What do you want? Don't you know the rules?"

But Granddad Khlypavka is not one to be easily frightened. He steps up closer, politely removes his cap, and greets the man: "Good health to you! Tell Vasyl to come here, my good man."

"Which Vasyl?"

"Hanzha, of course. My countryman from Tarasivka. Our former head. I brought him a parcel."

"Parcels are taken to the door on the right," the face explains before disappearing and shutting the window behind it.

"Oh, woe is me—he's an important man! I should have offered him a slab of salted pork fat at the outset," the old man chastises himself. "Why didn't I think of it?"

He finds the door to the right. There are people behind that door as well. They explain at length to the confused old man that the "prisoner" Hanzha has been transferred to a prison in Poltava.

"Prisoners who have been sentenced are not kept here."

The old man stands around by the prison for quite a while and then sets off to see his son who works at the train station.

"Here you are, my son, do it however you can, but get this parcel to Poltava. Take it to the prison and give it to Vasyl."

And his son had to deliver it. He did not do it right away, of course, but only when the opportunity arose. Thank God it was winter, and nothing spoiled.

And so the day will come when the guard at the Poltava prison will open the cell door and pass Vasyl Hanzha that heavy bundle. And Hanzha will empty a mountain of treats on his blanket.

"Come and get it, fellows; treat yourselves . . ." And then he will add more softly: "You see, they haven't forgotten about me."

He will stand and watch as the fellows parcel out the treats, relishing the simple peasant fare.

And one of them, busily eating, will ask in amazement: "Why aren't you having any?"

"I'll have some later," Hanzha will reply. And then he will take a little turnover and chew it for a long time, staring fixedly at the barred window, and his emaciated face, overgrown with grimy bristles, will reflect an implacable sorrow . . .

And at that time, a vicious storm was raging over his village, over Tarasivka.

Putko arrived in the morning. Mytrofan Onysymovych himself. He immediately ordered that the collective be called together. And when the terrified members gathered in the village hall, Putko rose from behind the table and eyed them with a disgruntled look.

"So what's going on here, my little doves? The class enemy is conducting a furious campaign against the kolhosp, and you're sitting around doing nothing? How am I to understand this?"

Not wishing to take off any outer garments even though it is warm in the room, he is still in his sheepskin coat and cap. Sweat is pouring down from under his cap, but he has made up his mind to stick it out. So that the collective in Tarasivka will understand fully how dissatisfied he is with them.

"How many signed-up members are there now, Comrade Tverdokhlib?"

"Twenty-nine households," Volodya replies guiltily. During these past few days he has grown dark and thin, and if it were not for his belt, he would be in danger of losing his trousers.

"Twenty-nine!" Mytrofan Onysymovych snorts derisively. "It's enough to make chickens laugh! Other villages have one hundred per cent already. What will the Party say when it hears about this shameful figure? Am I to take it to the provincial capital? Oh no, my little doves, you'll report this figure yourselves, and you will be the ones who will blush with shame before the proletariat."

Volodya's eyes are terror-stricken, filled with a raw, naked fear. And the members of the collective—afraid to breathe—lower their heads. It is only the militiamen accompanying Putko who feel at ease, whispering and laughing among themselves. They, of course, can afford to laugh: their job is to haul former kurkuls to the regional centre.

The red splotches that appeared on Comrade Olha's cheeks when she heard Mytrofan Onysymovych's words are still glowing. "May I speak?"

"Wait until I'm finished," even though he had been just about to ask if anyone wanted to say something. But it is he who would have asked, whereas this woman raised her hand of her own accord. Moreover she had been Hanzha's sweetheart. We won't let you forget that, as long as you live, my little darling! You'll be kept under surveillance forever! "So, where was I when I was interrupted?"

"You were talking about the numbers," Volodya prompts him hesitantly.

"It's a disgraceful number, Comrades, disgraceful! I'm saying to you, as plainly as I can—we did not have the Revolution to have numbers like these in the region! So there you have it . . . And now, who wants to say something with respect to this matter?" he asks, as if he had forgotten that Olha had asked for permission to speak.

But no, he has not forgotten; he casts a stern look at her: "Did you want to say something?"

"Yes I did!"

Olha jumps abruptly to her feet and tugs at her jacket as if she were still wearing an army tunic, and not civilian clothes. "I want to say that you are not conducting yourself properly, Comrade. Who gave you the right to offend all of us? You're treating us like children!"

Putko looks so menacing that Tanya, seated next to Olha, curls up in terror.

His eyes bulging, Putko rises on his toes and—bang!—his fist slams on the table: "Stop it! That's enough demagoguery!"

The militiamen instantly fall silent and look expectantly at the Head of the Regional Executive Committee: should we take her away, or shouldn't we?

"Ask questions that are to the point," Putko says a little more calmly.

This means that she is not to be taken away just yet. Well, we'll just sit here and wait for the order. What is meant to be ours won't get away.

Olha turns pale with anger. "I will inform the Regional Committee about your behaviour! And please don't use the informal 'you' when speaking to me."

"Go ahead and inform it," Putko says as he sits down. He is probably aware that he has gone too far. He finally takes off his cap and wipes his damp hair with the palm of his hand. "Of course, I did not mean to imply that you've all banded together with the kurkuls, or that you've become opportunists . . ."

The room instantly becomes brighter, as if not one, but two suns were peeping in through the window. Even the eyes of the militiamen grow softer: what are you afraid of, comrades? We did not come here to take you away, and we won't take you away.

"So, then," Putko continues in a deliberately amiable tone, "from this day forward consider yourselves to be mobilized for universal collectivization. We will set about this task in a serious manner. We've talked about it, handled the villagers with kid gloves, played at demagoguery—but that's enough! Has the village been broken down into brigades?"

"Yes, it has."

"Everyone knows what they are to do?"

"Yes, they do."

"Then we'll begin today. We're calling a general meeting of the village tonight, at seven o'clock. The only item on the agenda will be universal collectivization; there will be no other items. Is that clear?"

"It's clear," comes the gloomy response from the ranks.

"That means that we're finished with this topic for the time being. We will now proceed to the second question: the dispossession of the kurkuls and their henchmen . . ."

"But we've dispossessed them already!"

"You didn't dispossess them! You only played at blind man's bluff with them!" Mytrofan Onysymovych responds maliciously. "You grabbed what you could readily see, but you left the roots in the ground, didn't you? Do you want those roots to stay there until spring, so that they can destroy our harvest? We won't let that happen!"

"Who is there left to dispossess?"

"We'll decide that right away . . . That's why we've gathered here. Comrade Tverdokhlib, take a pen and a sheet of paper, and start writing down the names of the families."

Volodya tears a page out of a notebook, dips a pen into the inkbottle, and waits silently, apprehensively.

Everyone freezes, afraid to breathe.

They are staring as if hypnotized at the pen poised over the blank sheet of paper.

"Well, why aren't you speaking?" Putko asks with a note of displeasure. "Name the families. Do I have to ask you one at a time, or what?"

The peasants grow even quieter. Everyone is praying fervently: don't let me be the first one! Because what will I say? Whom will I name? My neighbour? My children's godfather, or my in-law? And how am I to look people in the face if I do it?

"But maybe you'll tell us who they are, Comrade. It's clearer to those at the top where the remaining kurkuls are."

"You want to hide behind my back, do you?" Putko once again grows angry. "Well, I'll assume responsibility for telling you that it won't work. Come on, Comrade Tverdokhlib, you begin. Who in your village has adopted kurkul values?"

The pen in Volodya's hand jerks, as if taking aim at the person it will strike.

"Mykola Oleksiyovych Prykhodko."

"Well, write his name down."

"But he served in the Red Army!" Ivan does not so much shout as wail when he realizes that his brother's name is going to be written down. He leaps to his feet and presses his cap pleadingly to his chest: "My good people, tell him! Don't let an innocent person suffer!"

"Come now, let's go about this without any shouting! Comrade Tverdokhlib, how many horses does this Prykhodko own?"

"A pair."

"Oxen?"

"Also a pair."

"And cows?"

"Two cows, a bullock, and a heifer."

"What else does he have?"

"Twenty sheep . . . Two pigs . . . Seventeen beehives . . . And I've never counted how much poultry he has. His yard is chock-full of poultry."

"So, it turns out that he's a typical kurkul," Putko summarizes. "And, as for you," he turns to Ivan, "don't shed any crocodile tears here. Don't try to pull the wool over our eyes with talk about the Red Army. If he's turned into a kurkul after serving in the Red Army that's even more of a disgrace in the eyes of the Soviet authorities. Sit down, Comrade. Don't make me think that a class enemy has bribed you."

"But it's his brother," Volodya says softly.

"Family ties are of no consequence here!" Mytrofan Onysymovych glowers. "We decide strictly on the basis of class, and in-laws and brothers do not enter the picture. And it might not be a sin to take a closer look at you as well, Comrade Ivan."

"He's one of our activists," Volodya takes pity on Ivan. "He was the first to join TOZ; he has a pile of children, and he's poor."

"And what about the kolhosp?"

"He's also signed a declaration to join the kolhosp."

"Fine, sit down. But bear this in mind: if you're going to side with the kurkuls—you'll follow in their footsteps. Have you written the name down?" he asks Volodya. "Well, who else among you is a kurkul in disguise?"

A few more people are named. Those who up to now have been considered serednyaks and respectable householders. Those who a year ago were given diplomas of commendation, praised in the newspapers, and set up as models to be emulated by others.

And it is just as well that we did not pay attention to those appeals. That we did not try our hardest, did not toil like plodding oxen, did not tear away the last crumb from our mouths in order to become respectable farmers. Because if we had, we too would have been added to that list, to that terrifying piece of paper that you cannot hew your way out of even with the sharpest axe.

Your surname, your name, and your patronymic.

Three words and, in their wake—a long trek to Siberia.

So that white piece of paper is terrifying—more terrifying than a grave!

But Putko does not think that there are enough names. He still is not satisfied. In a village of three hundred householders only six are to be dispossessed as kurkuls? It does not seem that the matter is being treated seriously. Thoroughly. The named kurkuls are outnumbered by the militiamen who have travelled with him. Moreover, he knows that there are more kurkuls. There most certainly are more kurkuls; all one has to do is root them out.

Mytrofan Onysymovych's true sense of class consciousness— a sense that has never betrayed him—is a guarantee of this.

And he has still another idea, one that, it could be said, has a tactical orientation. It is not possible to bribe peasants with fancy words or to win them over without giving them something. Over the years, the peasants have learned to be suspicious of speeches of all kinds. Especially if these speeches are made by the authorities. Because the authority figure makes a speech and goes away, but the peasant is left to cry out in despair and to slap his foolish head for being taken in.

So it is not enough to try to convince the peasant—he has to be frightened. Threatened with a heavy cudgel. Like a stubborn child. So that the righteousness of our words will not only be heard by the mind, but also felt on the back.

These deep tactical thoughts force Mytrofan Onysymovych to try even harder to expand the list of candidates to be dispossessed as kurkuls.

"So, are you saying that there are no more kurkuls among you? You're hiding them?"

The silence is oppressive. The room seems to have grown darker. Has the sun gone down below the horizon, or has it been hidden by some clouds, that such a sudden twilight has descended?

"Fine . . . Then we'll approach this matter from another angle. Who opposed the kolhosp? Who shouted most loudly against it? Come on, Tverdokhlib. I want names!"

And once again Volodya's throat goes dry. And his tongue turns rigid. And with his unwilling tongue he names a few more people.

And among them is Hanna Martynenko. The one who is called the Nightingale.

He names her, and he does not besmirch his soul. It was she, the Nightingale, who riled up the village women doing their laundry at the the ice-holes. She had shouted so loudly that her voice echoed: "Why, I'll choke my husband with my own hands—but I won't let him join the Commune. So that he can roll around with other women under a common blanket? It can go to hell, that commune of theirs!"

"Did she really shout those things?" Putko asks.

"Well, that was the gist of it."

"Then write her name down: Hanna Martynenko, a supporter of the kurkuls, indulged in hostile agitation against the Soviet government."

"She was only against the commune."

"It's one and the same thing. For who is presiding over the universal collectivization? The Soviet government. So, if you are against the kolhosp, then you're against the Soviet government. Is that clear?"

"It's clear . . ."

But it is not clear to everyone.

Tanya, for example.

She cannot understand or accept in her heart that it is necessary to denounce Mykola Oleksiyovych and Palazhka Danylivna as kurkuls and to dispossess them. She is unable to clamber up to that class platform—the only true platform—where all pity is suspended, and all personal sympathies are suppressed, and the enemy is beheaded.

What kind of enemies are they? Danylivna is an enemy? Danylivna with a perpetually gentle smile on her kindly face? Oleksiyovych—with his work-hardened hands? A man who prides himself on having acquired all his wealth through his own back-breaking labour?

Why are they being denounced as kurkuls?

Or the Martynenkos. Those Nightingales who have never had an extra piece of bread in their home.

What kind of kurkuls are they?

What is happening?

Tanya, her eyes uncomprehending and sorrowful, looks at Tverdokhlib, at Comrade Olha, and at all the people sitting next to her: why are you all silent? Get up and say something! Tell him that all this is not true. That this is not how things should be done!

They remain silent. They do not get up. They do not utter a word of protest. Even Ivan Prykhodko, whose older brother's name has been put on the terrifying list, even he, after Putko explained to him "the class essence" sits still, and not a peep is heard from him.

They are silent. And is it not because all the people are already on the platform so cunningly erected by Mytrofan Onysymovych?

It is only Tanya who is still struggling. But in the end, she too presses her lips together. She presses them so hard that they turn white.

For who is she to protest?

The daughter of a priest, the wife of a kurkul, the sister of a man purged from the Party. And she herself, not that long ago, had been expelled from a Soviet institution.

So be quiet, you suspicious person, you uncertain element; be quiet and do not even breathe if you want to live in this world for even a little while longer. Sit silently with your small, insignificant truth, a truth that is meaningless when compared to the great class truth that is personified at this moment by Mytrofan Onysymovych.

So sit still, Tanya, and be quiet! Sit still and do not utter a sound! Thank your lucky stars that you were not appointed to the brigade that is to undertake the dispossession of the Prykhodko family. Or the Martynenko family. To destroy the nest of those nightingales that have charmed the village with their singing for as long as anyone can remember.

In any event, they will not have their throats slit, nor will their heads be cut off; they will simply be sent to Siberia. And, over there, people do manage to live somehow, and they probably will listen most willingly to the southern nightingales.

People will come to the hastily erected sod hut, sit down on a bench of freshly hewn planks, and ask in their native Russian tongue: "Come on, khokhols, sing us a song . . . the song that you always sing . . . About the wind that blows and blows, but does not reach your Ukraine."

And the khokhols will sing. Why would they not sing for these kind people who gave them refuge, who helped them build their sod hut?

They will sing.

About the wind.

About distant Ukraine.

They dispossess the kurkuls the very same day; they do not put it off until tomorrow. They load them into wagons in the clothes they are wearing and haul them away to Khorolivka—straight to the train station where cattle cars are waiting for them.

Hanna keeps shouting and hurling terrifying curses at everyone: "You will pay dearly for our tears! May you be damned! May the earth not let you walk upon it!"

Oleksiyovych does not shout. He sits on the sleigh, and his legs, like broken roots torn out of the ground, dangle from it. And when the horses start out, his feet trail over the snow like those of a corpse.

Danylivna keeps reminding Tanya: "Take good care of the heifer. And when spring comes, transplant the cabbage from the sheltered meadow."

Tanya nods her head, but her eyes are filled with tears, and she can no longer see Oleksiyovych, or Danylivna, or Vasyl. It is as if they are enshrined in a mist.

And they vanish in that mist.

Only their cottages stand darkly, their open doors like gaping mouths wailing for their owners.

And those inhuman cries are bloodcurdling, terrifying . . .

And, in the evening the villagers will gather at the village hall for a general meeting. They will all come, without exception, because Mytrofan Onysymovych's tactical manoeuvre will have succeeded.

And, when Mytrofan Onysymovych finishes speaking—and, after him, Tverdokhlib and Comrade Olha, and Ivan Prykhodko from the non-Communist group—he will rise to his feet, lean forward on the table with his powerful hands and ask: "Is it clear to everyone?"

"Yes, it's clear . . . Of course . . ."

"If it's clear, then we'll put a stop to the debate . . . I'm putting to a vote the voluntary entry of the entire village into the collective. Now—all those who are against the Soviet government, raise your hands!"

Oh, sure, raise them! Those who had raised them were already on their way to Siberia with their hands still raised.

"There are no opposing votes . . . Then the matter is clear— everyone belongs to the collective. I congratulate you. We still have to pick the administration; Comrade Olha will read the names of those who are candidates."

And Comrade Olha reads out a few names.

"Are there any dissenters? Fine, then we'll vote. All those who are against the Soviet government, raise your hands! There are none . . . It's unanimous . . . You now have the floor, Comrade Tverdokhlib."

And Volodya will get up, his eyes beaming, and say in a voice hoarse with excitement: "We have to name the kolhosp . . . Mytrofan Onysymovych advised us to name our collective after our dear leader and teacher, Comrade Stalin."

And the meeting will end, and the people will disperse in a heavy, silent thoughtfulness.

And then they will herd their cattle together, and bring in their equipment and their seed grain, only to take everything back again, because there will be an article written by Comrade Stalin, "Dizzy with Success," in which it will be written, black on white, that a kolhosp is to be formed on a voluntary basis.

And it will be in vain that Volodya, his face dark with grief, will try to persuade his fellow villagers; he will clutch at their hands and the hems of their garments, and beg them to reconsider and not destroy the collective that is so dear to his heart.

Only half a hundred families will remain in the kolhosp.

That's just what you deserve, Volodya! Do not abuse your power, do not herd people together by force, and do not twist the policies of the Party.

And so, for twisting the policies of the Party, Volodya will be severely punished; a statement of censure will be sent to the bureau of the Regional Committee. And Comrade Putko, looking at Tverdokhlib with eyes as clear as those of the First Secretary, will ask at that bureau meeting how he, Tverdokhlib, could have stooped to methods of collectivization unapproved by the Party, thereby violating the directives of our dear leader and teacher, Comrade Stalin.

And Mytrofan Onysymovych himself will not escape severe censure; however, it will come a little later. He and the First Secretary will be called before the Provincial Committee, and others, looking at them with righteously clear eyes, will interrogate them about how they could commit such errors. It is those same others who phoned every week; they phoned—pressing buttons and turning dials—and demanded a round figure. Just a nice round figure! A figure so round that it could roll all the way to Moscow.

But wise Mytrofan Onysymovych will not be the least concerned about that. He will not be concerned, and he will not be enraged. He will thank them for the harsh lesson, for prompting him what to do next, for giving him orders. And then he will ricochet to Khorolivka "to correct the situation."

And it will be spring, and the snow will disappear, and the ploughed fields, begging for seeds and the warm hands of the farmer, will turn black.

All this will happen; it cannot be avoided, it will not pass them by. But for now, Tanya, having seen her "kurkul" masters off on their long journey, returns to the house.

It is empty, bare. Only a bench, a bed, and a table are left. The rest has been taken away by the Commission for the Dispossession of Kurkuls. Even the <u>rushnyks</u> were torn down from the walls, because they belonged not to the teacher, but to the Prykhodko family.

As she sits, she starts thinking about Oleh.

Where is he now? What is happening to him?

"If it were just a matter of my wife, I would not hesitate for a minute—I would come and live with you. But I have children, Tanya—children!"

"How could you have married her, if you didn't love her?"

"Oh, Tanya! Life is so complicated . . . so complex."

She looked at his irresolute, miserable face, and she felt both sorry for him . . . and angry with him.

Maybe it was because he seemed so distressed that she had not told him. That she was pregnant; that she was expecting his child.

Her only words were: "Well, what can I say? You have a family, and you ought to return to it."

And she just smiled bitterly when he shouted: "So, you're telling me to leave?"

Stroking his soft, fine hair, she tried to comfort him as one would comfort an ailing child: "The pain will pass . . . Now, go."

Then she pushed him away, fearing that she would break down and cry out in despair.

"Go . . ."

And so he went, without understanding anything. He went away offended and never showed up in Tarasivka again.

Well, perhaps it was better this way. If something had to be ripped out, then let it be ripped all at once, without leaving behind so much as a single thread.

Tanya is standing in the middle of the room, and little Andriyko comes up hesitantly to her. When she strokes his head, he grows bolder: "Ma, draw me a little man."

He pulls her over to the window.

Tanya does not ask what kind of a man her son wants to see, but she draws one. Blowing on the pane, she draws a circle with her finger. The contours of a face, eyebrows, eyes, a nose, and a mouth.

But Andriyko is not satisfied with it. He frowns and glares at the little man.

"I don't want him. Rub him out."

"Why?"

"He's ugly. He isn't smiling. He's crying,"

Tanya takes a closer look—truly, it does seem that the little man is crying. On his face there is not a smile, but a painful grimace, like that of a clown who is forced to amuse people, hiding his broken heart behind a painted face.

"We'll draw a happier man right now."

She erases her drawing, blows on another spot, and makes a circle with her finger. But this man also seems to be crying more than laughing.

And the longer that Tanya drew, and rubbed, and blew on the pane, the sadder the little men looked.

II

It could not be said that the harvest was bad that year.

The year was like any other, with rain showers in May and thunderstorms in June—when heavy grey clouds spread over the blue sky baked by the sun, and steel blue sheets of rain swayed over the villages, groves, valleys, and the endless expanses of the steppes.

People hid under thatched roofs, under wagons, and covered their heads and shoulders with whatever pieces of light clothing were at hand, but the horses and oxen, remaining calm as the transparent watery whips lashed at their steaming sides, shuddered only when a thunderbolt flashed over their heads and rent the swirling sky with a deafening roar.

"Holy! Holy! Holy!" the women, turning pale, crossed themselves and chased the children away from the windows so that they would not draw the heavenly fire to themselves. Because the year before last, in a neighbouring village, people had been looking out at a storm like this, and when lighting hit, it raced right through the house. It did not set fire to the house, but it struck down the entire family. They all lay there in a row—the father, mother, and three little children—blackened like charred logs. And the thunderbolt was found behind the house—a stone arrow about six feet long, and still so hot that it could not be picked up.

"Holy! Holy! Holy! Don't let that happen here. Lord have mercy!"

Crosses were hastily marked on windows, doors, and ovens. But this did not seem good enough for some people, so they put icons in the windows—surely Saint Elijah would not raise his hand against Christ or the Mother of God!

The thunder ended, the lightning went away, the most terrifying part of the storm passed, and the children dashed outdoors into the sparkling, softly falling rain and, jumping on the wet grass and over the bubbling little puddles, screamed as if demented:

"Come down, O rain, come down,
Fall on Granny's cabbages!"

Come down, O rain, come down. Do not miss a single field, a single piece of ploughed, spaded, and seeded soil. Let the fruit of our labouring hands, of our exultant, bloody sweat, grow, flourish, and mature. The entire world rests on our backs, waiting for us to feed it.

Sow yourself over the earth, O rain, sow yourself over the earth; and you, O earth, bring forth your crops. Bring forth oats and rye, and wheat, and all manner of cereal crops. So that there will be enough for everyone—for those who shout, and for those who are silent—and may there be something left for us as well.

And the wheat and the rye grew; the grain ripened, ripened and bowed submissively to the sickle, the scythe, and the binder. To be bound in large, tautly bound sheaves, stacked in stooks of thirty or sixty sheaves, and then—hauled away on carts and wagons.

And the oak wheels squeaked and creaked, and mountains of sheaves flowed to the kolhosp threshing floor. And the threshing machine hummed day and night, and the golden grain flowed in an endless stream. So that, after it was winnowed, it could be poured into gunny bags and sacks, and placed on drays—in the first caravan of grain destined for the state.

The first caravan in the region.

Within seven days, the plan was fulfilled—exactly as mandated. It was not like it had been before—three hundred households, three hundred peasants, and everyone watching carefully, so as not to deliver the grain earlier than his neighbour. And hauling sheaves to an outbuilding, to a barn, and threshing with a flail until the New Year: I'll get it done, there's no hurry—there's no fire.

Two hundred and thirty households have joined the collective. Only seventy remain outside it. The most obstinate peasants. The most tenacious ones. Those who are not afraid of high taxes; no matter how hard they are squeezed, they stand their ground; they are not the ones who come crawling to join the collective:

"Sign me up, because I don't have the strength left to carry on. Be it this way or the way that it was—either way, I'm ruined."

"That's the way it is, uncle. What did you think—that we're going to treat you private farmers with kid gloves? Do you now appreciate the superiority of the kolhosp order?"

"Yes, I do. How can I not appreciate it when they've strangled us with such a high tax that our eyes have popped out of their sockets!"

But the remaining seventy farmers resist with all their strength. They hang on to their own land and do not want to join the collective—because "a collective is the work of the devil"; because only lazy people profit from joining—those wretched souls who have ever walked around with a big spoon, but a small spade.

Having had their fill of trouble with these independent farmers in years past, this year the authorities are wiser. They assign the private farmers two common threshing floors right in the middle of the field. And they sternly forbid them to haul their sheaves to their yards; they have to thresh them on these common threshing floors.

"But why should I haul them all the way there, when my house is right here?" the private farmer objects. "I'll take the sheaves home, do the threshing and the winnowing, put some grain aside for the next seeding, some for my family, some for my cattle—to make it to the next harvest—and the rest I'll deliver to you; I swear on the holy cross that I'll deliver it."

They do not believe him. Not a word he says, nor his vow on the holy cross.

"Tell this fairy tale to someone else, uncle; we heard the same story last year."

They force him to turn his wagon towards the threshing floor, to the threshing machine.

"Haul it over there, and don't even look back! First you'll give us what's owing, and then, from the grain that's left, you can measure off how much you need for sowing and how much you need to gnaw on."

And it does not matter if he wants to or if he does not want to, he has to turn off to the common threshing floors. The end of the world must be coming if a man can no longer be his own master!

He stops his cart on that threshing floor, dumps the sheaves on the ground, looks malevolently at the threshing machine that wails greedily as it spits out the chewed up straw, and gloomily waits his turn. In order to pour the grain that is still warm into sacks, to put the sacks on a dray, and then to haul them to the district storage depot. And to haul them not by himself, but in an organized caravan, so that even the blind can see how amiable and united we are in our desire to meet the first commandment.

Fine. They deliver it. To the very last kernel. They fulfill the designated quota for the private sector, and even surpass it, attaining one hundred and ninety per cent.

And their accomplishment is extolled in the newspapers.

Tverdokhlib brings a dozen newspapers from the district capital and distributes them to the activists. He instructs them to go from house to house in the village and read the article out loud— let the people listen and rejoice, let them hear how our village is being praised.

They listen.

About the increasing tempo of grain delivery.

"We have many regions where much less grain was delivered this year than in the past year, and yet they're complaining that they can't fulfill the plan. This means that hostile kurkul elements—former followers of Petlyura—have settled there."

"Imagine that! It seems that they still haven't dispossessed the kurkuls in that region."

"And what will happen to those farmers who stood their ground and refused to fulfill the plan?"

"There's something written about that as well. Listen."

They listen to the decree of the National Council of Commissars of the Ukrainian S.S.R. and the Central Committee of the Communist Party (Bolsheviks) of Ukraine mandating that the names of lagging villages and districts be entered on a board of dishonour.

"With respect to the blacklisted villages and districts, the following must be done:

1. Stop the delivery of all provisions, shut down state and co-operative trading completely, and haul away all goods and produce.

2. Stop giving credit, and begin an immediate recall of all the credit that has already been extended, irrespective of the due date.

3. Inspect the kolhosps vigilantly and cleanse them of all counterrevolutionary elements."

"That's referring to the farmers who are in the kolhosps . . . And if they do that to them, what will they do to private farmers?"

"There's something about them as well."

"In the village of Yurchykhy, a large group of kurkul henchmen was undermining the grain delivery plans. The travelling judge confiscated all their property and sentenced the entire group to prison for a period of two to five years. After the arrest of this group, the tempo of grain delivery immediately improved, and by January 1, 1933—the day of the trial—the private farmers delivered ninety per cent of their prescribed grain quota."

"Aha, so they did fulfill it after all."

"So would you!"

"Well, yes, that's true . . ."

They listen and then disperse. It cannot be said that they are very cheerful as they make their way home, but at least everyone takes away with him an appeasing thought: "Praise God, that I delivered my grain. I'll make it through to the New Year one way or another, and by that time our government may soften its stand a bit . . ."

But before they recover from the pain of this grain delivery, uninvited guests appear once again.

"Haul some grain, old man!"

"What grain?"

"The grain that you're supposed to deliver to the state."

"For God's sake! I've delivered it already! Here's my receipt."

And he dashes to the icon corner and pulls out some papers that are not even dusty yet. He smooths them out with trembling fingers and, almost in tears, says: "It's all written here. I delivered everything, to the very last kernel."

They do not even look at the papers.

"Go wipe yourselves with your receipts! So what if you delivered that batch? You now have to give us what is dictated by the next quota."

And the peasant cannot restrain himself; he dashes to the storeroom and spreads his arms over the door as if he were being crucified: "I won't let you in! You can hack me to death or bury me alive, but I won't give you anymore!"

At first they try to reason with him. They explain patiently that the grain is needed for the five-year plan, to help with the industrialization of the country. In order to build a prosperous future more quickly.

"It's all for your children, your own children, uncle!"

He will not listen. He will resolutely shake his head. "I don't need that joyous prosperity of yours—you can have it all. Just leave me my grain! Because what will I give my children to eat, if you take all my grain away from me?"

Getting nowhere by talking with him individually, they will try to influence him through the collective—to wear him down at a meeting. A representative from the regional centre will address them, painting a picture of the conditions, both interior and exterior, and laying everything out clearly, as if it were on the palm of one's hand.

"Do you understand now, Comrade Farmers, why you must fulfill and surpass the next grain delivery to the state? The plan is entirely and completely realistic."

Then a voice from the audience will ring out, sarcastic and gloomy: "The plan, of course, is realistic; it's just that there is no more grain."

And the persuaders will lose all patience.

"You say there is no grain? Not even a kernel? We'll take a look for ourselves; we'll search in all your bins and storerooms!"

But the peasants were not born yesterday. They had learned a thing or two during the period of militant Communism about the distribution of provisions. And what they learned, they did not forget.

While the arguing and persuading continued, they furtively—hiding from even neighbours' eyes—dug secret holes, lined them with straw, and filled them with grain. The grain that they had saved to last them until the next harvest.

The brigades no longer came up against doors protected by peasants' spread-eagled arms—the doors to the storerooms were now opened wide.

"Here, go ahead and look! I don't know how we'll pull through this year."

But the brigade members also were not born yesterday.

"Tell us, old man, tell us like a good fellow, where you've buried it. Because we'll find it ourselves—and it will be all the worse for you. We'll flay you so badly that you'll be black and blue all over."

"Go ahead and flay me," the peasant will say, waving his hands in despair. "Peel the skin off my back to make yourselves boots and jodhpurs, and take my children away with you along with my skin! Take them from me, so that I won't have to see them die a hungry death."

He will stand and watch as they search for grain. As they rummage inside his house and behind it; as they probe the floor, stab the frozen earth with pikes, and eventually find the carefully secreted hole.

"So, you say there is no grain?"

And the peasant will not utter another word. His wife will lament, the children will wail, but he will stand dumb like a corpse.

And it is only when they harness his mare to his wagon, place his sacks with the remaining grain on it, and move out of his yard, that he will leap forward, grab the sleeve of a brigade member, and ask: "With what am I supposed to seed the land now?"

And such despair will gush from his deadened eyes, such an inhuman grief, that the man's heart will contract. And speaking softly, so that no one will hear, he will try to console the farmer.

"Don't worry, Yukhym. When spring rolls around we'll give you some seed for sowing."

"So why are you taking it away now?"

"So that you won't use it as food for your children."

Do you hear, Yukhym? So you won't use it as food for your children! So that you will not take so much as a kernel when your children are bawling, their mouths split wide open with hunger: "Daddy, food! Daddy, bread!"

When you—no longer able to stand that incessant whimpering and, swollen and blue yourself, as if you truly had been skinned alive—will rip open your sweat-stained shirt and, with eyes bulging dementedly, shout: "Here, go ahead and eat me, but just be quiet!"

They bled the private farmers dry—and started in on the kolhosp members. Because a plan is a plan, and it must be fulfilled, even if you die in the process! Because Comrade Stalin, in his speech, "A Summary of the First Five-Year Plan," had said: "Instead of the 500-600 million poods of saleable grain that was stockpiled in the period when most farms were owned by individual peasants, the Party, through its efforts, now has the capability of laying in store 1200-1400 million poods of saleable grain every year."

Is it clear, Comrade Tverdokhlib?

Is it clear, Comrades—Village Communists and Komsomol members?

Is it clear, Comrades—Members of the Brigades and Members of the Staffs of Grain Storage Bins?

Not five to six hundred million, but one thousand, four hundred million poods of grain.

And what does this mean?

This means, in concrete terms, that Tarasivka is supposed to deliver twice as much grain as, let's say, it delivered in nineteen twenty eight when there was a bumper crop.

The quota must be fulfilled and exceeded!

Because Comrade Stalin could not have erred when he made that statement.

Comrade Stalin knows better than you or I how much Yukhym's, or Petro's, or Mykyta's crops yielded.

And it is useless to indulge in talk about rotten liberalism, to expound all sorts of hostile thoughts about the plan being unrealistic, to say that there will not be enough grain left for the spring sowing, and that if we fulfill and surpass this new demand for more grain we will all die of hunger! That doesn't matter in the least!

Because Comrade Stalin has stated clearly: ". . . It is incontestable that we have succeeded, and that the material status of the workers and peasants is improving from year to year. This fact can be doubted only by the most obdurate enemies of the Soviet government."

Is it clear to you now, Comrade Tverdokhlib? Is it still possible for you to doubt that the peasants, after giving away all their grain to the very last kernel, will have a better and more prosperous life?

But what did you do? Who permitted you to give twenty per cent of the grain to the kolhosp members as payment for the days they worked? You're not saying anything? It's just as well that you aren't! So listen to us now—you must immediately take away all that illegally distributed grain and add to it any grain that they might have grown on their private plots. And seal up all the mills until all the grain has been gathered . . .

Go and do this at once. And devote more time to reading what Comrade Stalin has to say.

And once again the village shudders in the feverish delirium of meeting grain consignments.

Now the authorities no longer distinguish between a kolhosp member and a private farmer—they go after everybody. They poke into the ground with pikes, crawl through attics, and topple over chimneys and ovens. And at night they strain their ears: is there a mortar thumping anywhere? Are any grindstones creaking—grindstones that have been made stealthily by the peasants themselves?

Groaning, wailing, and lamenting, Tarasivka fulfilled this plan as well. And it was written about the village that it fulfilled the plan honourably. It did not leave itself a single kernel of grain. It fulfilled the plan and, revelling in the happy life it was leading, sang merry little folk songs.

About dear Stalin, the father of the nation.

> "Out in a meadow sits Stalin
> Gnawing the leg of a stallion,
> 'Oh, how vile and coarse
> Is the meat from a horse!'"

About the prosperous life enjoyed in the village:

> "In the pantry there's a sickle and hammer,
> In the house there's death and famine,
> In the house there's only one sheaf of straw,
> But . . . he's a kurkul by law!"

About the bountiful payment received for work days:

> "Granddad sits on an old hempen cloth
> Putting in workdays—he's no sloth!
> 'It's a workday, granny, a toiling workday,
> So give me bread for at least this one day!'"

Give it to him, granny, give it! Help the feeble old man survive; don't let him die at least until spring, so that he'll have time to sow the fields with the grain stored in the kolhosp storehouse. For what will you eat, granny, if granddad does not have the strength to go out into the fields when the snow disappears, and the ploughed field warms up? What will you reap, granny, if granddad is not there, flinging out his experienced arm, making sure that the grain sprinkles evenly through his fingers? If his generous hand does not sow the seeds from which the life-giving cereal crops will grow?

Give granddad some food, granny! Feed him with pigweed, or even with oak bark if you do not have anything more nourishing, and then step outside with him to greet the spring.

Here comes spring now—warm and rosy, caressed by the sun, wreathed in flowers, and glorified by singing birds.

But why is she so unlike her youthful sisters of yesteryear? Where are her bright flashing eyes and flushed rosy cheeks? Where is her happy, carefree laughter, her nubile, supple figure, her light, lilting walk?

Barely able to move her swollen, log-like legs, she shuffles along the fences like a hundred-year-old granny, and when she extends her withered hands and opens her terrifyingly black mouth, instead of a melodious voice, a hoarse death rattle breaks out of her throat: "I need to e-e-eat . . . e-e-eat . . ."

And all the birds fly fearfully past her, and the flowers wilt and drop from her grey, dishevelled tresses.

She wanders from village to village in the vain hope that she will find some nourishment, a scrap of something edible. She drags herself to the house where Tverdokhlib lives; clutching at the walls, the window frame, she presses her deathly pale face to the grimy pane. She no longer begs; she just waits numbly and submissively, hoping that maybe here they will spare her a tiny bit of bread.

"Volodya! Volodya!"

"Huh? What is it?"

Volodya tears his heavy head away from the pillow and blinks sleepily in the darkness.

"Someone is moving about under our window."

Turning his face to the window, Volodya listens carefully, but does not hear anyone. Last night two people crawled into the yard, and when he went outside in the morning, they were already dead.

"There's no one out there. You imagined it. Go to sleep."

But just as he lowers his head to the pillow, just as he is falling asleep, he hears Marusya's frightened whisper in his ear.

"Volodya! There really is someone out there."

"Oh, what a nuisance!"

Volodya sullenly slides from the bed and pulls on his trousers.

"Take the gun with you."

"Fine."

Reaching under his pillow, he pulls out a heavy pistol and pads barefooted into the porch. He stands there for a while and listens; he can't hear anyone. Quietly shoving back the bolt, he opens the door, sticks his pistol through it, and then pokes his head out.

The moon has set, and dawn will soon be breaking. At one time, roosters would be crowing at this hour, but now there is an eerie, sepulchral silence. All the roosters have been killed, and all the chickens have been eaten. The village appears to have died, and the stars, twinkling anxiously in the heavens, squeeze out a last pitiful glimmer. And, in that faint light, in that uncertain shimmering, hungry shadows crawl about. Rustling under fences and past houses, they stretch their swollen hands towards the door.

"Who's there?"

Silence.

"Who's there?"

Not a sound—not even a breath.

Gripping his pistol, Volodya steps outside. He walks through the yard and stands silently for a while—there is nothing.

He goes back into the house and mutters angrily to his wife: "You hear things, and then you don't let me sleep. You shouldn't strain your ears so hard."

He gropes in the dark for the dipper and has a drink of water. Then he shoves the pistol back under his pillow, pulls off his trousers, and lies down.

But he cannot fall asleep. He senses with every nerve in his body that Marusya is not sleeping. He turns to her and pretends to touch her face accidentally. Yes. He's right—she's crying.

"Are you crying again?"

She swallows her tears and does not say anything. For Volodya that silent weeping is like a sharp knife stabbing his heart. It would be far better if she would wail out loud.

"Well, what could I have done? Tell me, what was I to do?"

There is not a word in reply.

"I couldn't do anything else. I couldn't! Do you understand that?"

Hearing his voice, his mother awakens. There's a rustling on the oven bed, and a sigh: "O-o-h, oh, oh." She's probably crossing herself and praying to God to send peace and tranquillity into their home, and to keep away the cruel hunger that is roaming from house to house, choking people to death.

But there is no peace. There is no tranquillity in this house.

Now their little son is crying. Marusya rushes to the cradle and picks him up. The child instantly falls silent and begins breathing noisily, smacking its lips. A short time later the cradle creaks, and Marusya's voice flows through the darkness.

"A-a-a . . . A-a-a . . ."

And there is more pain in the "A-a-a" of that lullaby than joy; more tears than happy smiles.

But still—what could he have done?

How can he convince his wife that there was nothing else that he could have done? Absolutely nothing, even though his own heart was breaking! When Marusya's father walked into the village office—swollen, distended by a deathly fluid—and when he stood in the middle of the room and looked at Volodya with eyes dimmed by cataracts, drained by hunger, and white like those of a dead man, Tverdokhlib felt a spasm in his throat. He was sitting next to Neshcheret, the current head of the Village Soviet, and his gaunt face was like an open wound oozing with compassion for his father-in-law.

"Fellows, give me back my beans!"

Neshcheret jerked his feet as if something had stabbed him in the back. He raised his brows in a pitying ridge and glanced at Tverdokhlib.

"Maybe we should give them back to him? There aren't so many beans there—just a sack—but they just might help them pull through to the new crop."

"Volodya, my son, give them back! My old woman can't even lift her head . . ."

It would not have taken much more for Volodya to cave in. He would have told the Komsomols to give back the beans that had been taken for seeding the new crop. But then it occurred to him that if he backed down now, everyone in the village—both young and old—would know about it.

"So-o-o-o, you see, he returned the beans to his father-in-law, but he's skinning us alive. So that's what Soviet power is like!"

Volodya's face turned stony and, swallowing painfully, he replied as loudly as he could, so that not only his father-in-law and Neshcheret could hear him, but all the people in the next room: "The beans were taken away from you lawfully . . . We won't give them back . . ."

His father-in-law did not plead any more. It was as if he had made the trip to the village office because he felt obligated to do so, but having carried out this most unpleasant task, was not the least bit interested in the outcome. He turned around without saying a word and walked away, the soles of his feet slapping on the floor. Volodya's eyes did not follow him; they were riveted to the spot where he had been standing—to the dark bold outlines left behind by the bloody puss seeping from those bare feet . . .

The father-in-law and the mother-in-law no longer visit either their daughter, or their son-in-law—they are dead. They died on the same day, right on Easter Sunday, exchanging Easter kisses with that faceless one that does not pass over either the old or the young.

Volodya did everything he could to ensure that they were buried with due respect. Others were simply picked up from the street, hauled to the cemetery, and dumped into a common pit. Their bodies were dumped, and then lime was poured over them, because the pit was not to be covered with soil until it was full. But Volodya placed his father-in-law and mother-in-law in separate coffins and saw them off on their final journey.

Marusya did not say anything to him when she found out about the beans. Not a word. She just wept silently, and became a shadow of her former self.

"Oh, life, may you be damned!"

Had he wanted people to die off as they were dying now? Had he thought about what would happen when he ferreted out all the grain in the village? He took it all away, to the very last kernel, to fulfill the new plan, and he even helped out in the next village that was disgracefully slow in delivering its grain.

In that village, the women had resorted to counterrevolutionary tactics. Overtaking a grain caravan, they threw themselves under the horses' hooves, under the wheels, and carted all the grain back to their yards. And what did they gain by doing this? The judges arrived, the village overflowed with militia, and there was a trial; some were sent to jail, others to Siberia. And the grain was taken away again and, along with it, the vegetables as well. And now that village was worse off than Tarasivka.

Volodya only wanted what was best. He tried to convince the kolhosp members—he did not feel sorry for the private farmers, let them all drop dead!—that they would be given a ration.

Mytrofan Onysymovych himself had assured him of this.

And then that same Mytrofan Onysymovych had categorically demanded that grain be gathered for sowing as well. So that all the land would be sown, to the very last inch.

He banged his fist on the table and sternly ordered: "Keep this in mind—if you pilfer any of the grain set aside for the sowing, you can say good-by to your Party card! Rid yourself of your alarmist frame of mind and go and do as you are told!"

And Volodya did as he was told.

Steeling his heart and gritting his teeth, he did it. He understood all too well that if the crops were not sown this year, the whole country would be lost.

The bourgeois are waiting for us to fail. We have to stand the test. We have to stand the test at all costs. Regardless of the number of sacrifices.

Because there is no class struggle, Volodya, without victims. It is the most merciless of all struggles. And there is no place in it for tears, or pity. Read about all this in the writings of Stalin. Read it and absorb it fully.

And so he reads. And he absorbs it all. But he is not able to convince Marusya. His backward and politically naive wife.

No, he is not able to fall asleep! And the morning is already pressing its pale face against the window. It is time to get up.

After a breakfast of gruel, Volodya goes outside. He is wearing a black jacket, jodhpurs, and boots. His pistol is at his side—in case of a class altercation.

His jodhpurs are lined with yellow leather—so that they won't wear out when he sits in a saddle.

"You see, he wore out his bottom at all his meetings, so now he's sewn himself one out of calf leather," the peasants laugh quietly. Surreptitiously, so that he will not hear.

Because the time has long since passed when Tverdokhlib was called simply Volodya. Now they refer to him only by his patronymic—Danylovych. And whenever they catch sight of him—even if he is still a long way off—they quickly doff their caps.

Even Granddad Khlypavka has eschewed his familiar tone in his dealings with the head of the collective.

Right now, catching sight of Danylovych, he comes out of the storehouse where the seed grain is kept, along with the flour for the tractor drivers and the hot lunches for farm workers. The old man removes his cap, and it is immediately evident that he does not use his position to his advantage. His hair has fallen out, and there is an unhealthy glitter in his eyes.

"I wish you good health!"

Instead of replying to the greeting, Volodya asks in a surly tone: "Is everything in order?"

"It seems to be," the old man puts his cap back on. "There's just one problem—people never stop crawling over here. Maybe we need to dig a ditch around the storehouse!"

"Keep chasing them away! That's why you've been placed here. So that they won't come crawling here."

"I keep yelling and waving my staff at them, but they just don't seem to understand. They insist on crawling to this place— may God forgive me—like mice. It's not too bad during the day, but at night shivers run up my spine, because first there's a rustle over here, and then someone crawls nearer from over there. One of these days they'll strangle me. The way they strangled that watchman in the cemetery . . ."

"We'll have to give you a rifle," Tverdokhlib decides.

"Of course, it would be a lot more comfortable with a rifle," the old man agrees. "But there's really no need to shoot them; by morning they'll have given up their souls to God on their own. Take today, for example—they picked up six more bodies . . ."

"Some of ours?"

"No, strangers . . . Why would our own people come here? Ours know full well that nothing will come of their crawling here."

"Well, that's enough," Volodya interrupts him. "Take care of things."

But as soon as he starts walking away, Khlypavka yells out after him: "Wait, I want to ask you something!"

"What is it?"

"Children, little tykes, gather here in the daytime—there's no stopping them. They try to dig a bit of flour out through the cracks. Should I shoot them as well, or what?"

"Stop your gabbing, old man!" Tverdokhlib flares up. "Do as you're told. If you insist on making bad jokes, we'll expel you from the kolhosp. At once!"

"Well, I just wanted to know. Forgive me if I said something that I shouldn't have."

And he goes back to the storehouse to get out of harm's way.

Because Volodya truly could expel him if he wanted to. Would it take much for him to do it? He has the authority, and so he has the power.

But the old man's heart is not made of stone.

"It's fine for you to lie beside your wife and give orders; but you should try standing here for at least one night and . . . They keep crawling and crawling over here . . . as if something is luring them on . . . and you can yell at them, or swear at them—nothing helps. If I didn't chase after them and shove them away, they'd gnaw their way through the walls . . ."

And, almost weeping, the old man shouts into the obscure darkness—a darkness filled with rustling and movement: "Well, what do you want from me? I'm swollen with hunger myself!"

And he does not close his eyes all night long.

And when dawn breaks in the east, Granddad Khlypavka—pale, wretched, and weakened—makes his rounds to find the newly "departed."

"Oh, you poor souls! What were your names? How can you be remembered in memorial services for the dead?"

And, when the drivers come by later to pick up the corpses and throw them into the wagons, he shouts: "What are you doing, you sons-of-bitches? Have you no heart? Did a she-wolf give birth to you that you're treating people like that?"

"Oh," he thinks, "the world is in its death throes! It's coming to an end! Beasts are being born into it—brutes who have neither pity nor conscience . . . And who is benefitting from this—this use of hunger to murder people? Who?"

Resting his withered hands on his staff, Granddad Khlypavka watches the wagons leave with the corpses. And he blinks his red-rimmed eyes, etched with sorrow and filled with the bitterness of incomprehension.

It is only when the sun begins to warm up, and people appear on the streets, that the old man feels some relief in his heart. Now there is someone with whom he can exchange a word or two. Greet them with a "Good morning" and ask them where they are going.

For instance, the teacher Svitlychna. She has just come out of Mykola Prykhodko's yard—he has returned, you see, from Siberia, and now probably regrets that he has come back. She is barefoot, and clad in an old skirt and a dark kerchief. It is clear at once that she is not on her way to school; she is going to work in the beet fields. She even has a hoe over her shoulder. She will weed until one o'clock or thereabouts, and then they will pour some mash into a bowl for her. And in that way, she will manage to stay alive until she earns the next bowl.

"But it seems that the mash is not doing you any good, my poor dear," he thinks. "Just look how skinny you've become. Your eyes are glittering in your gaunt face. Oh dear, oh dear. Even your legs have swollen, my darling. Is that why you're walking with such difficulty?"

He raises his cap and greets her graciously: "Good health to you, Oleksiyivna! Are you heading out to the fields?"

"Yes, I am," Tanya smiles wanly, with some embarrassment. She is ashamed that her feet are bare. But what can she do about it? Her feet are so badly swollen that she is scarcely able to fit them into shoes. And so, as soon as she leaves the school, she takes them off.

"Are the children sleeping?"

"Yes, they are."

"Then let them sleep in good health. And may good fortune be yours."

Tanya thanks him and continues on her way. She is hurrying so that she can fulfill the daily quota. Long before lunchtime, you see, children will drag themselves to the beet fields. And all of them will come with bowls and spoons. With stomachs bloated from pigweed, from chaff, from potato peelings. With unnaturally large eyes on emaciated faces, and with hungry mouths prematurely wizened.

They will gather at the field camp where the mash is being boiled in a huge cauldron, and, standing a little ways off, they will wait patiently until their mothers finish working and come to have their lunch. They will wait silently, even pretending that they are not the least bit interested in the huge cauldron in which the mash is bubbling and steaming. And when their mothers share with them their pitifully small portions, they will slurp the hot food greedily, and there will be no need to wash either the bowl or the spoon when they finish eating. They lick them clean, until they are dry and shiny.

Tanya's sons do not come out to the fields Alarmed by a rumour that children were being stolen and slaughtered for meat, she has sternly, most sternly, forbidden them to leave the yard. And so they always meet her by the gate.

Carrying the mash in an enamel cup, she runs all the way home from the fields to the cottage. And she does not run because she fears being late for school; all the way home she has to struggle against the temptation to taste or sip the enticingly fragrant food. She is afraid that if she does taste it, she will not be able to stop eating until the bottom of the cup is visible.

She spots her sons from a long way off—Andriyko and Yurasyk. They are standing by the gate, and each of them has a spoon. Yurasyk's spoon seems especially big; he hangs on to it more tightly than to any toy, never parting with it during the day, and even keeping it at his side at night.

When their mother finally gets home, Yurasyk immediately grabs the kerchief in which the cup is wrapped and dashes to the house with it.

The steaming mash is poured into three bowls: Yurasyk gets the most, Andriyko a little less, and the mother the least of all. The older son attends school already, and so he will get a bowl of millet porridge there—a hot breakfast. The younger one will not get anything more to eat. Except for pancakes made out of acacia blossoms, that fall apart, dry and bitter, in the frying pan, and soup made out of potato peelings. Tanya had furtively dragged home a whole sack of them from the pig farm.

Today Tanya brings home some <u>halushky</u> instead of mash. After dividing them up between her sons and eating a small portion herself, she takes them both by the hand and heads for the school. Andriyko is enrolled in the second shift, and she does not want to leave Yurasyk home alone. She sits him down in the last bench, and he stays there, as quiet as a mouse. All the children have become listless and withdrawn. They sit apathetically at their desks and do not go out to play at recess. Their eyes glitter with hunger— a hunger that wells up and dissolves into bluish spectral shadows.

So the janitor, Granny Natalka, does not have to restrain them at recess, shouting her customary "Watch out! Watch out, or I'll tell the teacher!" Granny Natalka herself can hardly move; she is sucked so dry by hunger that she is just skin and bone. Her face is drawn into a fist, her mouth is sunken, and her teeth, it seems, have all crumbled. Propping her cheek on her hand, she laments without tears: "What is happening, Oleksiyivna? They should at least take pity on the children! If the children die—who will be left to walk this earth?"

What can Tanya say? What does she, a simple village teacher, know about the thoughts and the intentions of those wise government leaders who have felt such a compelling need to create this hunger? She only sees that the people are suffering and dying, and, confounded, she cannot understand why all this is happening.

But, full of fear, she remains silent. She does not share her thoughts with anyone, terrified that for a single word, for a thoughtlessly uttered phrase, she could be proclaimed a kurkul, a follower of Petlyura, or some kind of enemy agent, and dismissed from her job.

And that would mean certain death. A certain, cruel, hungry death for both her and her children. So she remains silent. She will remain silent as long as she lives; she will remain silent, trembling with fear all her life. She will remain silent even after everyone else speaks out, for she will not be able to believe that the change is real, that it will last. And when she is asked about her timorous silence, she will reply: "I've lived so long with such a great fear that I'll be quaking with terror even in my grave."

And so Tanya does not respond to the old woman's lamenting, to her tearless grieving; she walks by silently.

And all Granny Natalka can do is go home and pour out her despair to Granddad Khlypavka: "What is happening in this world of ours, old man?"

But Granddad Khlypavka has more important things on his mind, more important than empty chatter with the old woman.

A while ago he had stopped Neshcheret and asked him who the most powerful man in Russia was nowadays.

"Petro, who is our tsar now?"

"Well, Stalin is. But why?"

"Oh, it's nothing. I just asked for interest's sake."

So, it is Stalin.

The one whose portrait hangs in the village office.

The leader, the teacher, and the father.

Oh, you've drifted a long way off from your little children, daddy dear, a long way off. You sit there, daddy, and you don't see how your evil, hypocritical servants are destroying and killing your children. It's into the kolhosp—and then straight into the next world.

Is this the way things should be done, daddy?

Granddad Khlypavka is deeply convinced that Stalin knows nothing about what is happening. That if one could get to see him and open his eyes, he would immediately come to the defence of his people. He would order that they be fed and kept warm.

So Granddad Khlypavka decides that he will go to see Stalin. Somehow or other he will get to see him, and he will fall to his knees before him.

"Father, save my Ukraine, because there will soon be nothing left but graves and crosses."

And so, Granddad Khlypavka prepares to undertake the long trek to Moscow.

He does not divulge his plans to Tverdokhlib or Neshcheret; he fears that they may not let him go. He only asks that someone else be given the job of guarding the storehouse. He takes some cattle-food—two round pressed linseed cakes—and puts them in a bag along with three fistfuls of dried bread—bread that he and his old woman had been hoarding for the unthinkable day when things might get even worse.

And he says to Granny Natalka: "You'll get by one way or another, Natalka. I'm not going for my own sake—I'm going to save the people."

"But when will you return?" Granny Natalka wails. "In those foreign parts the rooks will pick your bones clean."

"Even rooks won't peck at someone as old and unappetizing as me," Granddad Khlypavka jokes grimly.

And Granny Natalka stands at the gate and watches the old man walk away.

And she wonders sorrowfully if they are fated to ever see each other again in this world.

No, they are not.

One night, not long from now, Granny Natalka will wake up, thinking that someone has called her. Softly and gently, like her deceased mother used to call her when she was still a child. And Granny Natalka will know that it is Death that is calling her. Death has slipped unnoticed into her cottage and, hovering over her, covers her, like a black shadow.

"O Lord, don't take my soul!" Granny Natalka prays. "Let me live until morning. My floor isn't swept, and my cottage isn't whitewashed. I'll be so ashamed to be laid out in a coffin in a house like this!"

And God takes pity on her and tells Death to depart.

And as soon as dawn rises on its spindly legs and creeps over the ground, lugging its swollen stomach in front of itself, Granny Natalka will get up, mix some clay and lime, and set to work patching her cottage. She will carefully whitewash the walls, outline with ochre the earthen embankment abutting the cottage, and spread a fresh layer of clay on the earthen floor.

And then she will light a fire in the stove, heat some water, take a bath, put on a new shirt, and lie down on her bed.

She will lie down, cross her weightless arms on her wasted chest, and say: "Now, my dear Death, you may come."

And Death will approach her once again.

She will lean over granny with her swaying, transparent face, and ask in a hollow voice: "What is your last wish, granny?"

Granny will champ her toothless gums and hesitantly say: "Oh, dear Death, I truly would like to taste some white bread."

And Death will shake her head; she has no bread.

"Then I would at least like some millet porridge."

Once again Death will shake her head; the famine has devoured all the porridge.

Well, if there isn't any, then so be it; she can die without it.

"Ask for something else!" Death will say in despair.

Granny will move her bloodless lips and look kindly at her: "Don't fret yourself, my darling; don't trouble your heart. I don't need or want anything."

And Death, extinguishing granny's life, will gently lift her soul out of her emaciated body, draw her eyelids over her eyes on her waxen face, and tiptoe out of the cottage.

And Granny Natalka will lie there, having fallen silent forever in her neat little cottage that she has tidied up as for a feast day, and that sparkles now like an Easter pysanka under the tender rays of the sun. A good painter has painted it in cheerful colours and rolled it into the green grass, into the orchards flooded with white blossoms . . .

Granddad Khlypavka is travelling by train to the distant northern capital. His son helped him get to Kharkiv by speaking to a conductor that he knew on a passenger train, and the old man travelled like a gentleman in the compartment set aside for employees.

In Kharkiv the conductor said: "You'll have to find your way from here on your own, granddad. Go to the freight station and try to get on a train headed for Moscow."

Granddad thanked him, took his bag, and set out for the station.

For three days and three nights he tried to find a train headed for Moscow. For three days and three nights he crawled around the tracks, hiding from the militiamen chasing away hungry people, militiamen that were losing their voices and could no longer purse their lips to whistle.

"Get awa-a-a-y from here! Come on, get away from here, or you'll end up in jail! Right now!"

But why would they be frightened by the prospect of jail? What kind of a threat is jail to people who are prepared to crawl through fire or dive to the bottom of the ocean just to get a crust of bread! Who, weak from hunger, can scarcely drag themselves to the train station and, opening their empty mouths, cry day and night—without reaching the ears of God: "Bread! Bread!"

And then there is the rumour. A persistent rumour that in Moscow bread is being sold without ration cards—you can get as much as you want as long as you have the money. And even if you have no money when you get there, you still will not perish; where there is bread, there will also be alms.

And so people crawl to the train stations, storm the freight cars, and often a dozen or more peasants pack an empty car and crouch there quietly so as not to be noticed and chased away; they wait until the train moves and then whisper joyfully: "Well, we're on our way!"

They rejoice like little children without knowing that they are not going towards the Red Capital, but in the opposite direction, into the very country that they had abandoned as a living hell.

Granddad Khlypavka is luckier; he does not end up on a train heading back to where he came from. A railroad worker, taking pity on the old man, whispers to him that he should go to the sorting point where a string of freight cars is being prepared to leave for Moscow. And after many difficulties, the old man finally manages to clamber to the roof of one of the cars, where a good number of men like him are already lying.

The train does not start out until evening. And so they lie in the hot sun all day, like in a frying pan. Two of the men, unable to withstand the heat, die. The other men are ready to shove them off right there, but then they come to their senses—if the militiamen find the dead men, they will find the live ones as well. They decide not to push the bodies off the train until they are beyond the city.

When the train finally leaves the city and hurries into the peaceful twilight of the steppes, the men cheer up a little. They begin to stir and talk. Especially at night, so that they will not fall asleep and slip off the roof of the train. They cannot see the others; they can only hear their voices. Occasionally someone smokes, and a fiery dot glows and fades in the night darkness. It glows like the hope that drives these people.

"If only we get there!"

"We will. We've left the worst behind."

"Uncle! Hey, uncle! Is it true that the stores there are bursting with bread?"

"Yes, they are, but not for us."

"Do any of you know what we're travelling on?"

"On a train."

"May your stupid father ride on a train! We're on a train carrying grain, that's what!"

"Grain?"

There is a general commotion.

"You're lying!"

"I swear on the holy cross—it's filled with grain. The railway worker who helped me get on it, told me. All these cars are stuffed with our grain, the entire string of freight cars . . ."

They fall silent; they believe him. They sniff the car—hungrily, greedily.

Then they begin talking again. The neighbour to the old man's right asks: "Are you off to get some daily bread, granddad?"

And when Granddad Khlypavka says that he isn't, they do not believe him.

"Why are you going then?"

"To save the people."

The men all listen to the old man in silence, attentively, without interrupting him.

And they fall into deep thought.

"Well, granddad, may you succeed!"

"Crawl over here, closer to the middle! Because, God forbid, you might fall off."

During the night, two more men die. One of them takes an especially long time to die. He keeps raving about an Oksana, asking her for bread.

Then he grows silent.

He is done eating forever . . .

After making the sign of the cross over him and shoving him off the sloping roof into the eddying black abyss wailing fiercely around them, they move in closer to each other, thinking: "Who will be next?"

And everyone silently pleads: "Not me, Dear God! Not me! I have children waiting for me back home."

In the morning, the train stops for a long time at a station. The peasants listen without making a sound as workers move about down below, tap the wheels with hammers, shout at each other, and curse. Finally the car on which they are lying begins to move forward, slowly at first, and then faster and faster. The station buildings, surrounded by birch trees, sail by, and the hamlet of Mykolayivska is left behind.

"Well, fellows, we're in Russia now."

Some of the men even rise to their knees to get a better look at this Russia, to see what it's like. But then, disenchanted, they lie down again. There is nothing special about it, except that there are more trees and forests; the people are the same as everywhere else, but the villages look exposed, uninviting, and cheerless; the dark unwhitewashed cottages do not float in a sea of cherry orchards, nor do they peep through the trees with gleaming white walls.

"Uncle! Hey, uncle! Why are their cottages so dark?"

"Because they eat dark bread."

"We-e-e-ll . . ."

And a short while later, the speaker adds in a plaintive voice: "I'd eat even dark bread . . ."

"Be patient, we'll be in Moscow before too long . . ."

To Moscow, to Moscow, to Moscow . . . But as soon as the hungry men reach the outskirts, Moscow greets them with <u>NKVD</u>

patrols, pulls them off the cars and platforms, packs them into empty freight cars, and unceremoniously ships them back— Moscow does not want to accept guests like that!

Granddad Khlypavka slides down off the car in the nick of time and shuffles off into some nearby bushes.

He stays there until dusk. And when it turns dark, he decides to finish his journey on foot. He makes his way to the railroad tracks and limps along, heading for the lights that flood the northern horizon.

And so, Granddad Khlypavka would have got to Moscow, and he would have seen Stalin and kneeled before him, if it were not for a river, and the bridge that spanned it, and the implacable guard on that bridge.

The guard cocks his rifle and turns the old man back: "Get a move on, granddad, get a move on! This is a restricted zone!"

And Granddad Khlypavka starts shuffling back to Ukraine.

He walks for a long time through fields and forests, down narrow roads and wide ones, through villages, towns and cities, but he does not look around or try to remember things so he can relate them back home. His curiosity has long since been extinguished, and not even a spark remains in his faded eyes.

And the old man's conscience is troubling him, because he has not been able to get help for his people. It troubles him, gnaws at his heart, and further drains his already failing strength.

One morning he reaches a regional centre and manages to make his way to a square. He lies down under a post with a black loudspeaker on it and prepares to die.

Placing his bag under his head, he crosses his arms on his chest and turns his thoughts to God, praying for forgiveness of the sins he has committed both knowingly and unknowingly. And just as he finishes praying, and closes his eyes so that he will not see the faceless one take away his soul, something crackles and snorts above him, and a brisk metallic voice calls out a morning greeting.

"Good morning, comrades!"

May the devil take you! They won't even let you die in peace.

And Granddad Khlypavka, whether he wants to or not, listens to some bravura music and the latest news.

And then the voice in the loudspeaker changes, and a woman's cheerful voice warbles: "And now listen to a sketch about the happy prosperous life of the Ukrainian farmers who have joined the kolhosps."

The loudspeaker seems to clear its throat, and then still another voice, that of a man, begins speaking.

"The kolhosp village lives, flourishes, and gains in strength. Honest work has yielded astounding results. Marvellous grain crops grow bountifully and densely, and completely hide a kolhosp farmer from view. Their full, green spikes sway in step with the happy, animated, fortunate face of the kolhosp farmer, and they assure him: 'There will be a good harvest!' And because of this, as stated by our leader and teacher, Comrade Stalin, the kolhosp members will be even better off, and, instead of being middle income farmers, they will become rich."

The old man cannot stand such a shameless mocking of the truth.

He groans heavily, raises his head, and spots a militiaman approaching him.

"Sonny, be so kind! Shut up that barking dog, and let me at least die in peace."

And so, instead of standing before the judgement of the Heavenly Judge, the old man has to stand before an earthly one. And it is not his guardian angel that hovers behind him, but the same militiaman who dragged him away from the loudspeaker and the post, supporting him so that he would not fall.

"Well, granddad, did you utter counterrevolutionary words?"

"But how was I to stay quiet when that thing was so shamelessly spouting blatant lies!"

"So, you did say them . . . Write this down: the accused has admitted that he engaged in counterrevolutionary agitation against the kolhosp order."

And they lead the old man off to sit behind bars.

After about two weeks, Granddad Khlypavka feels a lot better; "living in a state-run guesthouse, and eating food provided by the state," he has regained some of his strength.

They feed him not all that badly, and he does not have to work; they just order him to keep the cell clean. It would be possible to live like this forever without any real complaints, but he cannot stop thinking about his native village, about his fellow villagers who are swelling from hunger. And so, after thinking about the matter for a long time, and after asking if prisoners are fed like this in all the jails, he gets hold of a piece of paper and asks a fellow inmate to write a letter for him to Tarasivka.

"What should I write, granddad?"

"Write the following, my son . . . Good day to those of you who are still alive; these greetings are being sent by Granddad Voron . . . I did not get to see Comrade Stalin—they didn't let me go to him. I'll tell you more about it when I see you, because right now, I'm in jail. But don't let this news worry you. Life isn't all that bad in here; the authorities are respectful, they don't beat us, and everyone gets a portion of bread and corn meal gruel three times a day. So, listen to the advice I'm going to give you, my good people.

"Stop whatever you're doing and head for Khorolivka or Poltava while you're still alive. Lie down under a post on which there is a radio, and swear at that radio for all you're worth. The militiaman will come running and take you to court. And from there you will be taken straight to jail. But don't be afraid of that, my dear countrymen, because today it is only in jail that you can survive; everywhere else there is only famine and devastation.

"Have you finished writing that? And now, give my regards to my old woman, Granny Natalka, and seal the letter."

And the letter is sealed and sent to the province of Poltava to Tarasivka.

And for a long time after that, Granddad Khlypavka asks every new wave of prisoners: "Are there any people from Tarasivka among you? My good people, have you by chance met anyone from Tarasivka?" And he is worried that his countrymen may have not done what he told them to do.

The old man does not know that Granny Natalka is no longer on this earth. He does not know that he is fated never to return to his native village and see his fellow villagers. Death—the same Death that, fearing the militiaman, stepped away from him in the square—seeks him out and finds him in jail.

Perhaps the guard has dozed off, or is fooled by Death, but he does not notice a tall, lean woman with a scythe on her back slip past him. She makes her way into the prison where everyone is sleeping and walks from cell to cell searching for the old man.

She finally finds him and, without wasting any time, waves her scythe over him while he sleeps. She waves it, cuts short the over-ripened spike of life and carefully scoops it up, so that it will not fall to the concrete floor, so that not a single kernel of unlived days will roll away.

And so, Granddad Khlypavka dies an easy death. And we will see him off on his final journey. To the most obscure corner of the city cemetery, where beggars, tramps, and prisoners have been buried from time immemorial. To a hastily dug hole.

We will cast a handful of soil into that hole: "May the earth rest like feathers on your bones, granddad!" We will stand for a while, bowing our heads over the silent little mound, and we will depart quietly, no longer thinking about Granddad Khlypavka, but about the man to whom the old man had hoped to bring his pure heart, his great hope, his fervent prayer for all his people. The man who had so cruelly repulsed him.

We will think about the horrifying crimes that this man has committed and will continue committing; about the rivers of blood and the oceans of suffering with which he will flood the earth under his rule. And about the fact that this man, thank God, is not eternal; what is eternal is the nation that he is trying to suck dry. And that the time will come when Death will cut down the abhorrent spike bursting with blackened blood and kick it away in revulsion.

And here we will pause for a moment and ask the spinner who spins the threads of human fates: "Will this man go unpunished?

Will he avoid an accounting for his abominable crimes by hiding in his grave?"

And we will think at once about God.

That if He does not exist, then He must be conjured up. That there must be a fitting punishment, that this evil man must not escape His judgement.

Let God ascend His Heavenly Throne and listen to Granddad Khlypavka.

And then He will ask: "How am I to judge him, if he has not died as yet?"

"Well, God, I'll wait."

"Well then, wait. And while you wait you can live in paradise."

So Granddad lives in paradise, but he soon tires of having nothing to do. So he goes once again to God.

"Give me some work to do, God, because I'm bored out of my mind."

"What kind of work am I to give you?"

"Give me a plough and a harrow, God, and a horse or a couple of oxen, and a scythe, a rake, and a flail. And assign me a small plot of land."

And God gives Granddad Khlypavka everything that he asks for. And Granddad Khlypavka continues to sow and reap until Stalin finally dies.

And when Stalin dies, the Almighty calls both of them to Him and places them in front of Him, Granddad Khlypavka on His right, and Stalin on His left.

And, as Stalin stands there, black from all his sins, the blood from his innocent victims will lap at his feet.

And Granddad Khlypavka will be quiet and gentle even in his great anger. He will not demand; he will only plead: "Judge us, God. Let it be as you say."

And God will ask him: "Of what sins do you accuse this man?"

"He wanted to destroy my nation."

And Stalin will stamp his feet angrily, splashing blood in all directions: "You're lying! I worried about the happiness of my people day and night! It was Beria! Beria!"

But Granddad Khlypavka will not even look at him.

"How can you prove your terrible accusation?" God then asks.
"Call my witnesses, God."

And the Almighty will call His angels and tell them to bring the old man's witnesses.

And men and women who died from hunger in the prime of their lives will come in; and it will be terrible to look at them.

And there will be thousands upon thousands of them.

And mothers with their infants in their swollen arms will come in, and the babies will be sucking with their dead mouths at withered breasts that do not have a single drop of milk.

And it will be terrible to look at these infants and their mothers.

And there will be thousands upon thousands of them.

And old people will stand before God, their arms and legs all tangled and covered with lime—and it will be terrible to look at these aged people.

And there will be thousands upon thousands of them.

And people, tortured and murdered in prisons and work camps, will come to stand before the Almighty.

And after seeing them, God will shudder and hide His face in His hands: "Take them away! I cannot bear to look at them."

And then Granddad Khlypavka will approach Him.

"Do not shut your eyes, O Lord—You are God, not a mere mortal! You teach us in Your Holy Writings: whosoever walks past a crime, is himself a criminal. Whosoever holds out a helping hand to a bandit, is himself a bandit. And who is to judge between us, if You turn away from us?"

Then God will remove His hand from His eyes, and painfully ask the witnesses: "Who caused your death? Who murdered you?"

And they will all turn towards Stalin.

"And what do you say now?" God will ask Stalin.

And Stalin will be silent.

Then the Almighty will turn to Granddad Khlypavka.

"I permit you, my good man, to pronounce a punishment for this cruel tyrant."

But Granddad Khlypavka will not do it.

"I did not bring him forth into the world, and it is not for me to judge him. Punish him Yourself, O Lord."

And God will ponder heavily.

And, after thinking about it, He will say: "Forgive me, my good people, because I am not the judge that you need. There is no punishment in the universe that would be commensurate with the heinous crimes of this man!"

III

The grain is ripening.

The aroma of a rich harvest inundates the land, filling its curved chalice to overflowing. It settles in a rich golden hue on sharpened scythes, binders, vehicles, and carts, on horses and people, and on the tufted sheaves, stacked in stooks of sixty or thirty, that rise in towering peaks. And it gilds the trembling arms that pick up the first sheaf and cast it into the drum of the threshing machine.

Villages, rising like phoenixes from the ashes, are being reborn out of the cruel, ruinous hunger. And the windmills that seemed to have been stilled forever are coming alive and waving their wings like birds of good fortune that, clinging happily to the earth, try to lift it into the heavens. And the grindstones, unsealed once again, are turning, and flour pours like vernal streams in cottages and yards.

Over there, kneading troughs are ready, and here, sleeves are rolled up, and still farther over, bake ovens are fired up. And even though the boards in the kneading trough have dried out and shrunk, it is not a problem—as long as there is something to put into them. And even though hands have grown unaccustomed to this work, it does not matter—as long as there is something to knead. To pull out pieces of spongy dough, shape them into white rounds, place them on an oven shovel and set them in the oven.

And now, be quiet—walk without stamping your feet; be still and do not breathe. Everyone must fall silent, be still, and await in joyous expectation, because the miracle of all miracles is happening!

And then they will take the first loaves out of the oven, and it will be difficult to say from where the radiance is emanating—from the warm golden bread, or from the eyes of the mothers and wives.

The hunger has passed, perished, like a horrible dream. And, slowly, people begin to forget how the children looked when their little arms and legs were skinny like sticks of kindling wood, how ghastly the older people looked when they were filled with that deathly water. The carts packed with corpses are forgotten, as are the wide common graves filled with lime, and the groaning that, rising to the heavens, flowed over the Ukrainian land day after day, month after month.

The hunger is forgotten so completely that the instigator of the cruel hunger—a man who always wore military attire as if forever prepared to fight, to shoot, and to slaughter—is sincerely called Father by millions of people.

They will carry his portrait, exalt him in songs, and name their sons after him. And so, thousands of little Josephs will grow up to become adult Josephs.

And when he dies, they will flock from all directions with heart-rending wails.

And they will be trampled in the press to get at least a petal, at least a little leaf from the funeral wreaths piled high on his catafalque.

Wreaths . . . not stones . . .

The calamitous times seem like a nightmare to Tanya. And why bother to recall them? It is better to cross them out of one's memory, to breathe the rich air of the present, to revel in the cheerful faces of the people, and to walk down a smooth path through the steppe with a bundle in your hand.

There is no reason for her to hurry; she rose very early in the morning, and the whole day lies ahead of her. She is coming back from visiting her mother. Her mother is all shrivelled; the skin on her face is gathered in wrinkles and covered with a greyish-green moss; her mouth is sunken, and she moves it incessantly—chewing the remnants of her life.

Tanya spent an entire day with her mother. She tidied everything up, and read a short letter to her from Fedor—he had been too lazy to write a separate letter to his sister!

"We are all alive and well, and we wish you the same. I congratulate you, mother—you have another grandson! He's a lively one, that's for sure, and when he grows up he'll be a fine plaything for the girls (he should be ashamed to write something like that to his mother!) but as for now, all he does is suck milk and then pee in his cradle—he'll probably be a fireman . . ."

Well, everything is fine with Fedor, and so it is possible, as the saying goes, to live and praise God. Tanya has no reason to be worried; she is, you could say, happy, but she feels somewhat uncomfortable, because Hanzha is walking beside her.

He had caught up with her on the road. Recognizing her, he greeted her joyfully and began asking about the villagers—who was still alive, and who had passed on.

There were, however, two people he did not ask about—Olha and Volodya.

He does not say much about himself.

He has spent time in prison, was released before his term was up, and was coming now from the district of Kryvorizhzhya, where he had looked up some pre-Revolutionary friends. They wanted him to become a member of a factory management team. He had already agreed to this, and was just dropping in to Tarasivka to get a few things; he was planning to go back the very same day.

Tanya listens silently. She does not try to counsel him or to persuade him to do otherwise. Sensing the unhealed sense of injury that burns within him, she keeps glancing at him surreptitiously.

His hair has turned completely grey, and his eyes are darker than they were before.

They climb to the top of a high, expansive hillock and stop for a moment. The village of Tarasivka spreads below them. Drowning in orchards and girded by a river, it lures you to it with its small white cottages.

"And there's our village," Tanya says pensively.

Hanzha does not respond. He tugs at his grey moustache as if he wants to tear it off, but is unable to. And, as he looks yearningly and unblinkingly at the village below him—the cottages, the orchards, the gardens, the streets—his entire life flows before his eyes, a life tied so closely to this land.

And he is not at all certain that he can break with it so easily.

Kyiv, 1966

Yevhen Hutsalo

Yevhen Hutsalo: Biographical Note

Yevhen Hutsalo, a prolific and popular Ukrainian writer and journalist, began his writing career in the 1960s as one of an informal grouping of young poets and authors known as "the Sixtiers." These writers came to the fore during the "literary thaw" that began with Khrushchev's denunciation of Stalin at the 20th Congress of the Communist Party in 1956 and lasted, precariously at times, until his fall from power in 1964. Freeing themselves from Stalinist ideology and the confines of "socialist realism," these writers, especially the poets, embraced the refreshing wave of cultural and political liberalization, and began writing in a lyrical and innovative manner that injected new life into Ukrainian literature and continued invigorating it even after the reimposition of state censorship.

Hutsalo was born into the family of a village schoolteacher in the district of Vinnytsya in 1937. After graduating from the Nizhen Pedagogical Institute in 1959, he turned to journalism, a field in which he gained wide acclaim and recognition.

He made his first appearance on the literary scene with a book of poetry that was published in 1960, and he continued writing and publishing poetry for the rest of his life. It is in the field of prose, however, that he left his most lasting mark in Ukrainian literature. He is the author of more than thirty collections of novellas and short stories, several of which are directed at both children and adult readers, and a novel written as a trilogy.

Hutsalo's prose abounds in finely drawn psychological portraits, detailed accounts of village and urban life, and lyrical descriptions of nature, and his masterful recreation of the vernacular speech of his characters holds immense appeal for native Ukrainian readers. In works depicting the dark side of life, he is always searching for the noble human deed that has the power to nuture optimism and hope in the most tragic and desperate situations. This faith in the basic goodness of human nature is subtly exemplified in "Holodomor: Murder by Starvation," the story included in this collection.

Hutsalo was awarded several of Ukraine's top literary prizes, including the Taras Shevchenko Prize in 1985. His works have been translated into most of the languages of the former Soviet Union, as well as into many Western European languages. He died in 1995.

Holodomor: Murder by Starvation

At that time I had not yet been born, but I can see, as if we were face to face, the peasant Pavlo Trokhymovych Muzyka. Not overly tall, his body is contorted, twisted like a bush, and his hands are also like bushes, as is his head. His eyes, sunken and swaddled in a film of mucous, look, for all the world, like two tiny, terrified spiders that, darting and scurrying unceasingly, never find any cracks in which to hide.

It is almost dawn; the grey fabric of the sky is embroidered with golden stars. A fragrant dew wafts from the elders, the burdock plants, and the wormwood, and now and then the birds of spring call out, their voices resonant, like tiny flutes. But their songs do not alleviate the predawn sorrow in the village.

The village is somnolent and still, as if drugged.

Pavlo Muzyka is walking towards the church.

The church stands on a high hillock, beside a pond whose dark azure waters slumber among dense willows.

On this fine Sunday morning no one is going to church, because no Divine Liturgy has been celebrated in it since the previous autumn. It has not been celebrated ever since the village priest disappeared. One day he was there—his neighbours had seen him. But the very next morning it was as if he had ascended into heaven.

And it was as if no black car had come for the priest, and as if no one had taken him away. And a day later, his house, with its shingled roof, burned down at midnight. It blazed like a candle. And it was as if no one had started the fire, as if the house had burst into flames on its own. And no one had rushed to the fire, and no one had tried to put it out; it was as if the villagers did not see that fire, as if everyone had become blind and deaf. And by morning the fire was out, and the ashes were cold.

Pavlo Muzyka walks past the charred ruins marked by a blackened bake oven, and heads for the church along a winding path, up an incline. He is going to the church as he has always gone, because an unfathomable power keeps urging him onwards. Maybe a Divine Liturgy will be celebrated today after all? Maybe another priest will appear in their village?

At that time I had not yet been born, but I can see Pavlo Muzyka walking up the incline to the church—and halting abruptly in amazement.

The door is open!

The door that has been padlocked all autumn and all winter. Perhaps a priest has actually appeared? Crossing himself with the tips of three fingers, Pavlo Muzyka cautiously enters the porch and, casting a backward glance at the village, slowly pokes his bushy head into the church.

And then something sucks him into the church, and Pavlo Muzyka disappears.

Fear grips the village. Pavlo Muzyka, walking from house to house and from yard to yard, is telling everyone that, the night before, thieves had robbed the church. They had taken away everything that could be removed.

"They've stolen our icons!"

But they had stolen not only the icons, but all the church paraphernalia as well. You would have thought that these things were of no use to anyone, and yet they had stolen them.

"And they had no fear of God in heaven!"

No, they had no fear; they stole the icons and did not expect any punishment to befall them.

"Were they strangers, or our own people?"

Just try and guess. You could suspect strangers, but you could also suspect your own people, because people everywhere had drifted away from their spiritual moorings.

"Let's go and find the thieves!"

In no time, feeble women and elderly grannies—those with enough strength to get up from their sleeping benches or to crawl down from their <u>oven beds</u>—gather around him like a clump of withered tumbleweed. Standing in their midst, the red-headed Pavlo Muzyka is a flaming ember, crackling and scattering words like sparks.

"Might it not be Vasyl Hnoyovy who crept into the church and stole everything? Let's go to Hnoyovy's home! And you may be sure that he didn't do it alone!"

In the distance, the pillaged church, its azure walls shining resplendently above the village, seems like the voice of the lofty and incensed heaven that is sending them forth to seek revenge and punishment. The mindless human tumbleweed rolls to the outskirts of the village where Vasyl Hnoyovy—a destitute wretch and horse thief, who used to pray and still prays to the god of the drinking glass—lives in a ramshackle hut plastered with mud and thatched with reeds.

A boy in a torn shirt and patched trousers is walking towards the mob; he is barefoot, and his eyes are blue thistles on a face pock-marked like a sparrow's egg.

"What's that under your shirt?"

His grimy feet, covered in warts, are rooted to the ground, and his eyes are terrified, as if wrathful wasps had alighted on his wild pupils.

"Come on! Show us what's under your shirt!"

And they grab him by his shaggy matted hair, tug violently at his collar, and thrust their clawing hands into the bosom of his tattered shirt.

"It's the Mother of God with the Divine Child!"

And truly, out of the bosom of the coarse linen shirt on the boy's gaunt chest, the Mother of God, holding the Holy Infant in her arms, ascends into the sunlight of the spring day. A radiant, otherworldly glow surrounds the tranquil holy faces, and their eyes are filled with kindness and mercy.

And at the same time—with a gentle reproach.

As if they are not able to comprehend how they ended up in the coarse linen bosom, how they have ascended into the light of the spring day, and who is standing before them now.

They are holy, righteous eyes that are continually asking and, at the same time, answering their own questions; eyes that are always forgiving—for it is in their unfailing forgiveness that their immortality lies.

"Where did you get it? Who are you?"

"I'm Marko . . ."

"Thief! Where did you get the icon?"

"I found it!" the young boy's voice rings out. "Over there, in the weeds."

"You're lying!"

"It's the honest truth!"

"Cross yourself!"

His childish hand flies upwards to make the sign of the cross and touches his forehead.

"He's a thief—and he dares to cross himself!"

The wave of human insanity seethes and comes to a boil; hands flail and grab the child. The boy jerks away, screams, and bites a hand; the icon of the Mother of God with the Divine Child flies into the weeds at the feet of the mob.

"He's a thief—a tramp!"

"A godless person!"

"A Judas!"

Angry voices buzz and swarm; the mob lunges forward and knocks the boy to the ground. Clawing hands tear at him. As if they have to destroy this evil right here and now—as if then there will be no more evil left on this earth. As if this is the last of all evils. As if there must not be a single seed left for breeding.

The icon cracks loudly under Pavlo Muzyka's knee, and the madness passes.

The people recoil in horror, avoiding each other's eyes.

The unknown boy—a heap of unmoving, crumpled rags drenched in blood—lies on the road with his legs curled under him. With bared teeth, his tongue lolling out of his mouth, and an eye ripped out of its socket, he looks ghastly—like death itself.

And the clump of human tumbleweed rolls away and disperses in all directions, as if it had never been there.

But Pavlo Muzyka remains on his knees beside the murdered boy for a little while longer, as if he cannot believe what has happened. As if he thinks the boy is being cunning, that he is deceiving him, and that at any moment he will jump up from the ground and run away. He is a thief—a thief and a tramp.

But the thief-tramp does not stir, and he does not breathe.

Pavlo Muzyka slowly staggers to his feet and, gathering up the shattered icon with trembling fingers, shoves the splinters into the bosom and pockets of his shirt. And then he backs away from the murdered child. He backs away, fearfully watching the child: will he get up?

The boy has pressed himself close to his saviour, the earth. And the earth, having liberated him, does not release him.

Harkusha, his face covered with a stubby growth of bristles, crosses the threshold and stands framed in the doorway. The master of the house, Pavlo Muzyka, is seated at the table; to his left sits his wife Mariya; to his right—his daughter Halya. With six unblinking eyes they stare at their guest, who is tottering, on the verge of collapsing.

The guest does not speak, and they too are surly, silent.

Finally, Harkusha makes a champing sound with his lips, swallows with difficulty, and says: "You're eating . . ."

"Yes, we're eating," the mistress grumbles.

"I smell meat," Harkusha sniffs the air.

"Of course. We slaughtered a pig, and now we're enjoying fresh pork." It sounds as if Pavlo is not speaking, but barking.

"A pig?" Harkusha says in disbelief. "What pig?"

"The one you didn't take away from us!"

Wrinkling his brow, Harkusha recalls: "But we did take a pig."

The mistress glances fearfully at their neighbour and then at her husband.

"O Pavlo, Pavlo! What kind of a pig are we eating? For the love of God, don't say such things, because he might end up believing you. And then they'll come to take away a pig, but where in the world do we have a pig?"

"Say it's a pig!" The master is angry now.

"But it's not a pig—it's a hedgehog. We're eating it with some fresh nettles. Halya caught the hedgehog in a clump of hazelnut trees, and I picked the nettles."

"Say it's a pig! Let him hear that and let him suffer."

"It's a hedgehog, a hedgehog . . ."

Harkusha continues to gnaw at his dry lips as if he were determined to chew them up.

"I heard the grindstone rumbling in your barn at night."

"When? Which night?" Mariya turns pale.

"It was your ears that were rumbling!" Pavlo Muzyka says, rising from the table. "Why would our grindstone be rumbling? Didn't you, along with Vasyl Hnoyovy and Mykola Khashchuvaty, make sure that you found all our grain and took it away?"

Clutching at the doorpost, Harkusha slowly sinks to his knees and, putting his hands together imploringly, as if in prayer, says: "Forgive me!"

"There's no forgiveness for you."

"Forgive me!" Harkusha crawls on his knees over the dirt floor from the doorstep to the middle of the room and comes to a stop under the main beam.

"We searched for your grain, but we didn't take it all, because we didn't find it all. If we had found it, we would have taken it, but we didn't find it. And now you grind it at night, so that no one will hear you. But I do hear you, because I can't sleep at night. And I can't sleep because I'm hungry. I feel as if I'm dying, but I just can't seem to die."

"Oh, go ahead and die. People like you should long since have been lying in the ground."

"I'd die, but I feel sorry for my children; they're swollen from hunger. How many of them do I have left now? Three—but I had five. Kateryna's gone, and so is Mykhaylo. And the ones that are left—Hrytsko, and Petro, and Yukhym—they're all sick. If only I had a bit of food to put into their hungry mouths."

"There's nothing!"

"Yes, there is! I know it! The grindstone was rumbling in your barn last week as well."

"Pavlo . . ." Mariya says pleadingly, touching her husband's elbow.

Muzyka jerks his elbow away as if he were scalded: "Why are you saying: 'Pavlo . . .'? There's not so much as a single kernel. Don't you know that? This Herod took all the grain that we stored in the ground, and now he comes to beg? Let him perish!"

"But the children . . ." Halya musters up the courage to speak.

"Let his children all croak as well, so that no seed of his will be left on this earth."

"You believe in God," Harkusha remains on his knees. "If you have God in your heart, take pity on my children."

"Don't even mention the Lord, because for the likes of you there is no God, neither in heaven, nor on earth."

"I'm guilty; I'm guilty before you and before all the people, but my children are not to blame."

"Get out of my house; don't provoke my wrath."

Rising to his feet, Harkusha bursts into tears.

"Get out, you beast!" Pavlo Muzyka roars, stamping his foot.

Stumbling, Harkusha makes his way out of the house. Halya wipes her eyes with her sleeve and turns away to the window; her mother's teeth are chattering uncontrollably.

"So, he feels sorry for his children; he's finally come to his senses. But did he have any pity for the children of others? Does it mean that other people's children can swell from hunger and die, while he goes begging for food for his own? Well, there will be no food, neither for him, nor for his children, because his seed is not needed on this earth. The earth is grieving today because of demented beasts like him, and tomorrow there will be even more of them.

"As for the two of you, didn't you know that this werewolf doesn't sleep at night? You wanted to have flour. Well, you'd better hide the grindstone, or he'll report it as well. Why are the two of you pouting like screech owls? Eat the hedgehog. And then, Halya, you'll go and see if there's anything in the bushes. Look for more hedgehogs; they make a good meal. Yesterday I saw a snake in the forest, so I'll go and catch some snakes; they can also be eaten."

A wave of nausea sweeps over Mariya, and she gags.

"Stop gagging! Yesterday two swallows flew into the porch. How could you let them get away?"

"They just flew out . . ."

"They just flew out," he mocks her. "Make sure that they don't fly away again . . . And if sparrows fly into the barn, catch them with your hands or your skirt, but be sure to catch them. Do you know what Pylyp the teacher does? He lives in the school, so how does he supplement the little that he has? He opens all the windows in the school, the sparrows fly in, and he beats them with a club, or catches them in a net. And then he has roasted sparrows."

After carefully shutting both the outside door and the one leading into the porch, Pavlo Muzyka walks back into the room.

"Get it, Halya," he says, and he glances anxiously out the window.

Halya climbs up on the bench and retrieves a small greyish loaf of bread from behind a peeling icon. Her father picks up a knife, cuts off three thin slices, places them on the table, and passes the rest of the loaf back to his daughter. "Hide it behind the icon; let the icon protect it."

Picking up their spoons, they begin eating the soup made from nettles and the hedgehog.

Far up in the distant heights the evening glitters with greenish stars, while down below the ground is covered with fog, white and frothy, like fragrant, fresh warm milk that is still foaming.

Pavlo Muzyka raps on his neighbour's windowpane with his knuckles, and the glass rings out like thin ice cracking on a pond. The house remains silent.

"They're either swollen from hunger, or grown numb from the cold."

And once again there is the sound of thin ice cracking.

After a while, the door leading into the porch sighs like an old man, and the outside door wheezes like the rasping chest of a consumptive. Then finally, Harkusha pokes out his gloomy face etched with a web of wrinkles—wrinkles that exude darkness, the darkness of a soul in which there is not a single ray of light. He struggles to recognize the man before him. And then his gaze drops to the man's hands, as if he hopes to see something in them; but the hands are empty.

It occurs to Pavlo that the man is close to death.

"Take pity on me, Pavlo . . ."

"I was just walking across the meadows," Pavlo says, pointing with his head in the evening fog.

"So, what's in the meadows?"

"Well, I glanced under the willows . . . Come on, let's go. I'll take you there, because you won't find the spot on your own. Or can't you walk anymore?"

"Why go there? Why?" Harkusha asks sharply.

"Come on, because no one else will take you there. I saw it with my own eyes . . . I'll take pity on you, now that you're begging for pity. Come on, let's go."

Walking along the boundary of the field, they cross the garden and go into the green meadows where the willows stand in the fog like a weary <u>kozak</u> army; but there is a deathly silence—not a single horse neighs. Coming to a small azure well in which the water is hardly gurgling, Pavlo Muzyka stops and points at a nearby bush.

"Your child's sitting over there. Isn't that your little Yukhym?"

Harkusha takes a good look. Yes, his seven-year-old son Yukhym is sitting on the ground, huddled against some branches. His round little head with its blond tuft of hair is resting on his left shoulder. He is sleeping. And his hands are folded on his knees.

"Yukhym," his father calls.

The boy does not stir; he must be sleeping soundly, for his father's voice does not rouse him.

"Yukhym!" Harkusha calls again.

"He doesn't hear you . . ."

"Why don't you hear me, my son?"

"He won't hear you! He's fallen asleep forever. You're too late. When I was walking by, he was still picking at something on his chest. And he tried to say something, but only his lips moved. But he did say something; he was talking, but very quietly. I went to get you, so that you could take your child home, because evening was falling. Well, that's how it is. We got here too late."

The father falls to his knees beside his son and lifts him in his arms; the boy's body slumps awkwardly, and the little head with its blond tuft falls backwards.

"My dear little Yukhym," Harkusha groans.

"He doesn't hear you; take him home to his mother. It's because of our sins, our mortal sins. It's because of our sins that we are pitied neither by God nor by man. We're paying fully for our sins. Was your little Yukhym to blame for anything? He wasn't guilty, but the punishment fell on him, an innocent child."

"You're the one who is to blame! You're the one," Harkusha's lips turn blue.

"I'm to blame?"

"I begged you for a bit of bread. Not for myself, for my children."

"How am I supposed to have bread for your children when you took all my grain away from me? I don't have any, not even for myself. Carry him home—he no longer needs any bread. His suffering has ended, but yours isn't over yet. Such a fine boy! You'd think he was still alive. And he looks a lot like you."

Pavlo Muzyka is truly grieved; he crosses himself, and then slowly leaves the meadow. He turns around. Harkusha is still on his knees, unable to get up while holding the child. And he is howling like a wolf . . .

Halya lifts the lid of the trunk and peers inside. Why has she felt so drawn to the trunk all day? Why can she think about nothing else?

She peers into the trunk, and her heart flames; her lips are wreathed in a smile, and she whispers softly: a nightingale in a cranberry bush.

Her hand reaches for a little chest, and out of it she takes a string of coral beads—a blindingly bright strand that winds sinuously, shimmering and twisting like a brilliant, colourful ray of light. And now this ray floods her soul, and sparkling embers flicker and flash in her heart.

Halya tentatively rests the string of coral beads on her chest and then fastens it around her neck. And she looks into a mirror that hangs between the windows.

The dark eyes that gaze out at Halya from the mirror are mournful, but she cares nothing about that! And she cares nothing about the unhealthy flush on her sunken cheeks. She wants to see herself in the coral necklace, and in order to do so, she must step a bit to one side and raise herself on tiptoe.

The necklace is like a rainbow in the heavens.

And adorned with that necklace, it seems to Halya that it is no longer she who is looking out from the mirror, but rather an unknown, beautiful girl—one who is both strange and familiar. Who is this girl? Can it truly be she, Halya? She finds it hard to believe, but, yes, it is she, Halya.

Hurriedly taking her mother's embroidered blouse out of the trunk, and finding her mother's green jerkin beneath it, she takes off her ragged old clothes and changes into the holiday attire. She knows full well that there are no good boots or shoes to be had; nevertheless, hoping against hope to find a pair, she continues rummaging in the trunk. There are none. Well, she'll just have to wash her feet with extra care.

The water pail is on the bench, but there is only a thin film of water in it. Well, she'll have to fetch some water. Her family has its own well under the willow tree by the gate.

Grabbing a pail, she rushes into the porch and bumps into her mother Mariya on the doorstep. Her mother is coming in from the garden; she is groaning and carrying the spade she has been using in one hand, and pressing her other hand against the small of her back.

Alarmed by the unexpected encounter, Mariya jumps back, whispering: "Oh, a thief!"

Halya laughs gaily: "It's not a thief, mummy; it's me!"

"Oh, it really is you!" her mother says, peering more closely at her daughter and finally recognizing her. "Where are you going all decked out like that?"

"To fetch some water. I'm going to bring some water from the well."

"You're all dressed up!" the mother can scarcely believe what she sees. "You're all dressed up to go to the well . . ."

"I want to go out!"

"You want to go out?"

"I want to have a good time—have fun with the girls! Oh my, how I want to sing!"

"What kind of good time? What kind of singing? What's wrong with you, my child?"

"I thought I heard the girls singing. Isn't it a holiday today?"

"Holy, holy, holy . . . What's wrong with you, my child? Come, let's go into the house. You must not go outdoors dressed up like this; it isn't a holiday, and people will think . . ."

"But the boys . . . Aren't the boys singing?"

"No they're not. Who has ever heard of singing in broad daylight? The lads in our village aren't singing."

And the mother sighs, shuts the porch door, takes the pail away from her daughter, and leads her into the house. She is close to tears, and her troubled heart is filled with grief and sorrow. What has happened to her Halya? Has something gone wrong with her mind? Because these days there are ever so many people whose minds have grown dim. O Lord, look down and take pity on us; do not punish us so terribly, for in what way is she to blame, this girl-child, who has not yet lived fully in this world?

"You're saying that the boys and girls are singing? Oh no, no one in our village has sung for a long time now. Come, let's sit down on the bed over here, and we'll sing. The two of us will sing together, because who else is there for you to sing with in the village? You've dressed yourself beautifully—as if for your wedding. If only you had blue and red ribbons for your hair. And if only you had boots with heels on them. And if only you could bathe in sweet flowering herbs . . ."

"I wanted to fetch some water . . ."

"You can't go outside; let's sing indoors for a while. Which song shall we sing? My mind is clouded over, and not even the tiniest star twinkles in it."

"Let's sing 'Don't warble, O nightingale . . .'"

"And they truly aren't warbling. They should have flown back by now, but they're late . . .

"Goodness, how warm your forehead is, and you're shaking, as if something had given you a bad scare."

Mariya wails in a sorrowful voice:

> "Oh, in a cherry orchard
> A nightingale warbled . . ."

And Halya joins in, nestling against her mother's shoulder:

> "Tweet, tweet, tweet, tweet, tweet, tweet,
> A nightingale warbled . . ."

The mother and daughter sing as if they are lamenting over a corpse—there is no joy in their voices. As they sing, they cuddle together and close their eyes, and when they open them, Pavlo Muzyka is there. Having walked in silently, he is now standing by the oven and listening, and the look on his face is one of astonishment, alarm.

Finally, the mother and daughter fall silent, and he says: "I almost thought I'd gone mad when I heard singing in the house. What's going on? Halya, why are you dressed up like that? Are you going out to an evening party? Evening is still a long way off; it's still daylight outside."

"Our Halya wants to go out and enjoy herself."

"A girl can enjoy her youthful days only once," he says thoughtfully. "But why is she all decked out like that?"

"Let her at least walk about the house in her fine clothes. Let her at least sing in the house. Because where are there any evening parties these days? Where are there any young women's work bees?"

"Yes, you're right . . ."

And he stares with dismay at his wife and daughter, who are clutching one another in a tight embrace.

Twilight is falling, and a new moon, like a kozak's grey forelock, shines in the sky.

Pavlo Muzyka lowers a pail on a rope into the well; he lowers it slowly, all the while casting his eyes about and listening carefully. His neighbour, the old peasant woman Yustyna, is seated on a bench dug firmly into the ground behind her fence. She sits there every evening, staring at the village. And her face turns dusky like the twilight, and then it blackens like the night until it grows even darker than the darkness itself.

A woman—not from the village, but a stranger—is coming down the road; she has a bundle in one hand and, with her other hand, she is leading a little girl of about seven, who is wearing a white kerchief that looks like the petal of a large flower.

They are walking through a village that they do not know, and they are frightened.

"Good evening," the woman traveller halts and greets Yustyna.

"God give you good health," Pavlo's neighbour replies.

"We've come from the station, from the train," the woman traveller says. "We're on our way to Petrivka. How far is it? We're travelling from Kuban to visit our relatives."

"You just go across those fields," Yustyna says, pointing out the way, "and you're in Petrivka."

"But why is it so quiet in your village? There are no people to be heard, and no dogs."

"Because it is quiet, my daughter; oh, yes, it's ever so quiet. But don't you know why it's so quiet? Don't you know what's happening in our parts?"

"No, I don't; I just got off the train."

"It's almost dark—and you're going to Petrivka? And with a small child at that? It's terrifying to be out in the fields or in the forest, be it night or day. Don't go! For the love of God, don't go!"

"It truly is scary when I look around."

"What did I just say? My house is right here. I live alone. Don't set out at night for Petrivka with your child. You can spend the night in my home and leave in the morning. There still are good people in this world, but in these times there are more evil ones."

And the woman travelling at this late hour turns and goes into Yustyna's yard.

Pavlo Muzyka pulls the pail out of the well, slowly carries the water to the house, and tells his family what he has seen and heard.

A woman was walking from the station with a child, and she was carrying a bundle—a bundle that might contain food and maybe even valuable possessions. She had come all the way from Kuban to visit relatives in Petrivka. It seems that she does not know what is happening in this part of the country, or else she would not have come here. Can it be that things are not like this in Kuban?

"She placed her trust in Yustyna."

"She's a stranger here; that's why she trusts her."

"We can only expect the worst."

And now, first one member of the Muzyka family, and then another, and then a third, dashes outdoors, listens to the darkness, and stares across the cherry orchard at the small ray of light in their neighbour's window. The flickering flame glows like a drop of blood on the oven's ledge. It is very still outside; if villagers from distant Petrivka called out across the fields, people here would hear them and be alarmed.

The moon—like a kozak's forelock—is already high in the sky when Pavlo Muzyka, waiting in the cherry orchard, finally sees what he had hoped to see: the woman travelling to Petrivka walks out of the porch into the yard and empties a wooden tub—she has probably bathed her child after the long trip.

"Young woman!" Pavlo Muzyka calls out.

She stops dead in her tracks, holding the wooden tub.

"Come here a minute; don't be afraid."

She can hear the man's voice, but she cannot see him. She stands rooted to the spot without moving a muscle.

"I want to help you; come closer, and I'll tell you all about that Yustyna in whose home you're spending the night."

And because the woman seems to be struck dumb, he moves forward, stepping out from among the cherry trees.

"Beware of Yustyna; get away from her. She's a terrible woman."

The young woman jumps back in fright and dashes to the porch. An instant later she disappears, and the door slams shut behind her.

Pavlo Muzyka waits, expecting to see her come running outdoors with her child and her bundle so that he can take them into his home and give them shelter.

The lamp in Yustyna's window continues to flicker, the stars twinkle above the village like salt spilled by carters, but no one appears.

"I probably frightened her," he finally realizes. And he goes in and tells his wife and daughter: "I spoke to her, but she got scared. As if I seemed more terrible to her than Yustyna. So how can we now save these two innocent souls?"

Mariya crosses herself, his daughter crosses herself, and the shadows cast by their arms leap on the walls like hunchbacked monsters.

"Did you shut the door tight?" his wife asks.

"Yes, I did."

Pavlo Muzyka takes the axe from the porch and places it under his pillow on the sleeping bench. These days he always sleeps with an axe under his pillow. And his pitchfork is always at the ready as well—either in the barn, or in the porch. And he never forgets where he keeps the hooked metal pole that he uses to fish out drowning pails from the well; it hangs on a hook behind the storeroom door.

Mariya blows out the small kerosene lamp, and the reed wick, glowing like a brilliant dot, gradually fades and finally goes out.

"Mariya! Are you sleeping?"

"No . . . I just can't seem to fall asleep."

"Maybe you should go to Yustyna's house right now—to save that woman and her child? Tell her everything—the whole truth—because I didn't tell her."

"I'm afraid to go . . . Maybe it's already too late."

"Tell her—Yustyna is a cannibal . . . Everyone knows that, but how is that woman to know?"

"Who will let me into the house?"

Mariya kneels by the bed, presses her folded hands against her chest, and prays before the icon of the Mother of God. The room is shrouded in an impenetrable darkness, and the Mother of God is not visible.

Halya may or may not be sleeping, but her breathing is quiet and even.

Pavlo Muzyka thrusts his hand under the pillow and touches the blade of the axe. Even though it is under his pillow, the axe is cold, and he picks it up and presses it against his burning forehead to cool it off.

"Oh," Mariya shrieks, halting her prayers. "Put it down! Put down the axe! Why have you picked it up?"

Pavlo Muzyka shoves the axe under his pillow and lies down on his back, and Mariya continues whispering her prayers, pleading for mercy from God. And then she falls silent. Sobbing, she remains on her knees, her hands pressed together imploringly on her chest. And she peers intently at the Mother of God, barely discernible on the icon.

Her husband, lying on the axe, has long since fallen into a deep sleep, but Mariya does not rise from her knees; it looks as if, lost in silent prayer, she is kneeling in her sleep.

And when Pavlo Muzyka opens his eyes in the morning, his wife is still on her knees, just as she had been last night.

"Did you spend the entire night on your knees?"

"Oh, let me tell you what I saw!" she turns to him with a joyful face.

"Where?" Pavlo Muzyka asks. And he glances at the icon of the Mother of God, the one that Mariya has probably kept her gaze on all night.

"I went outside for a walk in the dew, and I glanced over at Yustyna's cottage."

"Go on, go on . . ."

"And Yustyna was walking to the gate with that woman and her child."

"The woman and her child?" Pavlo Muzyka jumps up off the sleeping bench. "And what about the bundle?"

"What bundle?"

"The bundle that the woman had, of course!"

"She was carrying the bundle as well."

"Well, praise God!" he exhales deeply. "And the bundle as well, so it means that . . . Maybe Yustyna was scared—and that's why she spared her guests? And she didn't steal the bundle? Or maybe she's got enough of her own. What do you think?"

Mariya rises from the floor. "Could it be that people are saying all sorts of things about Yustyna without any reason? And we follow their example and repeat the same nonsense."

"Oh, I don't think so. People wouldn't flap their tongues without good reason."

"Oh yes they would . . . Have we seen her do any of the things that we say about her? No, we haven't . . . And don't you go outside just yet, so that you don't meet up with that woman. You must have given her quite a scare in the orchard yesterday. What if she recognizes you? If you stop to think about it, we're all terrifying."

Halya's mother is sending her to visit her godmother.

"What kind of a godchild are you? You haven't set foot in your godmother's house for such a long time! You have such a wonderful godmother—there isn't another one like her in the village. Maybe she's ill, or weak from hunger, so you should visit her. She's all alone in her misery. Here's a treat I've made for her; but don't carry it in your hands—tuck it away in your bosom. And be sure not to go through the cemetery; nowadays it's terrifying to go that way."

Halya takes the small treat wrapped in a white cloth, places it in the bosom of her shirt, and dashes out of the house.

It is spring. The blossoming cherry and pin cherry trees look like brides attired in wedding finery. The pear trees, also in bloom, resemble fragrant white clouds that have descended to earth from heaven. The branches of the apple trees are covered with swollen buds that are almost ready to burst into bloom. Songs flow from Halya's heart.

> "Oh, periwinkle growing so green,
> Spread yourself lowly over the lea;
> And you, O dark and handsome youth,
> Come, sit nearer to me."

The blue periwinkle is flowering in the orchards and the yards, and it seems that never before have its petals shone so brilliantly. But there are no young men to be seen. If only she would run into someone, have a good chat. But there is not a soul anywhere.

Halya most certainly will not go through the cemetery, because just thinking about the cemetery terrifies her. Even though it is a shortcut to her godmother's cottage, she will not go that way. She prefers to go down the narrow lane that winds uphill among the small plastered huts, but this path has sunk so far into the ground that it seems ready to fall into the ravine. As you walk along it, all you can see is the sky above you, a sky that looks like a river of blue flax flowing into the distance.

And when you emerge from this lane into the outskirts of the village, into the open fields, this river of flowering blue flax changes into a sea that floods the heights and cascades into far-off valleys, into the misty horizon.

> "Oh, dear periwinkle so green,
> Spread still lower over the lea,
> And you, O dark and handsome youth,
> Move still nearer, closer to me."

The thatched roof of her godmother's cottage peeps through clouds of blossoms—clouds of cherry and plum blossoms so light and so frothy, that even the slightest breeze could seize them, carry them up into the azure sea in the sky, and leave them there to float towards the distant horizon.

Halya's breast expands with joy. Is it because she has dreamt up an image like that? And she walks more swiftly, so that she will reach the yard as quickly as possible.

A few of the surrounding fields are green, covered with weeds or prematurely fallen fruit, while others are starkly black, revealing the unploughed and unsown earth. There is not a soul to be seen out in the fields. People must be ploughing and sowing elsewhere.

Halya stands by the gate, smiles at the windows, and waits. Maybe her godmother will glance through the windowpane and come out to greet her. The door is open, and any moment now, she will walk through it.

"Godmother!" Halya calls.

No one comes out of the cottage—and Halya's smile fades.

"Godmother!"

Halya steps slowly over the green knotgrass and peers into the porch. The kneading-trough is turned over in a corner, and a rake, pitchfork, hoe, and axe lie helter skelter on the floor. Who has toppled everything over and thrown things around?

"Godmother!" she says softly, as if calling for help.

There is such a mess in the cottage, that heaven forbid . . . The ashes from the oven have been scraped out onto the ledge, and near the stove the shattered remains of a clay pot and an earthen mixing bowl lie on the floor. The lid of the trunk is raised, and the trunk itself is empty. The weaving loom—her godmother had inherited it from her parents, but no longer wove on it—is tipped over and smashed. And the walls have been wrecked with something, or slashed with an axe. Who slashed the walls?

And the main beam is damaged; it looks as if it had been chopped with an axe.

What has happened here? Where is her godmother?

Halya wants to call her, but her voice is stuck in her throat, and she cannot make a sound. She tries to lift her feet, but they remain rooted to the floor. There is no doubt that thieves have broken into this cottage—a cottage that, having made its way out into the fields, stands apart from the village. It is thieves who have robbed her godmother.

But where is her godmother? Where? Why is there no trace of her? Why does she not answer her calls?

An unknown power carries Halya out of the silent, violated cottage. It seems to her that someone is about to chase after her. That someone is hiding in the flowering cherry orchard, among the blossoming plum trees. That someone will attack her right from the sky.

The fields are silent—it is terrifying how silent they are.

She does not run along the narrow uphill lane, but through the surrounding fields, and, forgetting her mother's warning, suddenly finds herself in the cemetery. The graves and the crosses are covered with flowers, bees are buzzing, birds are singing. There is peace and God's grace among the dead.

She glances over her shoulder to see if she is being followed, and for some time she walks down the path in this way, with her head over her shoulder.

There does not seem to be anyone.

Suddenly her heart stops—and sinks slowly, in utter terror.

Something is growling fiercely, threateningly. Where is the growling coming from? Where? Where is the danger? And which way should she run?

Halya's eyes sweep the entire cemetery and, quite close by among the graves, she spots dogs—a black, shaggy dog, a reddish one, and a spotted one. Their jaws hang open, their fangs are bared, and their tongues hang out of their mouths. They are not dogs from her village; they have come here from somewhere else, and any moment now, they will attack her.

But the dogs do not attack her. It is as if they do not notice her. Perhaps they are fighting, attacking each other? No, they are dragging something among the graves, biting at something—and they are not able to divide it among themselves. Some foot cloths—no, not foot cloths; some rags—no not rags. It is something that they have dug their teeth into, and they are going berserk as they try to tear it to pieces.

Oh, my dear Go-o-o-o-d! It's a human head!

These roaming dogs are ripping apart a human head in the cemetery . . .

Is it her godmother's head?

Halya stares insanely at the tattered human head that the growling dogs are gnawing. A forehead, streaked and bloody, with torn skin dangling from it. Gnawed cheeks; no nose, no lips, no eyes—just a horrible stuffing oozing out of the sockets.

Halya backs away on tiptoe without taking her stupefied eyes off the dogs that seem poised to attack her. And she finally musters up the strength to run.

Racing among the graves, the crosses, and the granite headstones, she scrapes herself on the shrubs and elder bushes that have overgrown the cemetery and sobs in a quavering voice: "Godmother . . ."

She reaches her own yard, rushes into the barn, hides in a corner among some mouldering sheaves of straw, and stares with wild, terrified eyes at the doorway. Will the dogs break into the barn? Will robbers get in? She shakes as if in a fever; the world grows dimmer in her eyes, and darkness floods her consciousness with an inky-black sleep.

Beyond the windows there is the gentle murmur of a soft night rain. It is a rain without any wind, without the moaning of trees, and without the howling that one hears when, in a single rush, everything begins to roar, both on the earth and in the sky. Occasionally, a flash of lightning illuminates the cottage, and then those within can see the small orchard freshly washed by the rain. And there is also the occasional clap of thunder—either over the village, or just beyond it, and at times, right above the cottage, and then the windowpanes rattle in their frames, or a plate trembles on the shelf.

Mariya is not sleeping; she is lying down, but her eyes are wide open. Sleep has flown far from her without closing her eyelids, and in her soul she feels that the nocturnal storm is thundering and flashing in her thoughts, in her heart.

"Do you hear it?"

Perhaps it is the rain whispering on the thatched roof.

"Mariya, are you sleeping?"

No, it is not the rain; it is Pavlo whispering to her from the sleeping bench.

"Yes, I hear it . . . Go to sleep, there's a storm . . . It's thundering," his wife responds, yawning.

"What storm? What thunder?" her husband hisses. "Listen carefully. Is that thunder? Oh . . ."

In fact, it is not rain or thunder. Something is thumping on the storeroom side of their cottage.

The sound is so muffled that it is barely audible.

"What is it?" Halya asks drowsily, and then she instantly falls asleep again, lulled by the monotonous mumur of the falling raindrops.

There is a thump—and then it is quiet; then another thump—and then it is quiet once again.

"God, it's terrifying. Who can it be?" Mariya gets out of bed and wraps herself in a blanket, as if wanting to hide in it. "Oh! There it is again . . ."

"Someone is trying to break in."

"Into our cottage? How will we . . ."

"Into our storeroom. Or maybe they're after our souls."

Pavlo Muzyka gets up from the sleeping bench and pulls the axe out from under his pillow.

"I'll go take a look . . ."

"Don't you dare!" Mariya leaps up in her white nightshirt and, rushing up to her husband, throws her arms around his neck. "Don't go!"

"What do you mean, don't go?"

He backs away from his wife.

"Because you don't know how many of them there are. Don't go! And you may be sure that they're armed."

"So we'll just wait for death to find us?"

"Maybe they'll go away . . . They're trying to get into our storeroom."

"So I'll wait for them in the storeroom."

"The storeroom is empty. What will they take from it? Don't go into the storeroom with the axe. Don't go!"

There is a flash of lightning followed by thunder, and both Pavlo and Mariya duck as if the ceiling is about to crash on their heads.

The thunder roars and rumbles, and the rustle of the rain can not be heard over its reverberations. It is as if the sky is tumbling down on the earth, or the earth is plunging into hell. It seems as if the thieves have not only dug their way into the storeroom, but that they are now in the porch, and that the door will open at any moment . . .

The storm abates before dawn; it is followed by an eerie silence, and their fears do not diminish.

"Do you hear anything?"

"No, I don't."

"Neither do I."

The sun rising above the village rolls like a red-hot wheel into their cottage. Pacing from window to window, Pavlo and his wife look outside, at the orchard, at the road. The earth, flattened by the rain, is gleaming; the fallen blossoms are like snowy white foam on the green grass; and droplets of water drip from the branches.

There is no one anywhere.

The husband and wife exchange glances, and then Pavlo picks up the axe and, gripping it in both hands, heads for the porch. Tucking her head into her shoulders, Mariya follows in his footsteps: if someone is to be killed, then let it be both of them.

Just as they open the door, Yustyna appears on the doorstep; heaven only knows where she has come from—it is as if she had stood there all night.

Startled, Pavlo swings his axe.

"Don't kill me!" Yustyna shrieks.

Pale and shuddering, Pavlo slowly lowers the axe. "What in God's name are you doing here?"

"I came to see if you were still alive," Yustyna splutters.

"We're alive. Why? Do you want to eat us?"

"God forbid! I'm asking because someone must have tried to get into your cottage last night. I could see from my yard that there's a big hole under your storeroom."

She points at the side of the cottage where the storeroom is attached, and they can see that more than one hole has been excavated.

"Maybe you're the one who did the digging?" Pavlo glares at his neighbour.

"Don't talk nonsense. Where would I get the strength to do that? So, did the thieves get into the storeroom, or didn't they?"

With Pavlo holding the axe at the ready, they fearfully enter the storeroom and look around at the empty corners. There is not even the scent of mice in it.

"The stupid thieves," Pavlo says. "They didn't know that the floor is made of boards, and so they couldn't break in. If they were among our closer neighbours, they most certainly would have known that. So it must have been someone from another corner of the village."

"As if you know from which corner of the village they came. Let's fill in the holes while Halya is still sleeping, because the child is already scared to death. It's best that she not know or see what almost happened to us last night."

Halya sees a human head rolling over the green knotgrass along the side of the road.

This human head seems to have lips—but yet, it does not have any; its teeth are knocked out, and instead of a nose there's a gaping hole; its eyes are gouged out, its cheeks have been gnawed away, its ears have been plucked off, its forehead is bruised and battered, and its hair is stuck together in wads.

People walk down the road, but no one looks at the detached head; no one looks at it—probably because no one sees it. The head stops in front of one house, and then in front of another one; it seems to want to turn back, but it does not; it keeps on rolling, leaving a bloody trail on the knotgrass.

Whose head is it? Whose is it?

Finally, the human head stops in front of their yard. Will it roll on, or won't it? No, it turns into their yard and rolls over the grass, crushing it and leaving flaming spots.

"Why, it's my godmother," Halya realizes.

Her godmother had waited and waited for her godchild to visit her and, weary of waiting, had decided to go and see her.

"How will she roll into the cottage?" Halya worries; she must get up quickly and open the door.

But before Halya can finish her thought, the human head rolls into the cottage right through the closed door.

Halya cannot believe that a human head can roll through a closed door, but the door did not creak, and the head is already inside!

Halya is terrified and wants to flee. But really, how can she flee when her godmother has come to pay her a visit? What a wonderful godchild she would be if she ran away from her godmother!

"Hello, godmother," Halya greets her.

But she cannot hear her own voice. Does she have a voice, or doesn't she?

"I'm so happy that you've come."

The torn lips in the human head scarcely move, and a scrap of tongue jerks around among the broken and missing teeth. But Halya is clever, and she catches on to what her godmother is saying. She most certainly is saying: "Hello, my daughter . . . Why don't you come to see me?"

"I did go to see you."

"Well, where was I? Why didn't I see you?"

"I didn't catch you at home."

"I didn't so much as step out of my cottage, even once. Where was I?"

Halya sees the dogs in the cemetery, the pack of ferocious dogs.

"I don't know," she whispers.

"Well, you can at least kiss your godmother. Or am I so hideous that you're revolted by me?"

"Why no, you're wonderful," Halya whispers.

"Wonderful? Then kiss me."

"I don't feel so well," Halya stays in bed and tries to put her off. "I just can't seem to get up."

"You're not lying, are you, my daughter?"

"No, I'm not," Halya lies.

"Then I'll kiss you."

"Oh, I have no time . . . There's no time, because I have to go up into the sky before it's too late . . . There are no embers in the house to start a fire and warm the oven . . . I'll get some from the sky."

Halya gets out of bed, gropes along the wall, and touches the ceiling—the ceiling that seems like the sky to her. But where are the fiery stars? She moves her fingertips here and there, trying to find them, but there are none nearby, only way over there, farther on. She stretches as far as she can and pulls the star down from the sky; but the star is not burning hot—it is cold.

"Look, godmother!" she rejoices beneath the sky.

She turns around, but her godmother is gone.

There is no detached human head in the cottage.

But her mother Mariya has come in. She is watching her daughter, her anguished eyes filled with black terror.

"Where's my godmother? My godmother was here."

"She isn't here."

"Look, here's a star from the sky; now we can start a fire in the oven."

"Of course, a star . . . Sit down, Halya, sit down. Don't try to climb the wall. Settle down. O Lord, why are You punishing all of us so severely, especially our unfortunate Halya? How has our child sinned against You?"

Halya comes down from the sky, passes the star to her mother, and feels on her forehead the touch of her mother's palm—a palm that is like a cool plantain leaf. And from the healing touch of that plantain, a soothing twilight swaddles her head; her eyes grow dim—and the plucked star fades in her eyes and seems to fly out of the cottage by itself.

"For whose sins are we being punished like this . . ."

"How many children does Harkusha have left? Even though they wander around the yard, I just can't seem to remember . . . Not so long ago, little Yukhym was found in the meadow—he was the third one to die. So there must be two left, because there were five. And the blockhead that's sitting over there among the elder bushes thinks he can hide from the world.

"Go ahead and hide, if you want to; go ahead. But you can't hide from me.

"Which one is it—Hrytsko or Petro? Hrytsko is the older one, and Petro is the younger one; he's only eight. Ah yes, it must be Petro, because he looks like his father, and Hrytsko takes after his mother . . .

"Why is he hiding in the elders? Oh, he's reaching into the bosom of his shirt and pulling out a small bundle. Where did he get that bundle? And what's in it? He probably stole it. If he hadn't stolen it, he wouldn't be hiding. Oh, he's looking carefully all around with those thieving eyes of his. Well, he's taken a look, and now he's untying the bundle, peering into it, and sniffing it; and now he's putting his hand into it and stuffing something into his mouth; he's chewing.

"What has he stolen? What is it that he's chewing? And he's grimacing. What an evil boy you are! Don't you know that there isn't so much as a crumb left in your cottage? That there's nothing to eat, and your father and mother, and your brother Hrytsko are swollen from hunger? So-o-o, you don't know how to share; you'd prefer to have your own family starve to death than to tear away some of the food from your own hungry mug . . . Whoever is able to, steals, as long as there's something to steal. But in order to steal, you have to be healthy. But who is healthy nowadays?

"Oh, he's taking out one fistful after the other from the bundle, and he's packing it in. And he's grimacing. Why? What a young whelp—he takes after his father. His old man took everything away from the people that he could take, and this little one is sweeping up the remains. If he keeps on stealing—he'll keep on living. If he steals and eats it all himself—he'll survive, but if he shares it with his family, he might die. Oh no, this one won't share anything. This one will survive. But I don't want him to survive, I don't want even a trace of Harkusha's seed to be left on this earth . . .

"See, he's had his fill—and now he's puffing and blinking; he'll have a snooze now, of course. May you fall asleep forever! But no, he isn't falling asleep—he's clutching his stomach and writhing! What's the matter? Did you eat too much? Didn't it go down the right way? Well, go on and writhe for a while, and that will teach you how to steal; the Lord sees everything. But maybe God up in heaven is so hungry and so weak that He can no longer punish people for being unjust? So suffer a bit; go on and suffer."

Pavlo Muzyka is sitting on a small hillock under a pear tree, smoking last year's leaves. Oh, his need for tobacco is so strong, but where is he to get any? And so he came up with the idea of rolling a cigarette out of leaves, and now he is choking on the acrid smoke.

Harkushka's whelp is no longer writhing; he's fallen face down among the elders, and he's just lying there. So he did fall asleep after all, once he ate his fill . . .

But no, he isn't sleeping, because he just jerked again. And now he's no longer moving; he's all scrunched up like a heap of rags.

The small, rolled horn of leaves is burning out slowly between his fingertips, and Pavlo Muzyka flings the stub away. He has inhaled so much smoke that his head is whirling from the fumes, and he feels dizzy. He is tempted to sit under the pear tree and let everything go on whirling, and let himself feel dizzy; it's as if you are living—but not living; as if there is a world—but there isn't one.

But what is happening over there, among the elder bushes, with the little thief?

Pavlo Muzyka pulls himself ponderously to his feet and shuffles his way along the boundary over a ribbon of grass to the elder bushes.

The little thief is clutching his stomach and lying on his side, and something is flowing from his open mouth over his chin to the ground. It isn't blood; it's some kind of yellowish-white liquid.

Pavlo Muzyka squats down to have a better look. What is gushing out from between his teeth? Well, who knows. The boy's eyelids are lowered, but from under them peep thin blue streaks that are still animated, not quite extinguished. Is he breathing, or isn't he? Yes, he probably is.

What has happened to the boy? What has he eaten? The stained little bag is lying off to one side by his bent elbow. What's in it?

"O-o-o-o-oh, it's millet . . ."

The golden grain sifts through his twisted, claw-like fingers.

"From whom did he steal the millet?" he ponders out loud. And then he touches the little boy on the shoulder. "Hey there, wake up! From whom did you steal the millet?"

The yellowish-white liquid runs out of the open mouth. The boy does not even moan.

"It must have been from some old granny. Who else? Some old woman must have saved the seeds for sowing, but instead, she gave up her soul to God, and then this thief visited her cottage. Well, the granny is sleeping, either on the oven bed or the bench, and the little thief begins rummaging. And he finds granny's seeds . . . to his own ruination. Haven't you died yet, my boy?"

Pavlo Muzyka waits for a reply. The boy's right eyelid slowly stretches upwards—and a bright blue eye stares at the peasant.

"He's looking at me."

The eyelid over the left eye creeps up in the same way—and now the little boy is staring at him with both eyes.

"He's dying . . ."

He spits out a smoky wad of saliva that is making his mouth feel bitter and picks up the bundle with the millet. He ties it up and hides it in his bosom. Then he gets to his feet and slowly shuffles to his neighbour's yard. He peers through a window to see if there is anyone in the cottage, but he cannot see anything from the outside. He knocks on the window frame and waits.

No one appears. Maybe they've all died in there? Or maybe they've gone to find some work in the kolhosp? And he knocks on the frame once again.

Harkusha, clinging to the doorpost with one hand, slowly makes his way out of the porch. He squints in the sun, unable to see anything.

"Who is it?" he asks, even though it is broad daylight.

"Why, it's me."

Harkusha, recognizing his neighbour by his voice, finally fixes his gaze on Pavlo Muzyka. A blazing rage stirs faintly within him, but he has no strength left for hatred; his mouth is hanging open, and his breathing is laboured and jagged.

"Over there, among the elder bushes," Pavlo Muzyka points to the edge of the yard, "that's where your boy is. It looks as if he's dead. Go and get him . . ."

And treading heavily, Pavlo Muzyka, the messenger of death, calmly walks away . . .

"Sleep, my daughter, sleep."

"The moon is shining in the window. Tell father to put it out, because it won't let me sleep."

"Your father will put it out, but you must sleep. He'll do it as soon as you fall asleep, but now you must sleep . . ."

"Will you put it out, father?"

"Yes, I will." Her father, lying on the oven bed, grinds his teeth in the darkness.

Sitting by her daughter, Mariya can sense Halya's flaming cheeks, her burning forehead, and the heat that has seized her whole body; it is as if living flames are blazing from her.

"The moon is shining so brightly that I can see far, far away," their daughter's jagged voice jabbers in an unending stream. "The fields beyond the village . . . the yellow stubble in the cobweb of the last days of summer, and on all the roads there are wagons and more wagons! And on the wagons there are sheaves of wheat and of rye . . . And now father is riding on a wagon; he's driving the horses . . . Father, do you see yourself on the wagon?"

"Why wouldn't I see myself?" Pavlo Muzyka grinds his teeth.

"You're hauling sheaves to the village. Sheaves of rye."

"I'm hauling sheaves of rye."

"It's so splendid! So very splendid!"

Halya, drifting into unconsciousness, falls silent, and her mother blesses her with the sign of the cross. "Let her sleep, blessed by the Lord."

But, in that instant, as if responding to the charms of that blessing, Halya emerges from the waves of forgetfulness. "The Red threshing floor in our village is so splendid! So much grain has been hauled in from the kolhosp fields! I've never seen such a threshing floor, so much grain on the threshing floor, so many people.

"The entire village has gathered, and everyone is threshing and winnowing, threshing and winnowing. And red flags are blazing, and banners are flaming, and on those banners everything is written so beautifully . . . And now, mother is standing by the winnowing machine; she's winnowing wheat. Father, can you see her by the winnowing machine?"

"I see her . . . I've hauled in the sheaves, and your mother is winnowing the wheat."

"It's all so splendid!"

Halya once again loses consciousness, and her mother leans over her mournfully, peering at the features of the beloved face— a face so dear and so tormented; and she prays silently over her— and it is as if that silent prayer once again awakens her daughter.

"And how splendid the Red Caravan of wagons is! The horses are decked out in flowers and red ribbons; there's red bunting over the caravan, the sacks are on the wagons. I've never seen such a Red Caravan, so much grain . . . Mother!"

In her voice there is so much of her former joyous exhuberance that Mariya shudders.

"I'm listening . . . I'm listening."

"Take a look. Who is on the third wagon from the end? Do you see it?"

"I see it . . . Who is it?"

"Father is on that wagon!"

"Yes, it is father in the Red Caravan."

"In an embroidered shirt!"

"We embroidered that shirt together for him."

"A Red Caravan—such a festive day . . . There has never been another like it in our village. The children are singing, and I'm singing too. Oh, which song am I singing? We've given so much grain to our country; we've given it all our grain . . .

"From beyond the mountains so high
An eagle flies on steel-blue wings . . ."

Halya is dreaming now, but her hands jerk spasmodically on her chest as if they are the wings of the steel-blue eagle, the eagle that is flapping its wings and flying out from behind the mountains so high . . . She falls silent, and her hands become still . . .

And then she cries out clearly in a distinct voice, a voice charged with suppressed fear: "Father! Father, are you sleeping?"

"No, no I'm not."

"Don't sleep, father . . . Do you know what awaits us tomorrow?"

"What awaits us tomorrow?" her father and mother ask.

"Did you hide a small sack of grain in the cellar?"

"Why, yes, we did."

"Hide it in another spot. Hide it in another spot, because tomorrow Vasyl Hnoyovy will come and find that bundle in the cellar. It's not too late to hide it in a safer spot. Because what will we eat if they take that from us?"

"They've already taken it from us, Halya," the mother grieves.

"They've taken it? When did they take it?" she flinches.

"Last year . . . after the Red Caravan. They ferreted out everything that anyone had, and they took it all away; and they found our little sack as well . . . You're recalling what happened last year. It all happened last year."

"O-o-o-o-h!" her voice quivers with despair.

"One and Only All-Merciful God!" Mariya prays silently. "Are You so far away in heaven that You are unable to take pity on our daughter? Look down at her and take pity on her; return her health to her—she's still so young—and punish the guilty ones. Or are You so high up in heaven that You are unable to see the guilty ones?"

In the sepulchral twilight of the dark cottage, the eager voice calls out again: "Father, are you sleeping?"

"I'll get my sleep in the damp earth . . ."

"O father, mother! I must be a seer and a prophetess, because such things are revealed to me about the future that I am afraid to talk about them . . ."

"What is it that's revealed to you?"

"Our grandfather is lying over there, covered with a sheepskin coat on the sleeping bench. You can see, can't you, how he's all curled up from the cold? Well, you must quickly take that coat off him and hide it, or else it will be gone."

"The sheepskin coat will be gone?"

"Tomorrow Vasyl Hnoyovy will tear the coat off grandfather and give it to Harkusha. So that Harkusha can haul beets to the sugar factory in grandfather's coat. And grandfather will freeze to death in the cold without his coat."

"Oh, daughter! Vasyl Hnoyovy has already been here. And he's taken the sheepskin coat from grandfather and given it to Harkusha. Grandfather is no longer with us, may the kingdom of heaven be his. He crossed over into the other world last year."

"Dz-z-z!" Seized by a blind despair, Halya shakes convulsively.

Pavlo Muzyka's head slips off his pillow onto the axe, and his lips touch the blade; he presses his lips to the blade as if he were kissing it—and is unable to stop kissing it . . .

At that time I had not yet been born, but I can see, I can clearly see Vasyl Hnoyovy.

As he walks, he squats from time to time; his knees buckle under him, and he seems to sink ever lower. His stomach caves in, his head shrinks into his shoulders, and his eyes sink into his horse-like face. And from his gaping mouth his tongue protrudes from behind an uneven picket fence of teeth. The tip of his tongue darts out, and then hides; it keeps darting out and hiding again. The narrow tip of his tongue is like a serpent's stinger. The stinger darts in and out, as if it wants to strike, as if it is desperate for nourishment.

Even dogs do not bark at him. They did not bark at him in earlier times, when there were so many of them roaming around, and they do not bark now, when they have disappeared. But they did not die from natural causes; starving people killed them off.

He walks from house to house, calling the peasants to go and work in the kolhosp. He calls those who are already lying stiff, like logs, on a sleeping bench or on an oven bed. And those who are so swollen that they are unable to move. And those who are still breathing. And those who still have the strength to hear him and to look at him, their eyes racked with pain.

"Come to do the sowing!" Vasyl Hnoyovy calls out to them. "And take your spoon and bowl with you. Do you want to know why you're hungry? Why you have nothing to eat? Because you aren't working. Because you haven't earned any food. Those who do not work, do not eat. Do you want to eat, and not work? Oh, no! That's not how we do things here. It's the capitalists and the lords who ate without working, because the proletariat worked for them.

"But our country is a country of workers. In our country everything belongs to the workers. In our country only the workers eat, and we don't give a damn for anyone from the nonworking elements of society. What you get is what you've earned; from each according to his ability—to each according to his work.

"Who would expect us to feed our class enemies? All the lords are to be dumped into one pit in front of the village office. Today is the Celebration of Mighty Labour. Whoever labours mightily will eat out of the kolhosp cauldron."

And it is not only Vasyl Hnoyovy who is calling them to work; Mykola Khashchuvaty is also calling them.

Mykola Khashchuvaty is a diminutive man—like a dog on its haunches, as the saying goes. But you won't find a more ferocious man anywhere. His skin looks plucked, and it is marked with scars and scabs. And all these scabs and scars are black, as if he had been set out to be baked on burning coals in a blacksmith shop and should have come out nicely browned, but for some reason, did not.

"How are you getting along, my saboteurs?" Mykola Khashchuvaty asks as he enters a cottage. "You're sabotaging, are you? You're lying on the oven bed—and sabotaging the kolhosp?"

"I have no strength to get up," comes the response.

"That's sabotage! "

"I haven't had so much as a crumb in my mouth . . ."

"I hear the voice of a saboteur."

"But my dear Mykola, my arms and legs are swollen . . ."

"Of course! They're swollen from inactivity and laziness. Do you think that the kolhosps will perish? Do you think that you'll bury them? The kurkuls will not succeed in doing that, nor will their supporters, nor will the saboteurs."

"But Mykola, we're poor wretches . . ."

"You're kurkul supporters! Listen! If you want to eat—off you go to the Celebration of Mighty Labour. And for your work, you'll be fed out in the fields, so be sure to take your bowls and spoons with you . . ."

It is no longer dawn, nor morning, but closer to noon when a few peasants—some coerced into coming, others shuffling along on their own—appear at the village office. In front of this office, there is a red banner stretched between two poles dug into the ground, and on it are printed the words: "Whoever does not work—does not eat."

Standing in the office, Kindrat Yaremny, the head of the village council, and Matviy Shpytalnyk, the head of the kolhosp, are playing chess on the sill of a half-opened window. It is not their first game, but their seventh or eighth, and the village head is simply unable to beat the kolhosp head, even though Shpytalnyk always gives Yaremny a one-rook advantage. If it were otherwise, Yaremny would not even begin to play.

Chess is a longstanding weakness of the kolhosp head. No matter where he is, he is always thinking about all sorts of combinations and sacrifices of the chess pieces. And so, at this very moment, he is delightedly pondering which piece should be moved to win his opponent's bishop. Finally, unable to contain his glee, he expresses his pleasure: "Do you want to see how I can win your bishop?"

"Are you saying you can win my bishop?" Yaremny is amazed.

"I'll just move this piece over here," and he shows him how he will do it.

Yaremny, breathing heavily, ponders the move. And suddenly his voice is illuminated with joy: "You're right! There's no denying it. You can do it!"

"But I can also win by moving my rook this way," and Shpytalnyk, with a beneficent look on his face, shows him how he can move his rook.

"Well, look at that!" Yaremny is genuinely amazed and, breathing even more heavily, considers this alternative move. "It's true; it can't be denied. You can do it!"

"But that isn't all," Shpytalnyk says even more graciously. And he moves his knight over the chessboard. "I can also move my knight like this."

"You don't say!" Yaremny is truly astonished. Furrowing his brows and wrinkling his forehead, he concentrates and breathes heavily. And then he shouts enthusiastically. "You're right, Matviy. I too can see now that you can do it with your knight."

"It's all within our control," Shpytalnyk says indulgently.

"Come on, tell me," Yaremny dreamily half closes his eyes, "will I be able to play like you one day?"

"Never!"

"Never?" Stung to the quick, Yaremny's eyes fly open. "Why not?"

"Even if I explain it to you, you won't understand."

Yaremny, his face overcast like a foul rainy day, remains silent for a moment, then mutters: "You're right."

Shpytalnyk glances at his watch, wrinkles his nose, and says: "Do you want me to give you two rooks?"

"Two rooks?" The smile on Yaremny's proud face makes him look even more haughty. "And you'll still win?"

"Playing against you—yes, I will."

"If you're going to win, I don't want to play any more," the village head says with a sour expression on his face. And he finally tears his eyes away from the chessboard and glances out the window. "It's time to launch the sowing; the people have gathered."

"It's time for the Holiday of Labour," Shpytalnyk agrees. "Even though not all the saboteurs have been rounded up, we won't be able to come up with any more."

They step out onto the porch of the village office, stand shoulder to shoulder, and look out at the green grass onto which the people have swarmed with their bowls and spoons. Shpytalnyk tugs at his wedge-shaped curly beard with his freckled left hand, adjusts the glasses on his nose, and then slips his hand into the bosom of his green hunting jacket. With a studied gesture, he thrusts his right hand forward.

"Here's to the Holiday of Labour! We have created conditions in which every talent of every individual is manifested in work, not for one's self, not for the exploiters, but for the collective, for the country of workers and peasants. We have created the conditions in which the worth of every individual of our new society is measured by the criteria of selflessness and self-sacrifice in the name of universal ideals and a magnificent future. The world revolution—this is the measure of our new man, this is what he lives for, and this is his goal. For we are striving to gain good fortune not only for ourselves, but also for the workers and the peasants of the world.

"Is there anyone among us who can look on calmly while nations on five continents groan under the heel of capitalism? Is there any mother who will not be overcome by grief when she thinks about the fate of a mother in Ethiopia or Abyssinia? Are there any children whose hearts will not ache when they learn about the miserable childhood of their peers somewhere across the ocean?

"Listen to me! Through your work you are not only advancing the socialist industrialization of your own country, you are also ensuring the inevitable collapse of the international capitalist system throughout the world.

"So, let's get on with the sowing!"

As he speaks, Shpytalnyk keeps flinging his right hand forward, especially when he talks about international capitalism and the heel of capitalism. It would seem that this gesture is intended to underscore the following assertion: even though international capitalism and the heel of capitalism are nowhere nearby, we can get at them from here, so let them be on guard!

Pleased with himself, the kolhosp head turns to the village head and winks conspiratorially: "That's how it's done! The movement of the bishop across the central horizontal line! It is not a move that is made one step at a time."

"Yes, indeed," Yaremny gives him an enraptured look. "It is not the move of a pawn."

The voices of Vasyl Hnoyovy and Mykola Khashchuvaty ring out, the sporadic shouts of other activists who are gathered in front of the village office crackle in the air, and the crowd seems to awaken and begins to move. It inches forward like a worm on a rotting piece of meat, but the determined voices urging them on do not let up, and now the crowd trickles more steadily down the road, away from the village office.

"Let's go." It is hard to tell if Shpytalnyk is asking a question or confirming a statement.

"Let's go," Yaremny says, stepping down from the porch of the village office.

"Where are you going?"

"What do you mean, where?"

"Ha-ha-ha!" the head of the kolhosp laughs heartily. "I didn't mean there . . . We'll play another game or two of chess. And I'll give you a two-rook advantage . . ."

"Two rooks? Let's go!"

And they disappear into the village office.

What is that rumbling? What is that banging? Where is the din coming from? And the rumbling and banging are not dying away. The din is not receding; it is drawing closer.

How is it possible to remain indoors? Halya walks out of the cottage and stands by the gate.

The racket draws nearer and nearer, and then some people come around the corner. They are not really walking, but rather shuffling along as a motley, ragged crowd, scarcely able to lift their feet. Who is the man at the head of that raggle-taggle column, the one who is walking backwards, continuously waving his arms? And the rumbling and the banging are keeping time to his waving arms.

Clattering, clanging, banging, shouting.

What is it? What can it be?

Vasyl Hnoyovy is walking backwards at the head of the mob.

His knees keep buckling, and he appears to be sinking into the ground. His neck and head keep sinking into his shoulders, his chest keeps sinking into his stomach, and his stomach keeps sinking below his waist. And he is walking and exhorting the people to follow him. Oh, someone in the crowd has fallen; they go around him, and when they have passed him, he is left behind, left to lie on the road and stare after them.

The village activists are walking on both sides of the crowd. Halya finally recognizes them. It is they who are creating the ruckus as they bang on frying pans, pieces of tin, baking sheets, and assorted scraps of metal. They are pounding metal on metal, and it is this orchestra that Vasyl Hnoyovy is conducting. A few people in the crowd are also beating spoons on bowls, but these players are few in number.

"Saboteurs!" someone shouts.

The crowd creeps along slowly, until it finally comes abreast of Halya.

"We'll reforge the saboteurs of the kolhosp movement!" Mykola Khashchuvaty shouts, almost foaming at the mouth.

Hnoyovy, walking backwards, flails his arms, and at this signal metal strikes metal, making a deafening din.

"We will not permit socialism to be sabotaged in the village!"

And at that moment Halya feels an urge to sing:

> "Down the road goes a beetle, a beetle,
> Down the road goes a beetle so black.
> Look at me, my pretty girl,
> See how briskly I can walk."

Where are they all heading with their bowls and spoons? They can scarcely lift their log-like legs, legs swollen so badly that a serous fluid squirts from them. And their faces are equally swollen, and on those bloated faces—their eyes look frozen. Their eyes look frozen, and hardly a glimmer breaks through their murky surface.

"Saboteurs! Those who do not work will not eat!"

Halya sings:

> "The roads to Poltava are in sight,
> And Poltava itself is in view . . ."

But no one hears Halya, because the metal and tin are clanging, and the indigent activists are shouting.

In the midst of this crowd, a woman whose legs are giving way tries to latch on to a back or an elbow, but she is pushed aside and sinks to her knees in the grey dust. The crowd passes her by, and she follows it with her pleading eyes: "Take me with you! Take me with you into the fields. I want to eat . . . I want to eat . . ."

And she holds out her empty bowl, as if hoping that they will either take her with them, or fill her bowl with food.

And Halya sings:

> "Rise up, all you persecuted and hungry
> Workers of the world . . ."

The woman left behind on the road hears Halya's animated singing and, turning around, looks at her with terror-stricken murky eyes.

Suddenly, Halya finds it all so ludicrous that she is overcome by spasms of convulsive laughter, and she shakes uncontrollably until they gradually die away.

"O-o-oh . . . o-o-oh . . ." she groans as if in deep pain.

The woman rises from her knees, casts a terrified look at Halya, and drags herself slowly down the road after the crowd that is shuffling out of the village to the din of clanging metal, shouts, and whistles.

"The head is coming . . . Both heads are coming . . . Shpytalnyk and Yaremny . . ."

Far off in the valley, a bay horse is pulling a carriage in which the head of the village council and the head of the kolhosp are comfortably seated. Both men are wearing army berets, and from a distance they look like district militiamen.

"Where are they off to?"

"They're coming here."

It is early evening. Here, in the kolhosp field camp, the workers are about to have a meal, either dinner or supper as the case may be. The sowers have gathered under flowering wild pear trees that are dropping their wilted blossoms, and around this green oasis lies the seeded earth, as black as spilled tar.

The sowers watch the carriage as it rolls towards their field station. It pulls up, the bay horse come to a stop, and the two administrative heads jump to the ground. Kindrat Yaremny walks up to the peasants in an authoritative manner, while Matviy Shpytalnyk stays by the carriage. He is holding a bright cherry-red box.

Everyone stares at it.

The village head peers into a large, charred cauldron. Vasyl Hnoyovy and Mykola Khashchuvaty are standing by it, at the ready. The peasant woman Hychka is behind them; blind in one eye, she used to prepare food for weddings and funerals, but now she cooks only out in the field for the peasants who work.

"Is it ready?" Yaremny calls out in a brisk voice.

Hychka the cook nods her head.

Hnoyovy grins. "Will you have some?"

"I'm not hungry," Yaremny replies. And then he says jokingly to Hychka: "So, tell me, did you prepare it using your left eye, or your right one?"

The cook frowns angrily and remains silent.

None of the workers laughs at the joke, but Khashchuvaty says: "Probably with her right one, the one that's alive."

Assuming a stern look, the village head stands at attention, thrusts out his chest, flings out his hand, and shouts: "Those who do not work, do not eat! Socialism is an accounting! Enjoy your meal . . ."

And he walks to the carriage with a springy gait.

The sowers crowd around the cauldron, stretching their bowls towards it, and Hnoyovy and Khashchuvaty, wielding ladles, dole out the corn meal gruel.

"Give me some!"

"Fill it up. You haven't filled it."

"Don't spill any!"

To one side of the cauldron, closer to the pear trees, another group has gathered—children and old men and women, who did not plough or sow, but who dragged themselves here from the village in the hope that there might be a crumb or a drop left for them. Among them is Yustyna. They are waiting for the ploughers and the sowers to receive their portions, and then they will come up and beg for a bit of food. It is not possible to approach the cauldron any sooner, because both Hnoyovy and Khashchuvaty have keen eyes and are quick to bring their ladles down on the backs of anyone who might push ahead.

And Harkusha is there as well. And if either Hnoyovy or Khashchuvaty should happen not to notice the approach of a sluggard who did not work and wants to eat for nothing, he spots him right away: "Hey there, Mykola, Vasyl! Why are you giving him gruel? Those who do not work do not eat!"

And then . . . suddenly . . . the hands stretched out with empty bowls freeze over the cauldron, and the spoons of those who have already received their portion remain suspended over their gruel. The ladles held by Hnoyovy and Khashchuvaty do not move. Hychka the cook gapes, so startled that it seems that her left eye may miraculuously regain its sight. They all exchange glances and look around.

Who is singing?

Who is the woman that is singing so cheerfully?

None of those gathered around the cauldron to get some gruel is singing, and yet the voice drifts and floats through the air—an enchanting, sun-drenched voice:

> "All the pear and apple trees were blooming,
> O'er the river floated clouds of mist.
> On the bank came strolling young Katyusha
> On the riverbank so high and steep."

"It's a gramophone," Harkusha grumbles morosely, pointing at the carriage.

Most of the people resume eating greedily, looking at their bowls and not paying any attention to the gramophone, but a few turn their heads towards the carriage. And truly, on the carriage stands a gramophone—that square bright cherry-red box that the kolhosp head had brought into the field.

> "As she walked, she trilled a song of love
> About a steel-blue eagle of the steppes,
> About the lad she loved so very dearly,
> About her one and only love . . .

Shpytalnyk and Yaremny beam with delight as they gaze with enraptured eyes at the record spinning on the turntable. Neither says anything, but both men cannot help but wonder if the workers are capable of appreciating the rare treat that is being accorded them, right here, out in the open field, at the conclusion of their labour. Probably not, because they seem to see only the bowls in front of their noses; the gruel has overshadowed the beauty of the singing, the beauty of art.

"We are Red Cavaliers
And we
Are lauded in epics
By eloquent poets . . ."

The peasant woman Yustyna stretches out her bowl, and Khashchuvaty ladles some gruel into it. Caught up in listening to the music and the singing, he is not paying attention to whom he is doling out the food. Some of the others waiting under the pear trees trail after Yustyna to the cauldron, and they also receive a portion of the thin gruel.

"Speed on, O steam locomotive,
Your destination is the commune . . ."

Barely taking a step away from the cauldron, old Yustyna falls to her knees, pulls a spoon out of her bosom and, with tears streaming down her face, begins slurping the gruel.

"Storm clouds gather on the border,
Silence grips our gloomy, somber land,
Atop the River Amur's lofty banks
The guards of our Motherland stand."

After cranking the gleaming handle of the gramophone, Shpytalnyk walks down the road to the pear trees where the peasants are eating. The sun's rays swarm like ants in his keen, unblinking eyes. Silver sunspots glance off his shiny, polished boots.

He stops in front of old Yustyna, but she is so immersed in her bowl that she does not notice him.

"Are you a kolhosp member?" he asks.

Holding the bowl in both hands, Yustyna looks fearfully and uncomprehendingly at him. She did not hear his question.

"Are you a kolhosp member?' he asks again.

"Oh yes . . . a kolhosp member, a kolhosp member," old Yustyna struggles to get her tongue around the words.

"And did you help with the sowing today?"

"No, I didn't."

"But only those who worked can eat here."

"I swear on the cross that I didn't work."

"And why didn't you work, if you're a kolhosp member?"

"I don't have the strength. I'm not well."

"You don't have the strength to work, but you're well enough to eat?"

"I'm eating so that I'll get my strength back."

"And why don't you eat at home?"

"There's nothing to eat at home; there's nothing for even the mice to eat . . . There even aren't any mice."

"There even aren't any mice?" he asks in astonishment. "Oh, you saboteur!"

And, with a swift kick, he knocks the bowl out of her hands. The bowl falls on the ground, and the remaining gruel trickles out. Old Yustyna, her mouth gaping widely, is stricken dumb, while Shpytalnyk stalks off to the carriage.

A small child crawls up on all fours to the spilled gruel and begins licking it off the grass.

> "We don't need even an inch of foreign soil,
> But we won't give the enemy an inch of ours . . ."

The gramophone falls silent, and the carriage, its wheels creaking, drives off with the village head and the kolhosp head.

The sun sets in a purple cloud.

"Look over there. He's come . . ."

"Who's come?"

"What do you mean, who's come? It's Andriy Synytsya. He just stands under the willow tree and stares. He walks for a while on the road and then comes back and stares at our windows. You should go outside and say something to him. But maybe you don't have to say anything. Just go outside with the axe, and you'll scare him, and he won't come here anymore. Let him go stare at someone else's house. You see, he's wearing an embroidered shirt and a cap with a visor, but he's barefoot. Why in the world is that Andriy Synytsya walking around under our windows?"

"Don't you know why he comes here?"

"He's looking for something. He wants to steal something. But what is there to steal?"

"He's not alone today . . . Hrytsko Nakorenok is hanging around with him."

Mariya peers through the window and stares at the road. It is true. Today Andriy Synytsya is not alone; he is with Hrytsko Nakorenok. They appear to have met unexpectedly and struck up a conversation, but their eyes are fixed on Muzyka's yard.

"You say you don't know why they're hanging around here? They've come to see our Halya."

"To see Halya?" the mother finds this hard to believe. "But where is Halya?"

"Oh, so I'm the one who's supposed to know. She's in the pantry getting all dressed up."

"Why is she getting all dressed up?"

"Are you saying you've forgotten why girls get all dressed up? For the young men."

"O dear mother of mine!" Mariya claps her hands in despair. "What's going on?"

"Something's going on, all right; it certainly is . . . Oh, and there goes our Halya now."

Halya, dressed in her holiday finery, is walking past the window, but her eyes, smiling happily, are already over there, on the road, on the boys under the willow tree.

"I'll run after her, yes I will. I won't let her go. Where does she think she's going?"

And Mariya, unable to run, takes small tottering steps as she tries to catch up to Halya on the road.

"Halya! Where are you going with the boys?"

"To Kozhanka."

"Kozhanka?" Mariya asks in astonishment. "Boys, why are you taking Halya to Kozhanka?"

"We're going to the sugar refinery," Andriy Synytsya replies.

"To the refinery? Why to the refinery?"

"We can get something to eat there," Hrytsko Nakorenok answers this time.

"What can you get to eat at the refinery?"

The boys do not respond, so Halya says: "You can eat mash there."

"And you believe the boys, Halya? And you're going to wander off shamelessly with them to Kozhanka? Who'll give you mash there? No one will give it to you. Are you listening, Halya? Let the boys go, if they're so keen on it, but don't you go. You're a girl—and you're going to wander off to another village?"

"She needn't be afraid to come with us," Andriy says.

"Mother! It's broad daylight . . . It's just across the fields; Kozhanka is right over there."

"So what if it's broad daylight? The mash is guarded; don't you know that? Who's going to let you get near the pit? What will you use to get the mash?"

"We know what," Hrytsko Nakorenok says.

"Boys, I want you to know that I'm not letting Halya go with you. But who listens to a mother these days? Nothing helps. Not even tears or prayers."

The youths and Halya turn and walk away. Mariya follows them with her eyes, until they disappear into a grove of tall poplar trees . . . They can no longer be seen, but she still sees them—not with her eyes, but with her maternal heart. She sees the three of them in the fields on the road to Kozhanka.

And then she waits all day—suffering the whole time. Why did she let Halya go? She ought not to have let her go. And why has she been gone for such a long time? Why isn't she home yet? She's a young woman now; she doesn't want to stay at home; she wants to fly away into the world. And so she has flown . . . There, in Kozhanka at the sugar refinery there truly is mash, but who will let them at it? If they let everyone get at it, there wouldn't be any mash left, and the refinery would be dismantled. And so the mash is guarded, and no one can come near it.

It is evening when Halya walks into the yard.

Her mother crosses herself joyfully and asks: "Well, were you in Kozhanka?"

"Yes, I was."

"Well, did you have some mash?"

"Yes, I did."

"Then why are you so sad?"

"Oh, mother, don't ask."

And Halya bursts into tears—such copious tears that her mother's heart breaks with grief. It may well be that someone has harmed her daughter . . . but at least she has returned home alive.

"Tell me all about it—how much you ate."

"I . . . I'd rather not talk about it."

"And where are the boys?"

"Andriy went home, but Hrytsko drowned . . ."

"Where did he drown?"

"In the pit that holds the mash . . . Oh, mother, if you had only been there to see it! If you could have seen what's happening there. There are all sorts of people prowling around the factory, but there are guards everywhere, and no one can get past them. And there are throngs of people near the pit with the mash. Some of them can no longer walk, but they managed to get there anyway. Some stand, and others sit.

"We sat under some bushes because guards had surrounded the mash, and we couldn't come near it. And then, one man couldn't wait any longer; he crept up closer to the pit, and other people followed him. The guards began to shout, but no one listened to them, and the two boys, Andriy and Hrytsko, ran to the pit as well. But I was scared, so I crouched on the ground, because now everyone was rushing headlong to the pit, and the guards were nowhere in sight—they must have been crushed by the mob.

"Some of the people jumped into the pit by themselves; others were pushed in by those behind them who were trying to get nearer to it. There was such shouting, such a commotion! And then Andriy came running back with a pail filled with mash; you see, he had made himself a pail out of cloth that he coated with wax. Both of us greedily attacked the mash and began gobbling it up; we ate and ate, but we just couldn't get enough. And then, when it was all gone, we remembered about Hrytsko; and someone told us that Hrytsko had drowned in the mash, and that another person had drowned as well. We became frightened and ran away; some men were running towards the pit from the factory, and the people scattered in all directions.

"When we reached the outskirts of the village, we sat down and waited. We thought that maybe Hrytsko had not drowned in the mash after all, and that any minute he might come running after us. We waited and waited, but he didn't show up, and so we set out for home . . . Oh, mother! I feel so sorry for Hrytsko! But then . . . maybe he didn't drown?"

"You're asking me, my child?"

The two of them stand and look down the road and at the nearby fields, hoping against hope that Hrytsko will appear. Maybe he did not drown after all? But there is no sign of him.

"I'll go and tell Hrytsko's mother about the great grief that has befallen her."

"Don't go, mother!"

"Why not?"

"Well . . . maybe he didn't drown."

"So I'll tell her that maybe he didn't drown in the mash, that maybe he is still alive. But his mother should know what has happened, because she's going to be worried sick about him in any event."

Mariya walks gloomily down the road, while her daughter stares intently into the distance, where the blue sky is stretched tautly on the tall poplars.

Perhaps old man Hnylokvas is not so old, but he looks like an aged, hoary man.

And he looks like an old man because he is badly stooped, because his hands drag along the ground, and his straggly hair resembles a mound of riddled March snow sprinkled with reddish manure. His dishevelled hair falls down over his forehead, obscuring his eyes, and so it seems that Hnylokvas never looks either to the left, or to the right, but rather, always stares down at his feet.

He is forever searching and looking for something. As he makes his way through the village, he hangs on to the reins of a small mouse-grey horse with protruding ribs that plods along beside him; and behind the horse creak the ungreased wheels of a funeral cart. Hnylokvas could ride in that cart, but he does not want to do that because he makes many stops, and it would mean that he would have to get in and out a lot.

He stops the cart in front of a yard, knocks on the gate, raps on the window, and calls out: "Are you still alive?"

An old woman comes out of the cottage: "Have you come for my soul already?"

"There's time enough for me to come for your soul . . . What's happening in your neck of the woods? Has anyone died?"

"How am I to know? I sit in my cottage, and no one comes to see me," the old woman mumbles. "There are times when I myself no longer can tell if I'm still in this world, or if I've already gone on to the next one."

"Oh, you're still in this one . . ."

"Then why is this world so much like that one?"

"Ask the village head, not me . . . So, when should I come to pay you a visit, granny?"

"To pay me a visit? Why pay me a visit?"

"To haul you off to the cemetery. I only want to help you."

"How am I to know?"

"Well, who's supposed to know if you don't? I have a job to do. Do you think I'd be doing this for nothing? I haul someone off to the pit, and I get half a pound of bread."

"How much?" the old woman can hardly believe her ears.

"Half a pound of bread. And they'll give me the same amount for you, as well."

"So much? They'd do better to give it to me; I haven't eaten any bread for ever so long. I might even live a little longer."

"They don't give you bread for just living."

After chatting for a while with the old woman who still yearns for bread and does not want to die—she does not even want to mention death—old man Hnylokvas moves slowly onward, and the ungreased wheels of his cart creak with a dry, hungry whine.

"Oh, I almost forgot," the old man says, slapping his forehead. "Why, to be sure, this is the cottage and plot owned by Marko Hrusha. We haven't seen each other for ages, and there's no one out in the yard just now. Should I drop in, or shouldn't I? Yes, I think I will."

Hnylokvas walks into the cottage, sees granny Yavdokha on the sleeping bench, and greets her dully: "Good day to you, Yavdokha."

Granny Yavdokha is lying on a pillow; she does not stir.

"Where's Marko?" Hnylokvas asks her.

Granny Yavdokha does not reply—she seems to be asleep. And then Hnylokvas glances up and notices bare legs sticking out from the oven bed.

"Marko, do you hear me?" he calls.

Marko Hrusha remains silent.

"Both of them," Hnylokvas mutters, "they're both dead. Let's see, half a pound of bread for Yavdokha, and half a pound for Marko—that's a pound already. Even though it's hard to do this work by myself, I don't want to share it with anyone. Lots of people have wanted to help me, but I wouldn't let them. Because what if I did? Would I have to give away my half pound of bread? And who is going to give me a half pound? Is someone rushing to give it to me?"

He touches the old woman's forehead. It is cold.

"You're a goner. And why? Because you were foolish. You didn't want to marry me back then—you married Marko instead. Well, has he managed to feed you? He hasn't fed either himself, or you. If you'd been with me, you'd still be living. But now, I'll have half a pound of bread because of you."

He removes a blanket from the plank bed, spreads it on the earthen floor, and shoves granny Yavdokha on to it from the sleeping bench.

"How light you are . . . I never held you in my arms, but I'm holding you now."

The old woman's heels thud on the floor, and her body thumps dully. Seizing the corners of the blanket tightly with both hands, old Hnylokvas drags it through the cottage, and then from the porch into the yard and to the cart. The old woman's head dangles, and her eyes are bulging.

"I'll haul you to the pit; I won't leave you in the cottage. Because you're so foolish . . ."

When he reaches the funeral cart, he once again has to embrace the old woman to lift her off the ground. But he has lifted heavier bodies than this—and Yavdokha is like a feather.

"And now I'll go get the old man, so that you'll be together, like a couple . . . I'll haul you away like a couple, and the two of you can marry the damp earth. But what a wedding you had back then—in a church, with a priest. I didn't go to your wedding, but that's what people said . . ."

Walking back into the cottage, Hnylokvas looks around at the bare walls.

"The two of you lived out your lives, but you didn't amass any wealth. The Lord didn't even give you children."

Gasping, he leans on the sleeping bench and growls at Marko's unmoving heels: "What a man! You couldn't die on the sleeping bench—you had to crawl up on the oven bed so that I'd have more trouble with you."

He grabs a leg with both hands, and just as he gives a good tug a feeble voice gasps: "Is that you, Karpo? Why are you yanking my leg?"

By now Hnylokvas is used to all manner of things, and so even this does not faze him. "So, you're still alive? You haven't died yet? I was pulling you down from the oven bed, but now you can get down by yourself . . . What's there for you to do on this oven bed?"

"What's there to do? I want to die, but I just can't . . . Yavdokha crossed over into the other world this morning, but I just can't," he says, straining to pull his feeble voice out of his chest. "Yesterday the two of us had a talk . . . We said that we'd die together. And she's over there already, but I'm still here. She did what she said she'd do, but I deceived her. Where is she?"

"I've carried her out to the cart."

Marko Hrusha closes his eyes and falls silent. Then he opens them again and says: "I just can't. I want to die—but I can't."

"You aren't trying hard enough."

"I want to die so badly . . . along with Yavdokha, so that we can be together . . . And I didn't know that you were such a fine fellow. You'll help us. You'll help us be together . . . You've taken Yavdokha to the cart, so lug me out to it too. To the cemetery."

"It's to the pit, not the cemetery."

"Let it be to the pit, as long as we're together . . . I'll die along the way. My heart tells me that I'll die along the way."

"And what if you don't die along the way?"

"Then I'll die in the pit."

"Just to be with Yavdokha?"

"Just to be with her."

Hnylokvas stands on the sleeping bench and looks up at the oven bed. Does Marko Hrusha still have his wits about him? Imagine babbling such nonsense. Maybe he's still conscious, but he's not in his right mind.

"Oh, I'm sorry to lose my half pound of bread," he sighs.

"Huh?" Marko Hrusha tries to open the soggy eyelids on his swollen face.

"I said that I'm sorry to lose my half pound of bread."

"You lost your bread?"

"I will lose it . . . I won't haul you to the pit. Don't even ask me to do it."

"Then help me get up, and pull me down from the oven bed, and I'll crawl to the pit myself."

"I won't help you."

"Take pity on me . . ."

"No, I won't. I don't want you to die at Yavdokha's side. It's enough that you lived your life out with her on this earth. And now you want to be together in the next world? And you're begging me to help you? Well, I won't."

Wheezing and gasping, Hnylokvas slides off the sleeping bench on his stomach. Marko Hrusha groans, moves about on the oven bed, and jerks his feet. But he cannot raise himself.

"You better die first . . . And then I'll haul you away."

Holding the reins in his hand and walking beside the funeral cart, he mutters angrily, and his words buzz like wasps: "Do you hear, Yavdokha? I've taken you away from Marko at last . . . Do you know how long I suffered without you? My whole life. Now let him suffer for a while without you . . . Oh, who is that over there under the apple tree?"

On a nearby hillock, a girl with her head slumped on her shoulder is sitting under an apple tree.

"Is she sleeping in the sun, or has she given her soul to God?"

Leaving the funeral cart on the road, Hnylokvas shuffles to the tree on the hillock.

"Are you alive, or are you dead?" he asks the girl who is leaning against the trunk.

The girl does not stir.

"Listen, who are you?" he peers at her. "Oh, it's Pavlo Muzyka's child. Her head is still warm—she isn't stiff yet. Should I wait here until she stiffens? But do I have the time to go back and forth? Well, my girl, I'll haul you away right now."

Hnylokvas takes a couple of small steps, bends over, grabs the unconscious Halya under the arms and, backing up, pulls her off the mound.

"She hasn't even lived as yet; she wasn't even married, and she's died already . . . Oh, she seems to be moaning . . . What are you saying, huh?"

Another moan escapes from the girl's chest.

"You don't want an old man to embrace you? But where is one to find young men to hug you? There are no young ones, so you just have to put up with me."

He drags the unconscious girl to the road and lifts her in his arms to put her in the cart.

Just then, as luck would have it, Pylyp the teacher appears out of the blue. His head sticks out from the collar of his unbuttoned embroidered shirt like a golden sunflower from behind a fence.

"Granddad!" he calls.

And he holds his hands in front of himself as if he were warding off an evil spirit.

"Help me, my boy," Hnylokvas says hoarsely.

"Where are you taking her?"

"To the cart, and then I'll take her away to the pit."

"But she's still alive!" Pylyp shouts. "Can't you hear her? She's groaning. Where are you taking her? She's still alive!"

"She'll die soon anyway . . . Come on, help me."

"Let go of her. Let her be."

"My boy, of what use to you is a living corpse? How much time does she have left to live? And I'm supposed to make another trip for her later? My horse can scarcely lift its legs. But if you're so keen on the dead girl, take her, may you go berserk. No one wants to understand what my job is like."

Leaving the unconscious Halya with the infuriated, wild-eyed teacher, Hnylokvas snaps the reins.

"Giddy-up! Let's go . . . Just try and please these people. You see, a defender has shown up. He sways in even the slightest breeze, but yet . . . And I've just lost half a pound of bread! Well, I'll haul you out to the pit before long, and then I'll get it back. Giddy-up! The day is long, the village is big, and there's so much work that it's hard to get it all done. Our people are so ignorant. Oh, how ignorant they are!"

Old Yustyna sits behind her gate and stares at the road and the village.

The road, winding under the willows and poplars, is blanketed with a thick layer of dust undisturbed even by bathing sparrows. The village is sleeping in broad daylight, as if everything, absolutely everything, has died off. The sun is so searingly hot that the grass is wilting, and the sky, reduced to ashes, is so barren that it is more ghastly than the earth.

Old Yustyna always sits behind her gate. Occasionally she sees someone, or hears something, or imagines something—and in this way she stays in touch with the world around her.

The little boy has hardly any hair; his shirt has pulled out of his pants, and his eyes are like thistles. His torn shirt does not hide his blue skin and protruding ribs.

"My child . . ."

Startled by the old woman's voice, the child freezes in alarm.

It's scary to go past the old woman, and it's equally scary to try to flee. Because this is the Yustyna that everyone talks about.

"What's your name, my child?"

Her voice is gentle—and the gentleness in her voice alarms him even more.

"Yurko," his numb lips whisper.

"And whose little boy are you?"

"I'm Horpyna's boy . . . Horpyna Khrushchykha."

"The Horpyna who lives by the church near the ravine?"

"Yes, near the ravine . . ."

"Your mother's lucky to have a little boy like you." Old Yustyna is happy; she is delighted to chat with the little fellow. "But why don't you stay close to home?"

"I'm going to see my grandfather Ilko. I want to visit him, because he's very old," the little boy's tongue loosens up. "Maybe he'll give me a treat."

"You're a splendid little fellow," and a faint glimmer of a smile lights up her dark face. "Has your grandfather prepared some treats for his grandson?"

"I don't know."

Old Yustyna's face becomes overcast.

"So, you say your mother is Horpyna Khrushchykha? And your grandfather is Ilko?" And she sighs. "Your grandfather is no longer among the living; he died, and Hnylokvas hauled him away to the pit yesterday . . . There will be no treats for you . . ."

Little Yurko turns numb at her words.

"No treats?" he asks sorrowfully after a moment.

"How is he to get them for you now?"

"But my mother and I didn't hear anything about my grandfather . . ."

"Come a bit closer," old Yustyna pleads.

Without thinking, the saddened Yurko takes a step forward, but then hesitates and stops. Even though the old woman's voice is kind, he is still scared.

"Come on, don't be afraid; I'll give you something."

Yurko comes up closer—and then stops abruptly again. Because what will this woman give him? What? Her blue-veined hands are resting on her knees, and there is nothing in them. Maybe she's just luring him on; just look how slyly she's squinting.

And he is about to dash away, when this terrible old woman reaches into the bosom of her shirt.

Mesmerized, Yurko watches her hand, forgetting that he was about to flee. What is she searching for in her bosom? Why is she taking so long?

"You won't have a treat from your grandfather, so you can have one from me . . ."

She takes her hand out of her shirt and slowly opens her fingers. On her withered, wrinkled palm lies a white egg. As if it had just been laid in her bosom, as if it had just been laid there, and aunt Yustyna had brought it out at once into God's world.

"Take it, my child."

And she holds out her hand with the hen's egg in it.

Yurko looks at the egg as if it is a miracle. As if it is a miracle that could disappear just as quickly as it appeared. But . . . maybe as soon as he dares to take the egg, aunt Yustyna will grab him by the hand? And then . . .

In despair, his eyes full of tears, he looks at aunt Yustyna as if pleading with her to take pity on him, not to deceive him.

"Take it, my child, take it," old Yustyna repeats gently.

And Yurko, without thinking about what he is doing, steps forward, stretches out his hand—and the warm egg is on his palm.

"Auntie . . ." he wants to say something—but he does not know what to say.

"Eat it in good health, my boy . . . Grow up strong and healthy."

"Auntie . . ." his voice buzzes, and his tongue is tied in knots.

"As things stand now, you're nothing but skin and bones. Go ahead, take it . . . Your grandfather Ilko won't be giving you any more treats." And old Yustyna, clutching her back, gets up from the bench. She grimaces, as if she feels a wrenching pain.

Yurko is terrified. Will she grab him and drag him into the house? The door to the porch is wide open. He wants to lift his feet off the ground—but he can't.

"O-o-o-o-oh . . . auntie . . ." His teeth are chattering.

"What is it, my child? What is it?"

"O-o-o-o-oh . . . auntie . . ."

Finally, tearing his feet from the ground, he takes to his heels. Clutching the egg, and terrified of tripping and falling, he flees from the terrible aunt Yustyna. And it seems to him that she's running after him, that she'll catch up to him any moment now, because her bony feet are thudding behind him.

"Oh, oh, oh!"

He stumbles on a willow root and crashes to the ground, where he huddles in terror on a patch of dusty, bitter camomile. And there is silence all around. No one is thudding behind him on bony feet. Only a sparrow twitters nearby.

And then he notices that the egg in his hand is broken, and the yolk and egg white are trickling through his fingers. With his heart contorting in pain, he licks his fingers and the shattered shell. Then he licks the droplets from the camomile plants and the spurred rye. And, having licked clean all the plants, he looks around diligently to see if there is anything else that his tongue can lick. There is nothing more.

He gets up and looks all around to see if old Yustyna is anywhere nearby.

The road is empty; the sun is beating down mercilessly; it is scorchingly hot.

Maybe he should go back? Maybe aunt Yustyna will give him another egg? Maybe she has another one in the bosom of her shirt?

O-o-o-oh . . . it's too scary . . . Yurko sits down in the shade of a willow tree. Maybe aunt Yustyna will come down the road, and then he will approach her. But the old woman does not appear, and Yurko drifts off into sleep.

Teklya Kuybida lies on the oven bed and listens to the nightingales. But maybe there are no nightingales singing in her orchard? Maybe the ringing and humming are all in her head? The trilling flows in like a wave—and dies away; it rolls in like a sonorous wave—and fades away. Ashes of the predawn light are strewn throughout the room.

"Mother!" Teklya calls.

It is quiet; no one answers. Where is her mother? Why does she not respond? Teklya thinks hard, and then she remembers and whispers: "Why am I calling her? My mother is gone, may the kingdom of heaven be hers; she died on the Feast of St. Mary the Protectress."

Her mind clouds over, and not a single thought flashes through it. And then, suddenly she sees her father before her. She awakens and calls out joyfully: "Father!"

She opens her eyes, but her father is not there. Only the nightingale's song soars in from the outdoors and reverberates through the room.

"O Lord, why am I calling him? Father crossed over into the next world shortly after mother. She called him to her, and so he did not live long in this world without her . . . I must put their graves in order—adorn them with irises and periwinkle."

A smiling face, like the rising moon, floats into her consciousness.

"Tymko!"

Tymko is listening. He smiles but remains silent.

"Oh, where were you so long? But you're home at last!"

Opening her eyes, she extends her hand to greet her husband —and he vanishes as if he had never been there.

"They've taken you away, yes they have . . . Where have they taken you? Are you still alive, or have your bones turned to dust already?"

The nightingales warble in the orchard next to the cottage, there are fewer shadows in the room, and any minute now the windowpanes will blaze with the golden sun. Teklya wants to raise herself; she leans on her elbow, but it gives way under her, and she falls back and lies face up, trying to gather her strength. After resting for a while, she leans on her elbow again—and once more it buckles under her.

"Stepanko," she calls out.

She listens, but does not hear her child.

"Stepanko, where are you? Help your mother get down from the oven bed. Are you still sleeping, or have you woken up?"

The child is probably still sleeping, even though it is time to get up. Maybe Stepanko can go to the river and catch a fish. It is not possible that all the fish have already been caught; there must be some left in the river. Or maybe he can find a nest of wild duck eggs in the reeds.

"Stepanko, my child."

And suddenly a dreadful thought sears her brain. Maybe Stepanko has fallen into a sleep from which he will never awaken?

Scalded by fear, she pulls herself up, moves over to the ledge, and slides down to the floor. The earthen floor chills her feet. Teklya looks at the plank bed, but her child is not there. And he is not on the sleeping bench, or on the chest.

"Where are you, Stepanko?"

Her mind fogs over, and her heart aches. She totters outside, but cannot see him anywhere. She peers into the storeroom, but he is not there.

"So while I was lying around in bed, my child went down to the pond on his own. Or maybe he went off into the forest . . . Oh, that Stepanko of mine can't sit still for a moment; he's always running off somewhere, he's always trying to find something for me or for himself . . . He takes after his father, after Tymko. That man never could sleep in or stay in bed."

Teklya Kuybida stops by the oven: "Should I light a fire, or shouldn't I? But with what am I to light it? And what will I cook? There isn't a smidgen of flour in the house . . . I must go to the kolhosp to work. Maybe they'll give me some flour paste; yesterday they were giving out flour paste for working in the beet fields."

At the thought of yesterday's flour paste in the beet fields, Teklya becomes more animated, and her mind begins to clear. If they gave out flour paste yesterday, they'll be giving it today as well. She must dress quickly and go to the beet fields. It is quite far to the fields, and it will take her a while to shuffle her way over there.

Where is her spoon? Her bowl?

She takes her spoon and her bowl and tucks them into the bosom of her shirt where they should be safe.

She leaves the door to the cottage unlocked; there is nothing in it for thieves to take, and Stepanko, who is out there someplace, roaming around, should be coming home sooner or later.

It is spring; nightingales are singing, there is a scent of apple blossoms in the air, and the rising sun is flaming and cheerful. Her head is swimming, and she does not delight in the nightingales, the apple blossoms, or the cheerful spring sun. As soon as she gets to the beet field, and as soon as she has a bit of warm flour paste, she will feel better.

"Teklya!"

Someone is calling her, but she cannot see who it is because the sun has blinded her, and now dark ants are crawling before her eyes, blocking everything from view.

"Teklya, stop!"

Standing in front of her, partially obscured by the frantic scurrying of the ants, is an old man.

"Your child is over there in the meadow . . ."

Teklya stops and listens to the old man. "Stepanko?"

"I think it's him."

"Well, so what?"

"Go and get him . . ."

Teklya stands silently and listens.

"He's lying there—he's dead."

The old man falls silent. Teklya does not say anything, and then, stupefied, she turns away and continues stumbling down the road.

The old man catches up to her and grabs her by the elbow. "Teklya! Where are you going?" And he points: "He's over there, in the meadow . . ."

"I'm going to the kolhosp, to work in the beet fields," she mutters.

"To the kolhosp? Why to the kolhosp?"

"To work . . . I'll get some flour paste to eat there . . ."

"Take your dead child from the meadow."

Teklya Kuybida frees her elbow and looks at him in alarm.

"I'll get him later. I'll come home from the kolhosp, and I'll get him then. I'm going to the beet fields now."

And, tightly clutching the bowl tucked away in her bosom, she walks through the village and its flowering orchards, down the road to the beet fields. She walks, and the dark ants swarm in her eyes, obscuring the entire world. Where is that field? Where is it? If only she can get to it. . . . If only she can make it there . . .

The old man falls to his knees, crosses himself, and bows his head to the damp earth; he crosses himself, and prostrates himself again and again . . .

From early morning, young children of all ages wander listlessly through the village. As they trot back and forth, their slow mincing steps evoke an image of hapless birds that used to soar in the open sky, intoxicated by the clear azure heights . . . until their wings were cut off. Their sunken eyes, distant and expressionless, have receded so deeply into their wan faces that they seem to have burned right through their heads with a heavy, leaden pain and are about to fall out and get lost in the dust or in the weeds—and then their empty bloody sockets will blink with a blind, deathly terror, scaring not only the living, but also the dead.

They gather in a gang, a pack that roams through the streets, wandering in from who knows where, and going off to who knows where. And then the gang-pack falls apart, because the sad and the wingless, the indifferent and the weary, fall away from it without ever knowing why they banded together, or what they are searching for.

They come to a stop not far from the house of Kindrat Yaremny, the village head.

Above the cottage with its smiling azure windows sway the branches of a trio of tall ash trees that, draping over it like a tent, filter the streaming sun's rays through their sculpted green leaves and transform them into rolling waves of silvery bubbles on the red tile roof.

The children settle down not far from the house; seating themselves on the knotgrass growing among the cherry trees, they gaze with mournful eyes at the smoke curling lazily out of the chimney.

Grey braids of smoke slowly wind over the chimney, spread over the tiled roof, and either drift off to one side, or float up into the sky. The children watch the smoke as if they have never seen anything more interesting and, all the while, they keep glancing at the closed door of the wooden porch.

They are waiting, hoping that the door will open at any moment.

But no matter how long they sit on the knotgrass, the door does not open.

One of the children can wait no longer. He jumps up from the ground, goes up to the gate, and peers at the yard through the picket fence, combing it with his eyes, waiting and hoping that someone will come out—that someone will come out of the house, and he will be the first one at the gate.

The children stare at the house and at the smoke above it; they breathe the air in deeply, sniff it, and their little heads swarm with dreams and visions.

"The village head is probably baking bread."

"I can smell dumplings with cheese."

"Biscuits with honey and poppy seeds."

"Doughnuts."

"Tarts filled with beans."

Why isn't the door opening? Why? Why doesn't the head's wife come out and bring them a treat? Maybe she doesn't see them through the window?

And a few of the children get up, walk back and forth, and wave their arms about without ever taking their eyes off the house. What if the door opened right now? What if the head's wife brought every one of them a slice of bread, or a dumpling, or a biscuit? Oh, if that should happen, it simply would not do to be late.

But no one comes out, and no one brings them anything.

And the smoke is no longer drifting from the chimney.

Maybe now?

Nothing. Nothing.

The children begin to disperse, and only little Yurko remains. He is patient and clever. He knows why the head's wife has not come out of the house, and why she has not brought them anything. It is because so many of them have gathered—a whole pack of children—and is it possible to find enough for all of them? But now everyone else has gone away, and he is left all alone, and he doesn't need that much, does he? He just needs a little bite, a tiny little bite, just a crumb to put in his mouth, just enough to experience the fragrance and the taste of bread.

And then the door abruptly opens—and the surprise of it takes his breath away. He stands on tiptoe, his mouth hanging open.

It's the head's wife!

She is wearing a cheery white dress sprinkled with blue flowers and green leaves; her blond hair is dishevelled on her overheated forehead, her cheeks are flaming, and her red lips are smiling, revealing sparkling teeth! It is because of him that she has opened the door! She is smiling at him! And Yurko moves towards her, to the gate. And he too is smiling joyfully.

The head's wife stands on the porch holding out a metal tub. She empties some dirty dishwater under a lilac bush, flinging the water so forcefully that the soapy foam lands in bubbles on the branches. And then, smoothing the tousled hair on her forehead, she disappears from the porch.

And the door closes behind her.

Dumbstruck, Yurko is hardly able to swallow the bitterness that wells in his dry throat and, clenching his litle fists and fighting back tears, he trails after the pack of children who can be heard nearby.

Oh, someone is singing. A girl's voice is warbling:

> "Oh woe to that seagull
> That poor little seagull
> Who hatched her nestlings
> Alongside the beaten path."

Who is singing so close by, behind the cherry trees in the side street? Blue, red, and green ribbons flash in her hair, and her embroidered blouse blooms with multicoloured figures. Oh, it's Halya Muzyka.

"Come here," she beckons to him.

"Why?" Yurko asks.

"You're my little son, and you've been lost. Where have you been? O my dear little child!"

And Yurko flees from her—who can say if she is blessed or demented? He flees from this young woman who wanders through the village frightening people with her songs and her chatter.

The grimy, lacklustre gang-pack of children ends up in the yard of granny Khymka. There is not a kinder and more caring old woman in the village, and there is not a child in the pack who has not dropped by her cottage, if not this week, then two or three weeks ago. She will always find something, share something. It may be a boiled potato, or a dried pear from the year before that had gone astray in her storehouse and had just turned up.

And so they all go to see granny Khymka.

Granny Khymka, her eyes closed and her arms folded on her chest, is lying on the sleeping bench.

"Hello!"

Granny Khymka is sleeping—and does not hear.

"Good day to you, granny!"

She does not open her eyes! My goodness but she's sleeping soundly in the middle of the day.

"Shhhh . . . Let her sleep."

And they all eagerly eye the nooks and crannies. Finally, one of them can no longer wait, and he peers into the oven, but the oven is empty; there is only a pile of ashes on the ledge. They look in the ash bin, but there is only garbage in it; they look in the wood box, but there is only brushwood in it, and it reeks of mouse droppings. Maybe there's something in the inglenook? Only some hurds of hemp. What about on the stove? On the stove there is nothing but the acrid smell of soot.

They search in the porch, but they do not find anything.

In the storehouse there are only cobwebs on the walls.

In the stable only the beams protrude like bared ribs.

"Granny Khymka, wake up!" Yurko begs.

Granny Khymka's eyes are closed, and her arms are folded on her chest.

"Shhhh . . . She's sleeping."

Granny Khymka is sleeping an eternal sleep, and the hungry children creep slowly from the barren yard like reddish-brown mice.

Yurko looks back once last time. Maybe granny Khymka will get up, come out after them, and taking pity on them, call them to her?

The beekeeper Myna involuntarily tucks his head into his shoulders—someone is knocking on the window. But maybe it just seems that way to him? The hour is late, and all sorts of nonsense beset one's head at bedtime.

His head, covered with bristly dark grey hair, sits on his narrow shoulders like a hedgehog among fallen leaves in an orchard.

Suddenly his head retracts still deeper into his shoulders.

Someone knocks on the pane once again.

"Do you hear? Do you hear?" Melanka says in a dull, frightened voice from the oven bed. "Someone's knocking on the window."

"Of course I hear it," Myna whispers.

"He'll knock for a while, and then he'll go away. Don't open the door."

"Oh, sure, sure, and he'll do as you say."

All at once the window frame shakes from a sharp blow, and the glass rattles. Myna huddles against the wall, as if his slight figure had been smeared over it by that blow.

"I told you to put out the light—not to keep it on."

"Oh sure, you said that—may you be struck dumb!" Myna gets up from the sleeping bench and, walking like a doomed man, goes into the porch. Standing by the door, he asks: "Who's there?"

"Fellow villagers," responds an unknown male voice.

"What villagers?" Myna asks again, expecting the worst.

"From the village office," another strange voice calls out.

"Come tomorrow, when its light outside."

"So you're about to tell the village councillors when they are to come? Doesn't the village administration have a mind of its own? Come on, open up!"

But before Myna manages to unlatch the door, two or three late-night visitors ram their way into the porch, twist his hands behind his back, tie them up, and shove his gaunt body into the house so hard that he trips on the threshold and tumbles to the floor.

"Just lie there like that! Who's in the house?"

"And where are the councillors?" Myna peers at his guests.

"We're the rulers and the councillors!"

Two of them remain silent, while the third one does all the shouting; it is obvious that they have agreed on this tactic beforehand. This third man is tall, and the kerchief that is pulled down low, to his eyebrows, makes him look like a woman—if it were not for the blond moustache over his plump lip.

O Lord, the other two are also wrapped in kerchiefs! So what kind of rulers and councillors are they? And Myna turns cold all over. He has heard a lot about men who go into the storerooms and cottages of other people, and now these men have pounced on them. O Lord have mercy and make them go away; have mercy and make them go away.

"Oh, so your wife's up there, on the oven bed! Get down from there, woman! Get a blanket and put everything from the trunk into it. The sheepskin coat, and the boots . . . Get a move on; you're lumbering around like a bear chasing sparrows."

Melanka slides down awkwardly from the oven bed. And now she is by the trunk, holding a blanket and opening the lid.

"There's nothing but junk in here," she mutters.

"It's not for you to judge!" And then he turns to Myna: "Is there any whiskey?"

"No, there isn't. What am I to make it out of?"

"Don't lie."

"But I know where there is some. Should I go and get it?"

The uninvited guests exchange glances, and for a moment it looks as if they might tell him to go and fetch the whiskey.

"We've seen wise guys like you before," the tall man breathes deeply and tugs angrily at his moustache. "You'll just run away. Tell us, where have you hidden your gold? Come on, fellows, lift him up off the floor!"

The men rush up to Myna, grab him by his bound hands, and start twisting them higher and higher, until he is almost bent in two, and his head is dizzy from the pain.

Melanka watches and crosses herself. "Oh Lord!" she gasps.

"Let him go, fellows," one of the men says. "Let him catch his breath. He's probably remembered where the gold is hidden."

Myna groans: "What gold? My father had a few gold pieces, but thieves took them during the Civil War. Didn't you hear about it? And now you've come here again for that same gold?"

"We're from Petrivka, so we didn't hear about it," replied one of the men who had not spoken previously. "How could we know?"

"Maybe our own villagers took them, and maybe it was men from Petrivka . . . And do you think that under this new government of ours it has been possible to pile up any gold?"

"You're a beekeeper! With so many hives!"

"Do bees lay gold? And after we were all chased into the kolhosp, I had no more bees. My bees were chased into the kolhosp as well, and they all died off there."

"Yes, they did die off," agrees one of the men from Petrivka, the one who up to now had remained silent.

"Do you think we'd begrudge you the gold if we had any?"

"Well, wouldn't you?" the man with the blond moustache asks mockingly.

"There's nothing to begrudge," Myna tries to extricate himself.

"Listen, you haven't seen us anywhere, have you? And you don't know us, do you?" the tall man asks, winking at the man from Petrivka.

"Where could we have seen you . . ."

"Don't say anything about us to anyone. If you so much as say one word, we'll burn your house down. Do you hear? Hey there, old woman, have you tied the bundle? Let's have it! So, you've tied it up yourself, and you're giving it to us yourself, and, since you're giving it to us, we'll take it, because no one refuses a gift . . . Do you understand?"

"We understand."

"And don't so much as step out of the house until morning. We weren't here, and you didn't see us."

"Blow out the lamp, old woman; we don't want any light."

Numb with fear, Melanka puffs at the lamp—and the flame goes out.

The husband and wife, hunched over and quaking with fear in the darkness, listen to the thieves' movements until their shadows slide out of the house into the darkness of the night. After rustling about for a while under their windows, the thieves do not head for the road, but take off through the garden; apparently they were going to make their getaway by cutting through the village gardens.

"Untie my hands, Melanka . . . Cut the rope with a knife."

Melanka finds a knife and cuts the rope.

Myna almost weeps from the pain and the indignity that he has been subjected to.

Melanka closes the trunk, and the lid drops with a dull, hungry sound.

"Did you recognize him, Myna?" she whispers.

Myna grits his teeth, trying to keep the pain in check.

Melanka shuffles around him in her bare feet and murmurs almost inaudibly in his ear.

"Huh?" her husband asks. He is hard of hearing.

"That one, the one from Petrivka . . . He isn't from Petrivka at all. I recognized him. He's one of ours . . ."

Groaning, Myna takes a step from the doorway to the sleeping bench—and stops dead; he is in too much pain to walk.

"Do you hear me? He's one of ours . . . I recognized him when he spoke. It was Vasyl Hnoyovy!"

"What did you say?"

"It was Vasyl Hnoyovy, and not someone from Petrivka. We have to inform the village council."

And suddenly the beekeeper Myna flies into a frenzy. He attacks his wife, pummelling her with his fists and ramming her with his knees.

"That's so you'll know, you stupid old woman . . . That's so you'll know, you stupid old woman!"

Melanka shrieks and raises her elbows to protect herself. Her husband seems to have lost his mind, to have gone berserk.

"You saw Hnoyovy? Did you see Hnoyovy? Tell me!"

Melanka just groans and moans.

"No, you didn't. You didn't see Hnoyovy! And Hnoyovy was not in our house. It was a man from Petrivka that was here. They were all from Petrivka! And I'll keep beating you until I beat that Hnoyovy out of your head! Until I beat it into your head that all the men were from Petrivka. So, tell me, who was here?"

"Men from Petrivka . . ."

"Will you remember that?

"I'll remember . . ."

"Then sit there like a mouse and don't even squeak! Don't you know what people are like these days? Have you forgotten? Well, have you? They'll burn our house—and they'll kill us . . . If word ever gets out to Vasyl Hnoyovy, we're finished! There isn't a worse cutthroat than Vasyl Hnoyovy!"

Collapsing on the sleeping bench, the beekeeper Myna whispers to himself through chattering teeth: "It would have been better if he hadn't said a word. But he had to speak up, and the stupid old woman recognized him, much to her own misfortune and ruination, and to mine!"

The open carriage, drawn by two roan horses, will long be remembered and talked about. And with the passage of time, it will be talked about mainly by those who will have managed to survive, who will have grown up and told their children and, later, their grandchildren, and all sorts of acquaintances and people that they will meet up with on their path through life. The story about the carriage will be embellished with all sorts of details that probably never existed, but just now, this carriage is driving into the village.

This open carriage, on its light, springy wheels, is entering the village, and the weary horses are slowing their gait. A man dressed in a bright suit and light canvas shoes is holding the reins; a breeze is ruffling his blond hair, and his grey eyes protrude from his plump round face like two fat, contented quails. Beside him sits a young lady in a silk, cream-coloured dress that ripples and caresses her attractive body like silky, creamy water. Her hair is as light as the man's, her fine dark eyebrows quiver like taut violin strings and, under these brows, her large dark eyes, in which a silent sorrow is frozen, seem even bigger, deeper, and more pronounced because of that sorrow.

The woman looks at the drowsy, unusually silent village—and it seems that she is afraid to look, as if she is taking care not to see what up to now has remained hidden from her eyes, but which will now confront her, striking terror into her heart.

A child, seeing the carriage and the two strangers in it, tags along behind it, stirring up clouds of dust with his bare feet.

"Dmytro Dmytrovych . . ."

"What is it, my dear?"

"It's terrible to look at that child. Just take a look . . ."

The man glances over his shoulder at the child trailing after the carriage.

"He's a child like any other child. What do you find so strange about him?"

"Why is he following us?"

"Just because." And Dmytro Dmytrovych smiles, casting a warm, loving look at the woman. "He wants to admire and take delight in a beauty like you."

"Oh, what a thing to say."

"But it's true! Has he ever seen anyone like you? I am unable to stop looking at you myself, so the same is doubly true for the likes of him. Just look. There comes another one now . . ."

Truly, another child is now dogging the carriage without lowering his sad, thoughtful eyes.

"Oh, and now there's another one . . ."

As the open carriage slowly makes its way into the village, more and more children trail after it; they move in a flock and send the dust clouds flying.

"It's dreadful, Dmytro Dmytrovych . . . Their clothing is so ragged, and they look so unfortunate . . ."

"You can't feel sorry for everyone . . ."

The children, as if under a spell, stare at the horses, the open carriage, and the splendidly attired man and woman, who seem to have appeared out of nowhere, and who are going heaven only knows where. They might be from the district capital, and they might be going to the railway station.

Suddenly the man draws in the reins, and the carriage comes to a standstill. And the flock of children stops a short distance behind it. The beautiful woman in the silk dress gets out of the carriage and walks directly to the youngsters.

She is crying as she walks.

Why is she crying?

And in her hands . . .

In her hands something gleams whitely; it shines and glitters, as if she were carrying a fiery chunk of the sun itself. The children look intently at the woman and at the sun that she is pressing to her breast, the sun that is transforming her into a sun as well.

But why is she crying?

Bread?

The woman is holding a white, wheaten loaf of bread.

A woman. Bread.

"Children," the woman calls out through her tears. "Come, children . . . Here's some bread . . ."

And she slices the loaf with a knife. The children cannot believe their eyes. The children cannot believe that the woman has come down from the carriage, that she is slicing bread, and that she is already holding a slice of white bread in her hand. The fragrance from the sliced bread is spreading throughout the village, throughout the world. Is it possible that she is about to give away this slice? To whom will she give it?

"Take it my child . . ."

And the slice of wheaten bread comes to rest on a grimy, chapped hand.

"Take it, my child."

And another slice comes to rest on a child's palm.

They stand as if struck dumb, drinking in the aroma. Is it possible that this woman will slice the whole loaf without any regrets?

She cuts off another slice.

"This is for you, my child."

They all receive a slice, except for a freckled girl who is still waiting, hoping against hope that she will also get one.

"What's your name, my little one?" the woman asks her.

"Katya," comes the whispered reply.

Katya timidly takes the last slice, and the woman is left with the crust.

"Do you have a little brother?" the woman asks her.

"Yes . . . His name is Mykolka."

"Take this crust for Mykolka."

And she passes her the crust, pats her gently on the head, and turns away. And then, weeping unrestrainedly, she stumbles back to the carriage.

The children stare at the wagon for a long time, and as they do so, Katya backs away from the group. She also watches the carriage and the woman who is seated once again in the carriage, but she continues backing away until she reaches a clump of bushes.

Making her way to a spot where the bushes are the densest, where even the sun's rays do not penetrate, she hides the crust in her bosom and raises the slice of bread to her lips. Her teeth are anxious to bite the bread, but her lips kiss it. They kiss it with a long, lingering kiss—a kiss that is sweet and intoxicating. And then they kiss it once again with another long kiss—and this kiss is even sweeter and more intoxicating! Tearing the bread away from her lips, Katya looks at it as if this slice has flown into her hand like a golden bird from heaven knows where, and as if it might just as unexpectedly burst into flight and disappear. She squeezes the bread more tightly, and then she once again raises it to her lips—and the third kiss is still sweeter and still more intoxicating.

"This is a gift from the Mother of God," Katya whispers. "It is the Mother of God who came down to earth and brought us this bread."

Ever so carefully, she bites into the outermost edge of the slice—and leans back with closed eyes. The strange healing strength of the bread makes her little head swim. Katya is afraid to chew the bread; she just touches it gingerly with the tip of her tongue. Her tongue brushes against it—and halts; it touches it—and faints with delight.

Can this actually be bread?

What a good idea it was to hide in these bushes. No one can see her here; no one can take away even a crumb!

But, regardless how large the slice, or how slowly it is eaten, there comes a time when it will all be gone, and Katya chews with deliberate slowness, fearing to swallow the last bite, because once she swallows it, there will be no more bread. After chewing the last bite, she swallows her saliva, touches the crust of bread in her bosom that she got for Mykolka and, crawling on all fours, creeps out of the bushes, looking around fearfully to see if anyone is nearby.

There is no one in sight, and so she sets out for home.

It seems to her that the crust in her bosom is burning her breast and glowing so brightly through her shirt that anyone walking by would be able to see it and snatch it away from her. This is why she is afraid of meeting someone, and so, when she sees a human figure in the distance, she hides either in the tall grass or behind some trees, and waits patiently until the danger passes.

And now she can see her cottage near the wild pear trees, and her mother standing by the well with an empty pail on a rope that she seems unable to lower into the well.

Katya comes up closer. "Mother!" she calls out, wanting to brag about the crust of bread.

But her mother does not hear her; she seems unaware that someone is speaking to her.

"Mummy dear!" Katya calls out still more joyfully.

The mother jumps back startled and looks at her daughter. There are bitter tears in the mother's eyes.

"Mummy, why are you crying? Mummy, don't cry . . ."

"How am I not to cry? When such a terrible tragedy has befallen us . . ."

"What tragedy, mummy?"

"Our little Mykolka has died . . . He died just now . . ."

"But it isn't possible that Mykolka has died," Katya whispers.

"He fell asleep—and didn't wake up."

Katya runs into the cottage. Her brother Mykolka is lying on a blanket on the bed with his hand tucked under his cheek. "Listen, Mykolka! Wake up!"

He does not hear her.

Katya comes up closer, and touches his cheek. "Mykolka, wake up! I've brought you some bread."

He is sleeping soundly—and he does not wake up.

Katya shouts right in his ear: "I don't believe you! You're pretending. Wake up!"

And then she backs away from him. Maybe he truly has died; maybe he isn't pretending that he is sleeping.

And she is the one who is to blame, because she had lingered too long in the bushes eating her slice of wheaten bread. And so, poor Mykolka has not lived to eat the crust given to him by that woman. If Katya had not tarried, if she had run home more quickly, Mykolka would have eaten the bread, and he would not have died.

She wants to cry, but her eyes are dry, ever so dry.

Suddenly, she finds it terrifying to look at the dead Mykolka.

Backing up into the porch, she sees the ladder leaning against the wall and crawls up into the attic. She will burrow herself in the straw up here, and no one will find her; she will hide here from death—the death that is stalking the village and killing people, just as it has found Mykolka and killed him.

She feels so sorry for her brother—so very sorry!

Her hand grazes the bosom of her shirt and touches the bread.

Hesitating for a moment, Katya pulls out the crust, looks at it in wonderment, and then lifts it to her lips and warms it with a protracted kiss. The bread smells even more intoxicating, even more tantalizing than the piece that she ate in the bushes. Oh, no, that slice did not have a wonderful fragrance like this one.

Rejoicing that she has hidden herself away in the attic from the world, that no one can see her, and that no one will take away this priceless treasure, Katya cautiously bites into the bread and chews it, fearing to lose even a crumb.

And it occurs to her that Mykolka could be eating this bread, but now she is eating it, and she wants it so badly, so very badly!

And an unbidden thought wanders through her head.

It is a good thing that Mykolka has died.

It is a good thing that Mykolka has died, and that, instead of having to give him the bread, she can keep it. Now she will eat the bread herself. From now on she will be her mother's only child, and she will never again have to share anything with her brother, because he has died, and he no longer needs anything. Nothing at all! From now on she is the only one who will get everything— everything that grows in the garden or in the orchard; everything that mother manages to get somewhere; and everything that someone brings as a treat. Mother will no longer be worrying about finding shoes for Mykolka, but just for her, for Katya; and maybe mother will even find her a kerchief, and a new little dress, because the one that she is wearing is worn and tattered.

It is a good thing that Mykolka has died. He will no longer beg for food or for clothes, and she will no longer have to share anything with him.

And, oh my, how tasty this bread is! How very very tasty!

Halya Muzyka crawls up the ladder into the attic and rummages in the remains of the crumbling straw. She searches feverishly while talking to herself: "Oh, mother was right."

Her fingers find something in the littered straw, and she cries out: "Oh, what a wise mother I have."

After a while, she comes down from the attic, her eyes sparkling with joy.

"I gathered some, mother," she says. "But how did you come up with the idea of scattering beans in the rubbish and in the straw?"

"I had to think of something," Mariya replies. "Now we'll boil the beans with pigweed and nettles, and we'll have something to eat. But if I hadn't scattered those beans there, you wouldn't have found any. I outsmarted them . . ."

"Outsmarted whom?"

"The men who came to search our cottage. They looked through everything and rummaged everywhere; they dug up everything and ran their hands over everything. But not one of them thought of looking in the rubbish in the attic. They think that they're so devilishly clever, but I outsmarted them."

While Halya is washing the beans in a dish, her mother goes outside to pick some pigweed. Before long she comes back in with a fistful of green weeds and says: "Andriy Synytsya was out there; he was asking about you."

"What did he ask?"

"He wanted to know if you were at home."

"And what did you say?" Halya blushes furiously.

"I said, that yes, you were at home. And he said: 'You'll have some guests soon.' And then he continued on his way. So, I guess you can expect some guests. But why?"

"How am I to know?" Halya smiles.

She lights the stove, puts the beans on to boil, and at the same time furtively tries to make herself more presentable, washing her face, combing her hair, and putting on an embroidered blouse. And all the while a soft song blooms on her lips.

Her mother watches her and wonders what is going on.

And then Andriy Synytsya crosses the threshold—in a cap with a shiny visor. His hair, black as tar, winds its way down from under the visor and falls in waves over his high, flat forehead. His lips are tightly clamped, and the veins on his neck are protruding. And his eyes, oh, his eyes . . . The young man's eyes are strange, as if clouded over by dark smoke.

Mariya looks at him and thinks: "Did he come to pick a quarrel?"

"Good day, auntie," he says.

"Good day. Well, don't just stand there. Come in and be our guest."

Andriy Synytsya walks up to the table and sits down in the place of honour under the icons. He sits down, coughs, and stares at Halya with such a heavy, unblinking stare, that the girl feels a chill of fear.

"Why are you looking at me like that, Andriy?"

But he just keeps on staring as he clenches and unclenches his fists, and does not say a word.

"How are things going for you?" Mariya enters into the conversation.

Andriy Synytsya does not seem to hear her.

"Oh my dear God," Mariya thinks fearfully. "He's changed; he's no longer the Synytsya that he used to be; he's a different man now. He used to be so talkative, but now he doesn't say a word. He used to laugh, but now he just glowers. I'm afraid, but it seems that Halya isn't frightened. And as luck would have it, the master isn't at home."

"What's new in the village, Andriy?"

He is silent.

"We're cooking a handful of beans, so you can eat with us. But we don't have any bread."

Not a peep from him.

"Oh Lord," Mariya thinks. "Can it be that the lad has lost his wits?"

Suddenly Andriy speaks. "Aunt Mariya, I've been thinking."

"What is it that you've been thinking?" Mariya is happy to hear his voice.

"Will you give me Halya's hand in marriage?"

"Oh my!" Mariya exclaims involuntarily. "But have you asked Halya already? Listen, Halya, has he asked you? Our Halya is still very young."

"Young?" he repeats. "How much longer is she going to live?"

"What are you saying?" Mariya asks in astonishment, "My Halya does not have long to live? But are you the one who knows how many years she has left? And is this how you come courting, in such a strange, unheard-of manner?"

Halya pretends that she is fussing with the food on the stove, but she listens intently to the conversation.

Andriy Synytsya falls silent and says nothing more.

"Who takes a wife nowadays? Who gets married? Who has weddings?"

"But there are weddings now, mother," Halya says softly.

"Only those who can afford it have a wedding now . . . The food, the drinks, the music . . . And the dancing? We've danced more than enough . . . Nothing but grief and tears."

And all the while she is thinking: "Yes, he has gone mad. In Halya's case, her madness comes and goes; it comes and goes. But what will happen if two people who have lost their minds get together? May the good Lord protect us and have mercy on us. Oh, my dear Halya, don't you know that I want good fortune to be yours? But there is no good fortune in our home, just grief and poverty."

"You have nothing with which to put on a wedding, Andriy, and we don't have anything either," Mariya says out loud.

"But I do have something," he glares at her with clouded eyes. "I have meat."

"Meat? What kind of meat? What have you slaughtered or butchered? There's nothing to slaughter, and there's nothing to butcher. Or have you borrowed something? But no one will lend you anything now."

"We have our own meat . . . I prepared it for the wedding."

He sits at the table, clenching and unclenching his fists as if he is trying to choke something—but without any success.

"There's no talk yet of a wedding, and you've already prepared the meat . . ."

"He really is sick in the head," Mariya thinks. "He truly has lost his mind. What wedding? What meat? He's swollen with hunger, and his legs look like logs, but he's decided to get married. And, instead of trying to find a girl who has all her senses, he's come to court a girl who is as daft as he is. What is this world coming to?"

And then she says bitterly: "Do you intend to come and live with us? Or will you take Halya into your home?"

"I live alone now, so why would I come and live with you?"

"Alone? But what about your younger brother Semen? And what about your mother?"

"What brother?" Andriy frowns. "I have no brother, and I have no mother."

"What do you mean?" Halya tears herself away from the stove. "Where are they?"

"Oh, Lord!" Mariya groans, expecting to hear dreadful news.

"I don't have a brother or a mother. And I never did."

172 | Yevhen Hutsalo

He gets up from the table and walks out of the house, tucking his head into his shoulders as if afraid that someone will strike him from behind . . .

The mother and daughter eat the cooked beans and pigweed in a heavy, mournful silence. First the mother sips a spoonful of soup, and then the daughter sips a spoonful; first the mother—and then the daughter.

And then Pavlo Muzyka, looking angry and out of sorts, walks into the house.

"Come in and sit down, and have a bite to eat with us."

"Was Synytsya here?" Pavlo does not so much ask the question, as hiss it.

"Yes, he was."

"Why did he come here?"

And he crosses himself before the icons.

"He came to court Halya."

"To court Halya? And nothing more? And you're still alive?"

And he looks in alarm at his wife and his daughter, hardly believing that they are alive.

"We're alive . . ."

"As soon as Synytsya walked out of our house, the village police and the militia seized him and took him away."

"The police and the militia?"

Pavlo Muzyka sits down at the table and leans his head on his black fists. He sits as if he is in a fog, and his lips are sealed.

"Well, tell us, Pavlo . . ."

The master of the house looks heavily at Mariya, as if he were weighing her down with a stone. Halya, turning ashen, does not say a word.

"What's there to tell you? They took him away."

"What did he do? He was courting Halya . . ."

"He was courting Halya? He hacked his brother Semen to death with an axe and stuffed him in the oven . . ."

"O my God . . ."

"And he drowned his mother Skeleta in the well."

"In the well? Why would he do that to his own mother? O my dear God . . ."

"Because he's gone stark raving mad . . . The neighbours saw him do it."

"He's gone mad . . ."

Suddenly Halya bursts out laughing, and begins sputtering through her laughter: "Andriy Synytsya has gone mad . . ."

"O daughter, my dear daughter," Mariya says.

"Andriy Synytsya has gone mad!" Halya laughs gleefully, and she is happier than her father and mother have seen her for a long time.

Leaping up from the table and placing her hands on her hips, she whirls around the room in a dance and sings: "Andriy Synytsya has gone mad! Andriy Synytsya has gone mad!"

Teklya Kuybida totters into their yard with a bundle on her back and comes to a sudden stop. It is hard to say if her legs are giving way beneath her because the bundle is too heavy, or if she is weak from lack of food, but she is wavering, and it looks as if at any moment she will walk out again, beyond the gate.

"Mariya!" she can scarcely draw her voice out of her chest. "Come here . . . into the barn."

"Into the barn?" Mariya asks from the porch.

She finds it strange that Teklya has come into her yard and, instead of coming into the house, is asking her to go to the barn. Oh, she is already shuffling her way into the barn. Maybe she is hiding from someone? Or maybe she's afraid of someone? Just think—she might be bringing trouble along with herself into their yard. As if they did not have enough trouble of their own.

"What's happened?" she asks Teklya in the barn.

Teklya Kuybida eases the bundle from her shoulders to the ground and tries to catch her breath. Mariya glances anxiously at the doorway to see if anyone has followed them. There is no one there.

"Where are you coming from, that your legs are so tired?" she asks Teklya.

"Oh, don't even ask . . . I'm dying of hunger, Mariya, and my Stepanko has already died. Maybe you heard about him."

"Yes, I did, may the kingdom of heaven be his."

"So maybe I can beg something from you to eat?"

"What can you beg from me, if we ourselves are swelling from hunger?"

"People say that you stashed away some grain."

"People say a lot of things."

"I'm not asking you to give me something for nothing, Mariya. Just look here . . ."

Teklya bends over her bundle, reaches into it, and pulls out something.

"Look . . ."

"What is it?"

"Don't you see? It's an embroidered linen shirt." Teklya gives the rolled up cloth a good shake, and Mariya sees a wrinkled woman's shirt that glitters with festive embroidery on the front and sleeves.

"It really is a shirt," Mariya is surprised.

She examines the shirt—and falls silent, because her tongue goes numb and lies heavily in her mouth like a grindstone.

"It's a fine shirt," Teklya gives it another shake.

"There are reddish-brown spots here, on the hem . . ."

"They'll wash out—and they'll be gone. Will you take it?"

"What do you mean, take it? Where did you get it? What do you have in that bundle? You're acting strange, Teklya."

"You don't want the shirt? Then take this rushnyk."

And she spreads out the rushnyk that she has pulled out of the bundle—a rushnyk embroidered with birds of paradise amid the lush flowers of a heavenly orchard.

"Look here!"

And Teklya grabs another rushnyk, even brighter and more colourful; it is not just a piece of embroidery—it is a work of art.

"Just look at this one!'

And still another rushnyk bursts out of the bundle, fluttering and quivering like a fantastic legendary bird in Teklya's swollen hands.

Stunned, Mariya stares at it, and a wave of fear sweeps over her. Fear because they have hidden themselves here in the barn away from peoples' eyes; fear because of the crazed, demented Teklya; fear because of the embroidery flaming in her hands.

"Why is it mouldy?"

"Mouldy? So, you don't want it? But this isn't all; just look how much I have. Take it; just don't be stingy with the bread."

The door opens, and Pavlo Muzyka stands like an ominous shadow on the threshold. Teklya should have been alarmed, but she is not; she even seems happy at the unexpected appearance of the master of the house.

"Come on in, Pavlo, and look at this," she says. "But shut the door, so that an evil eye does not come by and see us. Just look at what I'm showing your wife. Don't worry, there will be an embroidered shirt in here that will fit you as well. Here . . ."

And she holds out an embroidered man's shirt.

"Take whatever you want; I don't begrudge you any of it. Just give me at least a sliver of bread."

Pavlo's eyes appear to be glued to the embroidered man's shirt.

"Mariya," he says, "do you see it?"

"I see it, Pavlo."

"Whose shirt is this?"

"It's yours, Pavlo."

"Take it, take it, my good people," Teklya says happily. "Oh, thank goodness that you at least like the shirt. And I don't need much payment for it—just a bit of bread."

"It's mine," Pavlo's lips twitch as he examines the shirt carefully. "You embroidered it, Mariya . . ."

"I embroidered it for you, tenderly placing one stitch next to the other . . ." his wife is almost weeping.

She takes the shirt, kisses it, and presses it to her cheeks.

Pavlo approaches Teklya threateningly. "Tell me, you damn bitch, where did you find my shirt? Mariya embroidered this shirt for me ten years ago."

"So it's your shirt? You recognized it?"

Teklya moves towards the bundle as if she wants to grab it and rush out of the barn, but the furious master blocks her path.

"I'm not saying that it isn't yours. If Mariya recognized it, then it must be yours . . ."

"Come on, tell us where you found it, before I kill you right here, on the spot."

"Why would you bring a sin down on your soul? I'll tell you," Teklya says humbly. "But just look at this, just look."

She picks up the sack, shakes it, and the contents fall out.

"Just look at these rushnyks, just look at them . . . And look at these tablecloths!"

Rushnyks, wrinkled tablecloths, women's blouses, men's shirts, and all kinds of treasures scatter at their feet.

"Take them; they're all yours. I don't need any of them. Just give me some bread."

"So are you going to tell us where you got them, or aren't you, you wretched cur!" Pavlo is ready to attack her.

"From the storehouse, of course, from the storehouse . . . It stands next to the ravine, and the water kept washing away the ground from under it until there was a gaping hole under one wall. And I could see what was happening; it's close to my place."

"Did you crawl into the storehouse?"

"How could I? There's a lock on the door! The water from the ravine washed the ground away, and all sorts of things began falling into the clay. And when I went there to get some clay, I found all kinds of treasures like these in the puddles. It was a sin to let them go to waste, so I gathered them up and came to you with them."

"But the storehouse belongs to the kolhosp."

"Who is saying that it doesn't? Of course it belongs to the kolhosp."

Mariya shakes her head: "When they were forcing people to join the kolhosp . . . That's when they took this shirt away from me. Whenever they found embroidered articles in anyone's home, they took them away. So that everything would belong to the kolhosp. And they carted everything away to that storehouse. After that, I never saw any of these things again. And now that I've seen them—my heart is bleeding. Just look at these embroideries— they've rotted in some spots, and turned mouldy in others."

"They've socialized them," Pavlo mutters.

"Huh?" Teklya seems to snap out of a stupor.

"I said that they've socialized them."

"Oh, dear me, dear me," Mariya presses the shirt to her breast. "There's so much grief—and there's no end to it in sight."

"There's such a gaping hole in that storehouse that a lot more is going to fall out, and thieves won't have to crawl in to get it. But if this shirt is yours, take it. Take whatever you want."

"Come on, pick it all up!" Pavlo thunders at her. "Pick up all these rags!"

Teklya squats and begins picking up the embroidered pieces and stuffing them back into the sack. She would like to understand what is happening, but she cannot comprehend anything, and so she pulls in her head, as if expecting a blow.

"Have you got it all? And now, take it away from here!"

"Where am I to take it?"

"Take it back to where you got it . . . I don't want Shpytalny or Yaremny to put me in jail. To put me away because of you. I didn't take these things, and I didn't steal them, so why should I be put in jail for them . . . for these things that belong to the kolhosp. Take them away."

"But they'll turn mouldy and rot there, Pavlo," Mariya says.

"What's it to you? Let them turn mouldy and rot . . . They belong to the kolhosp!"

"But it's your shirt . . ."

"And I'm saying that the shirt also belongs to the kolhosp. Let it turn mouldy and rot. Give it back to her!"

Pavlo Muzyka snatches the embroidered shirt from his wife and thrusts it at Teklya.

"Take it! Get out of here!"

Mariya weeps, and is blinded by her tears. And when she finally opens her eyes, neither her husband nor Teklya with her bundle of bitter embroidery is in the barn. It is all like a dream— a dream that is now burning her head and searing her thoughts.

The old man Karpo Hnylokvas taps Khrystyna's window with his cherry tree whip and listens attentively.

All is quiet.

He peers in through the pane—it is as misty inside the cottage as it is outside. It is as if the rain is falling not only out in the open, but also in the cottage; as if a grey cloud has been blown in under the ceiling.

"Domka!" he looks around at the garden and the orchard.

"Domka . . . Is she sleeping, or is she gone?"

His lame feet sinking into the ground, old man Hnylokvas walks into the cottage, because he has to do what he has to do.

"Domka!" he calls out inside the house.

There is no one. Puckering his face because of a nauseous smell in the cottage, Hnylokvas goes up to a flowered curtain that separates the sleeping nook from the rest of the room and yanks it to one side.

"O Lord . . . Khrystyna . . ."

On a narrow sleeping bench in the corner lies a woman; she is covered with a blanket, and her hands are clenched on top of it. Her fingers are so thin and yellow that if you were to light a candle and place it in her hands, she would truly look like a corpse. Her nose and chin are sharply outlined, her forehead is like a slab of wood, and her yellow, transparent skin is stretched so tautly over her face that a light touch would cause it to crack. Her almost transparent eyelids are drawn over her eyes. She looks like a cadaver. If only she would move her lips or raise an eyebrow.

"She's gone . . . Khrystyna, do you hear me? Tell me, are you gone already?"

Khrystna remains silent.

"Yes, she's gone. The devil take it."

Feeling dizzy, he gropes in his pockets for something to smoke, but then, remembering that he has forgotten to take both his flint and his tobacco, he groans angrily.

"My heart's gone numb for lack of tobacco . . . Oh, it's you, Domka!"

Domka appears in the cottage unexpectedly, like a divine spirit.

It is as if the wind has blown her in. Scrawny and bent in two, withered and light, she does not look like a living person, but rather like the casing of a human being.

"I was calling you . . ."

Domka does not walk; she appears to float in the air, held aloft by a little white cloud that is lifting her upwards. And that little cloud is her grey hair that, tousled like wool that is ready to be spun, looks like the feathery tufts of late summer flowers. And, under those tufts her eyes are wisps of vapour—bluish vapour framed by flowery tufts.

"Why have you come?" Domka asks. "There's nothing for you to profit by here."

"Well, I just dropped by . . . to see you."

"Why me?"

"Oh, to see if you'd give me a drink!"

And he coughs.

Domka looks in stunned silence at Hnylokvas who is stooped over in front of her like a bush with knotted, twisted roots.

"Where am I to get it? There is none."

"I know that it isn't possible to beg even a spoonful of heated tar from you," he thumps his whip on the floor. "I just dropped by . . . Isn't it time to take Khrystyna to the pit? It must be. She's neither breathing, nor moving. How long has she been lying there like that?"

"Khrystyna's alive!" Domka shrieks.

"Alive? How many years has she been lying there like that?"

"For a good many years—so many that they can't be counted; since the civil war."

"Since the civil war!" Hnylokvas scratches the nape of his neck with his wiry fingers. "She should have been taken away a long time ago."

"But she hasn't died. She's just sleeping," Domka wrings her hands in despair.

"What kind of a sleep is this? How long is it possible to sleep like this? When will she wake up? Anyone else would have buried her long ago, but you . . ."

"I take care of her. I feed her," Domka sobs, "and she sleeps."

"She sleeps? And she doesn't talk? Does she ever say so much as a word in her sleep?"

"She sleeps, and does not speak at all. But the day will come when she will speak."

"Do you really believe that? Oh, Domka! We're in the midst of a famine that's killing off people like a plague, and you're taking care of a corpse."

"Not a corpse . . . It's my sister! And she has children."

"And where are those children?"

"With various relatives. How could I look after both Khrystyna and her children?"

"Even her husband Sava has abandoned her. Where is he?"

"He's run away, and it's just as well that he has . . . There is no godliness in people now. It used to be that there were souls, and in those souls there was a spark of the divine, but now there are neither souls, nor anything divine in them."

"How do you feed Khrystyna when you have nothing to eat yourself? When you yourself can barely stand?"

"I manage one way or another . . . and others help me. It all depends."

"She's going to die in any event!" Hnylokvas shouts. "How strange are your deeds, O Lord!"

Infuriated, he stamps out of the cottage.

Domka, trying to keep up to him, mumbles: "Khrystyna is still alive, because her soul still lives in her breast."

"But the revolution liquidated both priests and souls! All that is the opiate of the people . . . I've hauled away ever so many bodies—probably no one has hauled away as many as I have—but I've never once seen a soul. There's been nary a one that has run after the cart, or showed up by the pit, or in the cemetery. Now, as for the corpse, it can always be seen, because a corpse is a corpse. But the soul? What is it like—does it even exist? It's the priests who have dreamt up the soul to suck people dry. And our people are so stupid that they're perfectly happy. Oh sure there's a soul. A soul that will live in the next world, in the heavenly kingdom."

He thumps his whip on the ground. "There is no kingdom of heaven—and there never will be, so we have to live as best we can on this earth."

"Profaning God will not lead to anything good. God helps those who believe."

"God? Where is that God? There is no God, just as there is no soul."

"God will punish you for saying that."

"He'll punish me? A famine like a plague is upon us, and the earth is groaning. So, is it God who is punishing us? Punishing both the guilty and the innocent, and even the little children? What did the children do to be guilty in the sight of God? And if it isn't God punishing the innocent, then why doesn't He defend them? In what way has Khrystyna sinned against God that He has put her into such a deep sleep that she's been sleeping all these years? Oh, Domka, if only God existed and could see what is happening!"

"Don't defile your lips with blasphemy." Domka is furious, but she speaks so softly and calmly that it almost seems as if she is not angry. "God is not guilty before Khrystyna, and Khrystyna is without sin before God. She was exhausted, and she fell asleep. She was a prophetess. Maybe she saw something so terrible in the future that the fear overpowered her and put her to sleep— and so she's sleeping."

"She's waiting until it passes, ha-ha-ha!"

"I've looked after my sister, and I'll keep on looking after her. To be sleeping is not the same as to be dead. A sleeping person will awaken, but a dead one never will. And when she awakens, we'll hear what she saw and heard there."

"Where?" Hnylokvas grumbles.

"Why there, where Khrystyna is sleeping."

"Why, oh why, are our people so stupid?" Hnylokvas is amazed.

"Who's stupid?" Domka does not understand.

"Our people are stupid!" he croaks. "And you're stupid as well."

And he goes back to the cart standing on the roadway, picks up the reins, and whistles at the horse. The cart is covered with a sack, and a pair of spindly legs stick out from under it.

Domka follows the funeral cart with her eyes and crosses herself.

"My sister is sleeping, but she knows everything, and she sees everything. She sees absolutely everything. And her soul is not sleeping; her soul is suffering, just like the soul of any living person, and she's taking it all in, she's taking it all in . . .

"And she will wake up! And when she wakes up, she'll tell us everything that she has seen. Oh yes, she will. That Hnylokvas talked a lot of nonsense, saying that there is no soul. Well, maybe he doesn't have one; his kind never did have souls, and they don't have them now. But Khrystyna has a soul; I talk with her, and how could I if she didn't have a soul? And I'm no murderer of souls, no I'm not . . ."

Yustyna, Mariya's neighbour, her eyes full of pity, looks at Halya, shakes her head and says: "You and I, Mariya, we had our good times as girls; it would be a sin to deny it. And we've lived out our lives. But what has she seen? And she's ever so thin, like a candle."

Halya Muzyka truly does look emaciated, thin enough to be a candle. A warm breeze ripples her hair, turning it into feeble trembling flames, and her dress undulates on her breast and around her legs. She is standing nearby, under a willow tree by the side of the cottage, singing softly:

> "My beloved has gone away
> Far beyond the Desna River.
> He said: 'I'll return, my dear girl,
> I'll return the following spring.'"

"What keeps her body and soul together?" Mariya sighs as she sits next to her neighbour by the fence. "Why has the Lord punished her? A dark night falls in her head, and then the dawn breaks; then night falls again, and then the dawn comes . . ."

"She's such a splendid girl! I look at Halya—and I'm reminded of her grandmother, your mother . . ."

"My mother departed for the next world so that she no longer would have to suffer in this one."

"And I even recall Halya's great grandmother; Halya also resembles her."

"Yes, and she died one year short of a hundred."

"Halya takes after you, Mariya, and after her grandmother, and her great grandmother . . . You're like three drops of water! Your dark complexion and hazel eyes, and your singing."

Having finished the song, Halya begins to sing it from the beginning again, as if the song has cast a spell on her:

> "My beloved has gone away
> Beyond the Desna River . . ."

Her mother smiles sorrowfully: "She sings well. I don't sing as well as Halya. She hears something once, and she instantly picks it up—that's the kind of ear she has. And she's been that way since she was a tiny little thing. No matter how long a song may be, once she's heard it, it stays with her—she never forgets it. She herself probably doesn't know how many songs she has in her heart."

"Like a nightingale . . ."

"Oh, there's no comparing her to a nightingale!" Mariya disagrees with Yustyna. "A nightingale knows only one song, and it sings that song all night long. It flies away across the sea and then returns with the same song in the spring; it doesn't learn the songs that it hears over there, it doesn't make them its own. But as for Halya . . . She's equal not only to a thousand nightingales, but to a whole cloud of them! And if Halya flew away across the sea, don't you think she'd return with new songs? She would learn the songs they sing over there, and she would make those foreign songs her own."

Halya sings:

> "A maiden waited and waited
> And then she came of age . . ."

The orchard greenery and the foliage of willows and poplars surround the women like dense viscous water tossed by a wind as it scatters the sun's shimmering rays on the trembling leaves. High up in the heavens a stork floats by; he floats by leisurely, keeping his distance, as if afraid to draw too near to the village with its somnolent people—the village where so many have died. But it must be that he hears Halya's song as he passes over

Mariya's yard, because he remains suspended for a moment in the heights before making a large circle over the yard, and then another one before continuing on his unknown heavenly path.

"I taught Halya all the songs that I knew," Mariya said. "And now she knows far more songs than I do, more than the entire village knows. She not only likes to sing songs for her own pleasure—she likes to pass her songs on to others. But to whom is she to pass them on?

"My, oh my! Who has ever seen anything like it—she can barely walk, but she keeps on singing. She has no strength left, and no health; she's wasting away and is on the verge of starvation. And yet how can we save ourselves? I pray to God, our Lord, to send death to me, but it's a sin to ask for something like that for one's daughter. Yes, it's a sin, even though it might be best for all of us if we died, because then our suffering would finally come to an end."

"There's no need to ask God," Yustyna responds. "Our life has become such that, before we know it, He'll take pity on us and end our suffering . . . But I feel so sorry for Halya! Here's what I've come up with. Let Halya go with me to Petrivka tomorrow."

"Let Halya go with you to Petrivka?" Mariya asks in surprise, involuntarily recalling the terrible rumours that have been spread about Yustyna in their village—that she's like this and like that, and that she's a cannibal. But she is so weak that she does not even have the strength to be disturbed by these recollections. "Why should she go to Petrivka? And why are you going?"

"I have a brother who works on a tractor there, or have you forgotten?"

"No, I haven't."

"Well, I decided to go and visit my brother, and I'll take Halya with me . . . They give Sava food for driving the tractor, so he isn't hungry. Do you suppose that he won't treat Halya? Of course, he will."

There is such a somnolent emptiness in Maria's heart, that she feels no fear.

And Halya goes on singing beside the house.

The faded downy moustache on old man Sava's gaunt, sharp-nosed face resembles steppe feather grass glittering with a silvery sheen in a gentle breeze. The shirt on his gangly body appears to be hung on wooden pegs. His shirt, trousers, and boots are soaked with engine oil, with gas. And fume-like smoke seems to be issuing both from him and his tractor.

"Well, did you fill your belly?" old man Sava asks.

His work has darkened his face. It shines like a well-polished boot, and his teeth gleam brightly like choice white beans.

Halya smiles gratefully. "Do you want me to sing for you?"

"You'll sing?" Sava the gangly old man is surprised. "Why?"

"For the barley gruel and the flour paste."

"Go ahead and sing, my dear."

As he smooths his feathery moustache with his fingertips, Sava's chiselled face becomes not so much more attentive as more impenetrable.

Halya holds out her left hand and places her right one on her willowy waist. And her voice rings out:

> "Oh, on the mountain a fire burns,
> And in the valley a kozak lies,
> A kozak hacked and slaughtered
> And covered with a burial shroud."

Old Sava listens, caressing the girl with a bitter, mournful gaze, and when she finishes her song he says emotionally: "Oh, what a voice, and what a song! How can I ever thank you? I simply don't know how to thank you."

Hearing these words, Halya stares at his hands, embroidered with knotted veins. What will those strong, work-hardened hands do? They reach once again into a canvas bag wrapped in a sack covered with patches, and they bring forth a crust of bread.

"This is for you, my child. Take it."

Halya reaches for it—but is afraid to take it. Can it really be for her? Is it possible that uncle Sava can be so generous? He's a tractor driver, a real tractor driver. Aunt Yustyna has not deceived her; she has not brought her to Petrivka in vain.

"Thank you," Halya whispers, hardly able to believe her good fortune as she presses the crust to her breast.

"Eat it in good health."

Gaining courage and glancing boldly first at the village of Petrivka with its glistening white cottages scattered on the nearby hillocks, and then at the tractor standing darkly at the edge of the field, Halya moves her bare left foot to one side and sings:

> "Oh there's a din, mother, such a din
> Where the kozaks are marching,
> And the narrow road is ever so green,
> The road on which they are marching."

Old man Sava's fingertips graze his fluttering feathery moustache, and stealthily touching his eyes to wipe away a bitter tear, he slowly bends over the sack under which his bag is hidden.

Halya watches every movement of his hands with ravenous eyes. What will those hands pull out of the bag?

It is white, ever so white, and pure as snow . . .

In his grimy hands gleams a lump of refined sugar!

But maybe it isn't refined sugar? Yes, it is! But maybe it isn't for her? Yes, it is—uncle Sava is holding it out to her.

"Thank you," Halya mumurs.

"Eat it in good health, my child."

Halya hides both the crust and the lump of sugar in the bosom of her shirt and, faint with happiness and out of breath from her unexpected success, she moves her left foot to one side. Her lips open, and she is ready to sing again.

But old man Sava pats her on the shoulder and says: "There's no need to, my daughter."

"There's no need to?"

"No, there really is no need to," uncle Sava says sternly. "Because my bag is empty."

"But I'll sing for nothing!"

"There's no need to, even so. You sing splendidly, but I've heard all I want to hear now."

"But I . . ."

"If you want to," uncle Sava says kindly, "come again some other time, either alone, or with aunt Yustyna. And in the meantime, my bag will fill itself out a bit; at the moment it's a trifle lean . . . And now you'd better go, because I have work to do. Aunt Yustyna will spend the night in Petrivka and set out for home tomorrow. Are you afraid to go home alone?"

"No."

"Your village is right over there, beyond the green rye. You know the way, don't you? You won't get lost, will you?"

Sava places his rough hand on her head, and such a wonderful feeling of peace and well-being sweeps over her that she does not want to go anywhere; she would like to remain here under the protection of the old man's hand.

"Don't be afraid; go now."

"And if I get frightened, I'll just start singing, and you'll hear me, right?"

"Sing, my child, sing."

Old man Sava goes towards the tractor, and Halya, diving into the green rye as if into green water, disappears.

And, because she is instantly overcome with fear, she hums a song under her breath. At first she hums softly, because it isn't really scary yet, and if she looks back over her shoulder, she can see uncle Sava by the tractor . . .

> "A kozak loved a young maiden,
> He loved her, but did not marry her.
> Oh, it's so sad, so sad . . ."

Now she can no longer see the village of Petrivka, and a hillock has hidden uncle Sava from view. The young gleaming rye is denser and taller; it glimmers with the blue sheen of cornflowers. The delicate spikes, forcing their way upwards from the sharp leaves, have whiskers just like the feathery moustache of uncle Sava. When will the rye ripen? . . .

> "A kozak loved a young maiden
> But did not marry her . . ."

And suddenly an invisible bird grazes her soul with its sharp wing as it flies by—and Halya turns numb with fright.

Was there something there, or wasn't there?

Did it just seem to her that something flashed over there, in the rolling rye? Way over there, off to one side. Turning and staring, her eyes intense and terror-stricken, Halya looks all around and then moves forward with small, hesitatant steps. Should she sing so that uncle Sava will hear her? Should she sing loudly, ever so loudly? But it isn't possible for him to hear her, is it? When he's so far away, behind those hillocks . . .

> "Three kozaks came riding
> To visit a young maiden . . ."

She glances backwards, and stops short in alarm.

In the distance, a swarthy young man bobs up from the green rye, plunging up to his waist in the rolling waves. His dishevelled embroidered shirt flutters on his chest, and the coal black hair falling over his forehead sparkles in the sun's rays.

How did he come to be here, out in the fields? Who is he? Maybe he's from Petrivka, but then again, maybe he's isn't. He might even be from her own village. But she doesn't know anyone like that.

Oh, he's raised his hand, as if beckoning her to go to him.

Could it be someone she knows, someone that she hasn't recognized as yet? Why else would he be following her? Why else would he be calling out to her?

He is smiling. But his smile is forced, and his lips are twisted, as if in pain. Halya wants to return his smile, because the young man is handsome, but her heart is on guard and numb with fear.

His gait is strange as he walks towards her through the rye, as if he is struggling in swirling water. And as he draws nearer and nearer, he appears to grow in stature, and his swarthy face, that seems to have grown wooden, turns even darker.

Yes, she's sure now that he is a stranger. He truly is handsome, but he seems different somehow, peculiar.

And why is he silent? Why doesn't he say anything? Is it normal for a young man to approach a girl without smiling, without saying something? With such terrifying eyes? Why is he glaring so menacingly, when he is surrounded by such an unblemished expanse of fields? By the bright, azure cupola of the heavens?

And what is that shiny, dangling thing that he's carrying?

Oh, my heavens! There's an iron chain in his hands—hands that are scarred and covered with warts.

"Give back the bread!"

And the chain, like a twisting snake, lunges into the air above Halya's head, ready to grasp her neck in a deathly noose. With a despairing shriek Halya bolts to one side and races down the path, her heart pounding so hard that it sticks in her throat and she can't breathe.

"Give back the bread!"

The words echo behind her.

The groaning shout flails Halya's back; she desperately wants to run faster, but the young rye beats against her chest, the air has turned into a wall, and her feet stick to the ground. The thumping behind her is not going away—it is coming closer, and it seems that at any moment now the iron chain will encircle her neck.

She tries to scream. She wants to scream loudly enough for people to hear her, so that they will rescue her from this attacker who wants to choke her to death and take away the bread and sugar that she got from uncle Sava.

"Oh-h-h-h!" she screams for the whole wide world to hear.

But the whole wide world does not respond to her despair.

Stumbling, Hayla falls headfirst into the rye—and she does not have the strength to rise to her feet again. What will be, will be, and she shuts her eyes and presses her lips to the ground, breathing in the choking dust.

The meadowlarks are singing.

Streams of silvery trills resound up above, and at first Halya does not even realize that it is the meadowlarks that are singing, because is it possible for the whole wide world to be singing like a meadowlark? It is hard to believe that she has not heard this music until now. The healing music pours into her heart and washes away her blind terror.

Clutching at the bread and sugar in her bosom, Halya wrenches her head from the ground, sits up and, seeing only the rustling rye all around her, listens to the meadowlarks that seem to be singing ever more zealously, ever more resonantly.

Raising her head, she peeks cautiously over the rye that rolls in expansive waves. There is no one anywhere, only the empty green sea, only the festively clear azure sky above the green sea.

Why had she become frightened? Why? Maybe she had just imagined the iron chain. Maybe there was no such chain, and maybe that young man did not want to strangle her with it to take away her bread. But no, he must have seen uncle Sava give her a treat of bread and sugar.

But maybe the young man in the embroidered shirt was just an illusion?

Oh no, the young man in the embroidered shirt had not been an illusion. He was ever so handsome, ever so swarthy, and his hair was as black as tar. It was just that he had a scowl on his face, and his eyes were terrifying . . . And it's all because he's hungry and not well; he's sick. He begged for some bread to shore up his strength, and she had not given him any.

Where is he?

Halya rises to her feet in the murmuring rye and, surrounded by the singing of the meadowlarks, looks all around. Maybe his tufted head will bob up somewhere. It is nowhere in sight. But what if . . . what if he has died from hunger?

After deliberating for a moment, Halya reaches into her bosom, takes out the crust of bread and holds it out in front of herself; she holds it in such a way that is can be seen by the meadowlarks, the sun, and the whole wide world. And that young man who watched her and ran after her should also be able to see it.

There are only the glistening waves of young rye.

Halya pulls the lump of refined sugar out of her shirt and holds it out as well. Look! Surely you can see—here's the sugar, and here's the bread! And she sings:

> "Vasyl is walking with his scythe,
> And a sweet voice drifts toward him . . ."

He does not see; he does not hear . . . He has gone beyond the Desna River . . .

Her hands fall at her sides as if wilted, and Halya slowly floats through the green sea towards the horizon, to her faraway village that has adorned itself with apple and cherry orchards.

The funeral cart creaks along on its ungreased wheels, and the mouse-grey horse nods its heavy, drooping head and keeps trying to raise it, as if fearing that it will drop off and fall to the dusty village path. As he walks with a halting gait beside the cart, Karpo Hnylokvas's elongated face also hangs down to his chest, and he jerks it upwards time and time again, as if he too is afraid that his head will drop off.

"Karpo! Karpo!"

Hnylokvas does not hear the call.

And then Yustyna, who is sitting on a bench by the fence, no longer shouts, but groans piercingly: "Oh-h-h! Oh-h-h-h!"

Hearing that groan, Hnylokvas stops and looks at the old woman with muddy, clouded, sleepy eyes.

"Why are you groaning?" he asks. "Are you still alive?"

"Come here for a minute," Yustyna pleads.

Hnylokvas, whip in hand, shuffles up to the woman. "What's wrong?" he asks hoarsely.

"I'm sitting here and waiting for you . . . Are you hauling someone away?"

And she nods at the funeral cart from which dark twisted fingers are protruding.

"Yes, I am . . . Maybe I should haul you away as well?"

"Where are you hauling him?" Yustyna asks.

"To the pit, where else?"

"Eh-h-h-h, I don't want to go to the pit," Yustyna replies gently, happy that Hnylokvas has come by and is carrying on an amiable conversation with her. "I want to be hauled to the cemetery, not to the pit."

"Right now?"

"Well, not right now, because I'm still breathing."

"Well if you're still breathing, go ahead and breathe. So why did you call me?" Hnylokvas says angrily without really being angry. "Because I have work to do; the village is big. It takes a while to go this way and that way, and here I have to stop and talk with you. You're stupid, Yustyna."

"Yes, I really am stupid," Yustyna agrees softly. "Here, take this . . ."

And reaching for a little grey bundle in the weeds under the bench, she hands it to him.

"I went to see my brother Sava in Petrivka, and he gave me a little bit of fish to moisten my throat. Here, take it."

Hnylokvas takes the bundle; there is a plate wrapped in the cloth, and the bundle smells of fried fish.

"So, will you take me to the cemetery?" Yustyna asks.

"I most certainly will!" and he hugs the bundle to his chest.

"Just be sure that you don't haul me to the pit, because Holy God sees everything, and He won't forgive you."

"Aha, to the cemetery," Hnylokvas promises, because it is not hard to make a promise—especially in exchange for fried fish.

"I'm stupid, yes I am, but don't think that I don't have some brains in my head," Yustyna is pleased with herself. "I wanted to come to an agreement with you beforehand, and I've already come to terms with the gravedigger Nykon; he's promised to dig a grave for me. I'm not asking him for a big grave, because why would I need a big one? I'm small to begin with, and now I'm withered as well, so I won't take up much space, right?"

"Right . . . But tell me what you want, because I have work to do," Hnylokvas reminds her, ready to hurry away, because he knows Yustyna won't be giving him any more fish.

"All I want is to be with my family, that's all. By my father and mother, by my grandfather and grandmother, by my sister Kylyna, and my brother Ilko."

"Isn't it all the same where you're buried?"

"No, it isn't!" Yustyna objects mildly. "I told the gravedigger where he is to dig my grave. Our family was together in this world, and we want to be together in the next one; we want to be with our kin, because it's always easier with your own people, no matter where you are. Being in that pit is like being in the kolhosp, and I don't want to belong to the kolhosp. After all, I'm an independent person, don't you know that?"

"Oh yes, I know you're independent."

"So why should I join that mob? I don't want to!"

"Oh my, you're such an independent person, Yustyna!"

"Yes, I am. Yes, I am. I don't want to go into that pit; I want to go to my own people, to be among my own. Just make sure that you don't deceive me, Karpo. I've given you the fish, and I've reached an agreement with you; deceiving me would be a grievous sin."

"So tell me where that sin is . . ."

"And the judgement of God," Yustyna reminds him. "Even though there is no human justice, there will be God's justice."

"Well, you just go ahead and wait for it. Go ahead."

"And so I will," Yustyna promises. "If I don't see any justice in this world—and I'm barely able to move around already—then I'll see it in the next one, because what else is there to do up there? You just lie around and wait, and there's no work to be done, nor is there a kolhosp of any kind, and the days and nights run together and become one and the same . . ."

"Well, I have work to do."

Hnylokvas walks over to the funeral cart, tucks Yustyna's bundle in beside the twisted fingers of the dead hand sticking up into the air, and jerks the reins. The old horse tosses its mane and tail to shake off the flies and gadflies, and the ungreased wheels begin to squeal.

"Well, I don't think he'll deceive me, because I gave him the fish. And there's no one else that I can bribe with a treat."

Vasyl Hnoyovy straightens up over the stump on which he is chopping wood and, holding the axe, looks at the woman who is coming towards him from the gate. The woman's head is wrapped in a white kerchief that makes her swarthy face look like a large black lump of coal, and on this lump her eyes blaze like fierce embers.

"Good evening," the woman greets Vasyl, peering at him intently.

Hnoyovy flings his axe to the grass and asks angrily: "And who are you?"

"Good evening," the woman greets him again. "Don't you recognize me?"

"Nowadays a lot of people wander through the village."

"But I'm Horpyna."

"Which Horpyna?"

"Have you forgotten Horpyna? I'm from Zabara; I'm your wife's sister—Olya's sister."

"Horpyna?" his jaw drops. "My wife's sister?"

"Have I lost so much weight that you can't recognize me?"

"Well! Is it truly you, Horpyna, or are you a ghost?"

"Yes, it's me; I just look like a ghost," Horpyna says, and she passes her hand over her dry eyes as if she were wiping away tears. "And how is dear Olya?"

"She's not well . . . Why have you come here?" And, without waiting for a reply, he cries out in amazement. "Why, you're still young, but you look so old!"

"Yes, you're right. I do look old. Is Olya in the house? Then I'll go inside and see her."

"But I told you that she's ill, and so she's lying in the storeroom, because she smells so awful . . ."

Horpyna goes into the storeroom, and Hnoyovy picks up the chopped wood and grumbles: "Anyone else would have stopped feeding such a wife long ago. She's made up her mind to die, so let her die, but I, fool that I am, keep on feeding her. I have nothing to put into my own mouth, but still I . . . She should be taking care of me, but I have to look after her."

He carries the wood into the porch and stops in front of the door leading to the storeroom from where women's soft voices can be heard.

"I wonder why she's come here from Zabara? And just before nightfall at that . . ."

He lights a fire and places a cast iron pot of water on the stove; a bone with some meat left on it protrudes out of the pot.

"She's come at nightfall, so that means she intends to spend the night here. Ha! Back there in Zabara, she must have decided that I would feed her! She came here to eat, because she has nothing of her own left. But do I have anything? Does anyone give me something, or do I have to find it for myself? I get it before they count all the ribs."

And Hnoyovy works himself up into a fury, as if that wretched Horpyna were already eating all that he has, tearing food away from his mouth.

"Nevertheless, she's a fine young woman. If she were fattened up a bit, if she put some flesh on those bones of hers . . . But what can she put on those bones when there's a famine, when the wind can topple her over."

The fire burns in the stove, and the aroma of the boiling meat is beginning to fill the room. Hnoyovy walks in deep thought from window to window—he is hoping that an evil spirit does not bring someone to his home just now. The thoughts that are turning in his head are heavy, like furrowed earth under a plough.

"When will they finish talking in there? They're like magpies!"

He adds a handful of millet to the pot, throws in a peeled onion, and swallows his saliva.

"I have to be my own housekeeper, may the Queen of Heaven forbid such a thing . . . Oh, come in, come in, Horpyna," he says, seeing his guest on the threshold, "because supper will soon be ready. Did you have a talk with Olya? Both she and I are so unfortunate. Why has such misfortune befallen me? Sit down on the bench. There's nothing to be gained by standing on your feet. You must have something to eat to regain your strength, because you look as if you're starving."

"Thank you, Vasyl," Horpyna says gratefully, "for your sensitive heart. I don't remember when I last had something hot to eat. The way things are in life, you don't know what you'll lose and what you'll find. Do you know what our late mother used to say about you? She told Olya not to marry you, because you have an unfeeling heart. But how can your heart be called unfeeling, if you're taking care of Olya now that she's bedridden? And you aren't begrudging me some food."

"Oh, your mother said a lot of things!" Vasyl says angrily, as he picks up the boiling pot with a rag and fills two earthen bowls. "She said a lot of things—and went off to her grave, because that's the easy way out. And here am I—left to suffer and take care of Olya . . . Take your time eating, because you'll burn your mouth. Let it cool off, and then take a bit at a time; don't eat too much all at once; you don't want to make yourself ill."

They sit facing each other across the table. Beyond the windows, the evening is gloomy.

"So, you aren't married yet?"

"Who thinks about getting married now . . ."

"And, as for me, I didn't have any luck with your sister! Sure, if times were different, I would try to have her cured, but nowadays? Well, go ahead and eat . . . You know, Horpyna, I'm looking at you, and I feel sorry for you, because good fortune has passed you by as well . . . Well, I'll take her something to eat; let her moisten her throat with the soup that I've prepared."

Horpyna sits and waits for him to come back, and when he finally returns, there are tears in her eyes.

"People say awful things about you! But you're a good man!"

"Who says awful things about me?"

"Everyone . . . Even Olya."

"Everyone? Even Olya?" he lifts his bristling eyebrows. "Go ahead and eat, go on. What did Olya say?"

Horpyna rubs her face with her fist, sobs, and says: "She says that you live by stealing."

"That's what Olya told you?"

Closing her lips tightly and bitterly, Horpyna nods.

"Is that what she said?" Karpo wants to know. "Tell me!"

"She said . . . That it was by stealing . . . That you go from village to village . . . If you don't steal in your own village, then you go to other villages . . . Along with others just like you."

"And did she see me do this?"

"She says that she knows . . ." And Horpyna nods at the bowl of food. "She told me about this meat as well. She said that you didn't have a cow of your own, and that you didn't slaughter anything, but yet you're eating meat."

"And isn't she eating it?" Hnoyovy shouts. "I just took her some—and she's eating it! So why is she eating it, if she's judging me, huh? Let her not eat it! And with what am I to feed her? You can't get rich in a kolhosp."

"That's true; that's true."

Hnoyovy places his fists with their swollen veins on the table.

"So, Olya says that I live by stealing? Yes, I do! Because otherwise I wouldn't be able to survive. And she wouldn't be able to either. She squawks, but she takes all she can get."

"But how can you do it? You're an activist . . ."

"Well, who knows about it? Maybe my wife, but that's about it . . . I take from those who have something. But if people don't have anything—I don't take anything from them. You better eat now; go ahead and eat."

"I am; I'm sipping the soup . . . I feel sorry for you, Vasyl. People are so terrible now."

"People are terrible, but I'm even more terrible," he responds arrogantly, indignantly.

"Someone will catch you . . ."

"No one has caught me so far—and no one will . . . What else am I to do? Oh, that Olya! She's sick, just two steps away from death's door . . . She eats, but she rebukes me. But how would she live if it weren't for my stealing? That's the kind of wife she is, and that's the kind of gratitude I get. Well, I'm thankful for one thing—that the Lord God didn't give me any children from a wife like that."

"It's a great misfortune not to have children."

"To have them die off? Listen, Horpyna, I have an idea . . . Go ahead and eat . . . build up your strength." Hnoyovy gets up and paces the room as if the devil himself were chasing him. Then he stops and says: "Don't go back to Zabara; stay here with me."

"I'll spend the night—and tomorrow I'll be off."

"Eh-h-h-h! Stay with me forever, and be my wife."

"What do you mean, be your wife?" Horpyna does not understand, and her spoon remains forgotten in her bowl.

"Well, what kind of a wife is she to me? You saw for yourself. She can't get up, or do the laundry, or look after herself. She's a cripple. But I still have my strength and my health. I can still provide for myself, and I'll feed you as well. Because what is there left for you in Zabara? You'll swell with hunger, and that will be that—until you die. I look at you, Horpyna, and my heart breaks with grief . . .You'll take care of me and look after your sister. And I won't treat you unjustly."

Horpyna can hardly speak: "Who ever heard of such a thing."

"Eh-h-h-h, that's nothing compared to what's going on these days."

"I would stay, but Olya—she's my sister. And I'll bring shame down on myself in people's eyes."

"Shame won't eat your eyes out. You'll be ashamed for a little while, and then you'll get used to it. Just don't think about it! And I'll feed you and clothe you. Because I still have my hands."

And he shows her his hands; they are long, lined with veins, and calloused, and his fingernails are grimy.

"But what if you're caught?" Horpyna asks. "You may be nimble, but there's always a chance that you can be caught by others who are just as nimble."

"You can't die twice, and you can't cheat death even once. Just take a look . . ."

Hnoyovy goes to the trunk, opens the lid, and grabs a fistful of all sorts of clothing and other merchandise.

"For whom did I get all this? For your Olya. Other women walk around in tattered clothing, in rags, but just look at all the new things that I have for her right here. But she no longer needs any new clothes. So you'll have all this. You'll wear out all these things . . . Just try on this kerchief."

Throwing the clothing back into the trunk, he passes Horpyna a flowered kerchief with tassels.

Hesitating for a moment, she timidly takes the kerchief and strokes it gently.

"It's nice," she whispers.

"Don't be afraid—try it on."

Taking off her white head covering, Horpyna wraps the flowery kerchief around her head and looks questioningly at Vasyl, as if she wants him to tell her if it suits her. There is no mirror in the room, and she is not able to see herself in the kerchief, to delight in how she looks in it.

"You look like a young engaged woman!" he praises her.

"Oh, go on," Horpyna blushes unexpectedly.

There is a rustling in the porch, a shuffling sound, and a low moan. A pail clangs. Then the door slowly opens. It is already open, but there is still no one there. And then, in the excruciating silence, a hand clutches the doorpost, a foot appears on the threshold, and finally the figure of a feeble, hunched-over woman comes into view.

"Is it you, Olya?" Vasyl blurts out. "You got up?"

Olya is a mere shadow of a human being. Her grey head sways on her spindly neck. A faint hint of a poignant smile trembles on her face, and her wasted lips quiver painfully.

"I wanted to be with you."

Clinging to the wall, she reaches the window beyond which the evening stands like thick dark hemp, and drops exhausted on the wide bench. She is gasping as if she has had to conquer a great distance, and not just walk across the porch from the storeroom.

"Do you hear, Horpyna?" she says. "You look wonderful in that kerchief."

"I'll take it off right away. It's Vasyl . . ."

"Don't take it off," Olya continues. "Keep it on. It's better that you get it than someone else."

"You're right about that," her husband says happily.

Olya puts her withered hands together as if in prayer and, with a tortured smile, says softly: "I was lying there, and here's what I've come up with . . . How much longer will I live? Only God knows, but it won't be long now. My heart tells me that it won't be much longer . . . You've suffered for a long time with me, Vasyl, and now you won't have to suffer any more."

"Olya, it's a sin to talk like that," her husband says.

"But I only want what's best for you. And so here's what I've come up with. Let Horpyna remain in our house—and you can live together."

"What do you mean, live together?" her sister and her husband cry out.

They are taken by surprise—she has either guessed what they were talking about, or eavesdropped on them.

"Like man and wife."

"Oh, Olya," her sister sobs. And she unwinds the kerchief from her head. "This kerchief belongs to you."

"Don't take it off! Don't!" Olya says to her. "You have the health to wear that kerchief, and I don't. Do you hear, Vasyl? Keep Horpyna here; let her be your wife. Do you hear, Horpyna? Let Vasyl be your husband. You'll get along. Vasyl may be a terrible cutthroat, but it is possible to live with him."

Clutching at the wall, she rises slowly from the bench.

"Where are you going?" her husband asks her.

"To my little corner . . . and that is where I'll die. And the two of you can stay here and talk; don't come with me. Have a good talk, and come to an agreement. Reach an agreement in a friendly manner . . ."

She shuffles across the threshold, and the door, sighing and groaning, creaks shut behind her.

"Uncle, give me something to eat."

"Where am I going to get something to eat?"

"You have food."

"Who told you that I have food?" Pavlo Muzyka is so incensed that the veins on his forehead are bulging. And he peers more closely at the boy who has wandered into his yard and is standing barefoot before him in a torn shirt and patched pants. The little boy's eyes, green as an elder bush, are gazing at him so sadly, so pleadingly, that hot tears are almost bursting from them.

"Whose little boy are you?

"Don't you know? I'm your neighbour."

"Hrytsko?"

"Of course I'm Hrytsko."

"So why don't you ask your father Harkusha to give you something to eat? Or your mother?"

"We don't have any food, and father is sick in bed," little Hrytsko shuffles from one foot to another. "Give me a little bit of food! If you don't, I'll die like my brothers died. I don't want to get food for nothing—I'll work it off for you. Either now in the garden, or later, when I grow up."

"Uh-huh, when you grow up. If you don't die," Muzyka grumbles. "You don't want to die. You want to live, don't you?"

"Oh, yes, uncle. I do want to live!"

"Ha-ha," Muzyka bares his teeth in a smile. "So stupid, and yet so clever . . . Maybe I should give you a bun?"

"What's a bun?" Hrytsko asks.

"It's bread that's white, ever so white, and fluffy, like down."

"Don't try to fool me, uncle," Hrytsko says. He swallows his saliva, and his face darkens. "You're talking about some kind of buns, but there are no buns anywhere. I haven't seen any. I've seen poppy seed biscuits, and plain biscuits, and sourdough biscuits, and fritters, but I've never seen any buns."

"So why are you concerned that I may give you a bun? I don't have a bun, and I won't give you one."

And then he mutters under his nose. "And even if I did have one, I wouldn't give it to you."

Muzyka disappears into the house, and little Hrytsko waits on the doorstep. Because even if this neighbour is stingy, even if he's so grim-faced that it's terrifying to look at him, surely he won't begrudge him a little bit of something, will he?

He waits and waits, but uncle Pavlo does not come back. Hrytsko's feet buckle under him and, falling into a somnolent state, he slowly sinks to the embankment abutting the house.

"Hey there, wake up, my boy!" someone is shaking him.

Hrytsko opens his eyes and sees Pavlo Muzyka standing before him.

"Here you are," he says, holding out a piece of hide to him.

"What is it?" Hrytsko struggles to his feet.

"Its hide from a calf. You can eat it."

"But how am I to eat it?"

"Oh, you have to be taught everything," uncle Pavlo grows annoyed. "You'll singe it in the fire, stick it in some water, boil it, and eat it. The hide is from a young calf, so it will cook up well. It was lying around in the attic, and I'd forgotten about it."

Little Hrytsko takes the hide covered with reddish hair and clutches it to his breast with both hands.

"Thank you, uncle. I'll singe it, boil it, and eat it. And I'll pay you back; I'll pay you back for your kindness, you can be sure of that."

"So, you want to live, do you?"

"Oh yes, ever so much." And Hrytsko, hunching over like an old man, totters off to his own yard.

Some time later, a fire burns in the caragana bushes; the calf hide is boiling in a pot hung over it on wooden pokers.

Pavlo Muzyka is not feeling well. He is sitting under a cherry tree, gazing out first at the road and then at his neighbour's yard. He is muttering to himself: "Harkusha's breed . . . He took my grain away from me, and now I have to feed his child. I should have left that hide in the attic; it wasn't begging me for food. But no, I had to give it away. But will anyone give me anything? No, no one will. They only want to take things from me . . .

"Oh, the pot is really steaming. Now this child will regain his strength to my own destruction. It's hard for good people like me to live in this world. You see, I begged God to get rid of Harkusha's children, to the very last one, and God seems to have listened to my prayer. There's only one left; this little Hrytsko is all that remains of my neighbour's family—of my fierce enemy's family. And now I'm saving this child myself. And he'll pay me back some day when he grows up. Oh, sure, he will—as if I'll ever live to see the day."

And Pavlo Muzyka regrets giving away the calf hide so badly that he is ready to gnaw his elbows in anger; he is prepared to go into his neighbour's yard and yank the hide out of the boiling water.

"The hide must be cooked already, because he's eating it now—may he choke on my kindness." And he finds it hard, too hard to watch the child eat! To avoid seeing him, he gets up and, shuffling off to the house like a gloomy shadow, hides inside it.

But his anger is so great that he is unable to stay indoors. An evil spirit upbraids him and, before long, shoves him outside again, into the gentle, early golden evening.

"O Lord! What's wrong?"

Is he imagining it, or is something writhing on the ground under the caragana bushes in his neighbour's yard? Writhing as if possessed. Over there, by the fire that is still giving off a bluish smoke.

"Is it the little fellow? What could have happened?"

He goes through the orchard and shuffles slowly to his neighbour's yard. He comes up closer. Yes, it is Hrytsko who is writhing on the ground, thrashing his feet, and clutching first at the grass and then at his stomach with outstretched fingers.

"Hrytsko, what's wrong?"

The boy does not speak; a mucous liquid oozes from his mouth.

Muzyka bends over and picks up the boiled calf hide from the ground.

"So that's how he's boiled it, and that's how he's eaten it! Who cooks hide that way? I told him to singe it, but he didn't. Because he doesn't have any brains. And he even promised to pay me back, to work for me when he grows up to pay for the hide that I gave him. So, how are you going to grow up now? How are you going to repay me? Do you hear me, Hrytsko?"

The child is still jerking on the ground, but he does not respond; he will never speak again.

Pavlo Muzyka tucks the hide into the bosom of his shirt.

"It's not right that something of value should go to waste."

The child is no longer moving.

"I'll go and find his father. Who told him about his other brats? I did. So let him hear about this one from me as well. And I'll watch him closely as I tell him, yes I will. There's no seed of his left on this earth now, and he himself will soon be gone. And I won't be me if I don't help him leave this world. And why not? Didn't he decide to rid the world of certain people? So when is the world to be rid of him and the roots he's put down? For it's a sin for people like him to go on living, a grave sin."

Pylyp the teacher stops beside a walnut bush and, holding his breath, looks at the old lime tree that stands by itself at the forest's edge. He does not want to scare off the little bird perched on a large broken branch covered with small withered twigs.

"Aha! It's a forest lark."

Yellowish brown, with a dark spotted breast, the forest lark patters over the dry branch and halts on its sharp broken tip. It sits and looks around, as if measuring itself against the expanse of the sky before soaring upwards and breaking into song. But it does not fly away; instead, it patters back down over the branch and reaches its thick end. It could hop over it, just as other birds do, but no! It stops on it—and then patters back again to the tip.

From its perch, it suddenly flutters to the top of the lime tree and disappears among the thick green leaves, as if it has gone into hiding. But it has not hidden itself, because it bursts unexpectedly out of the tree's green crown and flies high up into the heavens.

"Tweet, tweet, tweet!"

The forest lark whistles. It is not so much a song as a crackling sound, but that is what its spring song is like.

"Chirp, chirp, chirp!"

It whistles slowly, eagerly, and seems to be so inspired, that it probably hears no one but itself.

"Sing on, my little bird, sing on," the teacher whispers.

The forest lark flies down from the heights and alights on an ash tree, losing itself amidst the trembling figured leaves.

The teacher wanders through the walnut grove, and his heart swells with the inspired singing of the fortunate forest lark that, calling to its mate hidden in the thickets, praises spring and the rebirth of nature.

O Lord! What is that—over there, under the oak tree?

Pylyp stops abruptly and freezes. A man is sitting on the ground, leaning against the trunk of an oak tree, and his head, covered by a cap, slumps on his chest.

"Hey there!" the teacher gets up the courage to shout.

But the man does not stir; he does not seem to hear. Maybe he should pass by him, let him sit here, because you can meet up with all sorts of people in the forest. But the teacher conquers his fear and, staring unblinkingly at the hunched figure, walks up stealthily to him through the tall grass.

When he is still some distance away, the teacher realizes that he is looking at a dead man.

Then, when he comes up closer, he sees that, near the man, among the gnarled roots of the tree, there is a heap of mushrooms. In the lifeless hand there is a mushroom with a bite taken out of it. And by the man's foot there is a scrap of reddish paper, and in the paper there is a bit of salt.

The man must have come to the forest to have a meal of fresh mushrooms with salt. He picked some, began to eat them—and poisoned himself.

Who is it?

From which village?

When did he poison himself?

In his heart the teacher still hears the whistling song of the inspired bird. He must tell Karpo Hnylokvas about the dead man. Let him come to the forest and haul him away to the pit. But will he want to come all the way out here? Will he want to take him away? If he gets half a pound of bread, he might come, because he would be sorry to lose it.

But whose voice is that?

Is it really a voice, or is he just imagining it? The teacher listens intently, because it is not so much a voice, as a wail. Maybe it's a little animal over there in the bush? Oh, there it is again. Yes, someone is crying.

Why would someone be crying in the forest on such a fine spring day?

Turning his eyes towards the sound, the teacher walks cautiously to the bush from where the crying is coming and parts the branches with his hands.

On the black earth there is a little white wrinkled blanket, and in the blanket there is an infant. The child is lying on its back, and red ants are crawling over its chest and stomach. It must have woken up when the ants started biting it.

How did this infant get into the forest? Who left it here?

The teacher looks all around, as if expecting to see the mother, who must have left her child for just a moment; she has probably gone away and will be right back.

Thinking that she is close at hand, he waits for her. But no one appears. All is still; only the birds are singing.

And after some time has gone by, the teacher is emboldened to call out: "Hey, there! Is there anyone in the forest?"

There is only the rustling of the leaves, the singing of the birds, and the sun's rays that twinkle on the succulent emerald grass. No one returns his call. But it cannot be, it simply cannot be that the infant has been abandoned in the forest. That it was brought here and left to die . . . far away from its mother's eyes.

The teacher is terrified; he wants to yell, to cry out, but his voice chokes in his throat. Hoping against hope, he waits and waits. And the child, curling its tiny lips, whimpers and whimpers.

The teacher resolutely picks up the infant.

"Who left you here? Who?"

But what can the child answer? It is only a month or two old! It blinks its hairless eyelids, wrinkles its colourless eyebrows, sucks its lips as if searching for a nipple, and kicks its feet impatiently.

"Let's go to the village."

And the teacher, cuddling the infant, walks through the forest.

On the outskirts of the village, a cottage with a thatched roof stands on a hillock; its porch has almost sunk into the ground. Maybe someone here can tell him something; maybe someone here will recognize the infant.

The door to the porch is open, but the cottage is deserted. As if no one had ever lived in it.

The teacher walks slowly to a neighbouring house.

"Is there any one here who is still alive? If there is, say something."

No one responds.

"Don't cry, my child. We'll find your mother. She has to be around here somewhere."

An older woman is walking down the street towards him.

"Do you know whose infant this is?" the teacher asks, holding out the child to her.

The woman looks at the child in alarm and hastily crosses herself.

"It's not mine," she says, and continues gloomily on her way.

The funeral cart creaks, its wheels squeaking and thumping.

"Has it fallen asleep?" Karpo Hnylokvas asks, nodding at the infant in the teacher's arms. "Where are you carrying it? Put it on the cart, and I'll haul it away."

The teacher hears him, but he does not want to hear him, and he presses the child even more tightly to his chest.

"We'll find your mother, yes we will," he whispers, his lips taut and colourless.

He continues walking down the deserted village path, and whenever he spots someone near a cottage, he holds out the infant and asks: "Do you happen to know whose child this is? Who its mother is? I found it in the forest."

But no one knows; and no one says anything.

And then the teacher asks the infant: "Perhaps you'll tell me who your mother is? Let's go to my place, let's go . . ."

But the infant does not reply.

It does not know; it is unable to tell him.

It will never have a mother.

"Who abandoned you? Who turned away from you?"

The world is silent; it does not reply.

Olena Zvychayna

Olena Zvychayna: Biographical Note

Olena Zvychayna, an émigré author, was a passionate champion of individual and national freedom. Born in Ukraine into a well-educated family—her father was a lawyer, her mother a teacher—she was encouraged from an early age to develop her gift for languages and her talent for writing. She graduated with a gold medal from a high school in Kharkiv and continued her studies at an institution of higher learning.

Influenced by a grandmother who cherished the Ukrainian language and culture, and by parents committed to helping their compatriots, Zvychayna vowed not to publish any of her works as long as she was subject to Soviet censorship. Her marriage to a man who was actively involved in a movement to free Ukraine, and who was incarcerated several times as an "enemy of the people," further increased her resolve.

During World War II she was interned in a Nazi labour camp in Austria. Some years later she settled in the United States and began publishing her works in the late 1940s. Her stories describe life in Ukraine under Soviet oppression and Nazi occupation, as well as the experiences of people displaced by war. Drawing on her first-hand knowledge of the atrocities perpetrated by both the Soviet regime and the Nazi war machine, Zvychayna, with her deeply ingrained sense of justice and her profound empathy for the misfortune of others, was able to craft gripping stories that reveal, in all their devastating horror, the tyranny and cruelty of the occupiers, and decry the collaboration of individual Ukrainians convinced of the merits of the social and political ideologies of the oppressors.

Known as the"Harriet Beecher-Stowe" of Ukrainian literature, Zvychayna focussed her literary efforts on documenting human suffering at the hands of ideological extremists in positions of power. In an autobiographical novel written in collaboration with her husband (pen-name: Mykhaylo Mlakovy) she describes the fate of the unfortunate millions accused of being "enemies of the people" by the NKVD. Her short fiction about the Terror-Famine of the early 1930s during the period of forced collectivization in Ukraine draws vivid contrasts between the horrific suffering of the starving peasants and the privileged lifestyles of those who enforced the decrees of the Soviet state.

Little is known about Zvychayna's life, and few of her writings have been translated into English. Born in the early 1900s, she died in 1985.

The Market at Myrhorod
(1953)

Author's Dedication

This work is dedicated to the millions of Ukrainians
who were the victims of the artificial famine
inflicted on Ukraine by Moscow in 1932-33.

Author's Note

The Market at Myrhorod
was written on the basis of factual material,
and the names and surnames of the characters
in the story have been deliberately maintained.
One of the sons of the late Mr. M. S. Samodyn
lives in the United States.

The Market at Myrhorod
(1953)

"In Myrhorod there is no thievery,
and no cheating . . ."

Mykola Vasylovych Hohol
(Nikolai Gogol)

I

M. S. Samodyn

Did you, esteemed reader, know Mykhaylo Semenovych Samodyn prior to the Revolution of 1917? If you ever had the occasion to travel on the broad Kyiv-Poltava-Kharkiv highway in the district of Myrhorod, you most certainly must have met him more than once, especially in early autumn . . .

Do you remember the dignified manner in which he walked alongside his wagon—a wagon stacked so high with hempen sacks of wheat that it looked like a moving mountain? Did you observe how solicitously he plied his whip to chase away the annoying gadflies from the backs of his curly-horned oxen? How smartly he shouted in a deep bass voice: "Gee-up, to the left!" or "Gee-up, to the right!" and how affably he called out: "Hey, hey there!" to those oxen, urging them to move along a trifle more quickly to Myrhorod? And how he greeted you and everyone that he met with such traditional courtesy and such genuine respect!

Ruminating phlegmatically and swishing their tails to chase away the cursed gadflies, the grey curly-horned oxen pulled the wagons overloaded with wheat in a deliberate, confident, and stately manner and, plodding slowly ahead, one step at a time, continuously nodded their horned heads as if saying "yes, yes."

Every step brought them closer to Myrhorod where, behind the railway station, immediately to the left, the mill owner

Ostrovsky would greet the wagon-mountain hospitably and grind the sea of golden kernels into gleaming white flour.

As for Mykhaylo Semenovych Samodyn—the owner of the wagon, the curly-horned oxen, and the pyramid of huge sacks stuffed with wheat—his overall appearance, beginning with his sturdy, thick-set body, itself called to mind a large hempen sack tightly crammed right up to its knotted end with kernels of the choicest wheat.

His small dark eyes—deeply recessed under his forehead and twinkling with such lively sparks beneath heavy bushy eyebrows that they resembled distant stars peeping out from under a mass of glowering clouds—always looked with a gentle clarity either straight ahead or directly into the eyes of the person with whom he was conversing. Thick blond hair, dusted ever so lightly with the first signs of hoarfrost, a drooping <u>kozak</u> moustache, a friendly smile that revealed two rows of sound and densely planted pearly white teeth untouched by either a dentist or a toothbrush, and large, powerful muscular arms—these were the characteristics that in their totality constituted the living portrait of this native son of our fertile land.

Gentle by nature and reserved in his speech, Samodyn rarely quarrelled with his neighbours, and even more rarely with his wife. Lovingly rearing five stalwart sons who were to replace him on this earth—sons in whom he invested his hopes and around whom he planned his future—he never used hired labour on his exemplary farmstead.

In addition to caring for his family and his farm, he took a keen interest in what the newspapers had to say.

And, during long winter evenings, when raging blizzards howled like wild beasts, he repaired footwear. Sitting with his head slightly bent and listening dreamily to the duets that his wife sang with their daughter-in-law as they sat at their spinning wheels, he was often moved to sing along in a rich bass voice that was soft and dark, like velvet.

This is what Mykhaylo Samodyn was like back then, before the Revolution . . .

* * *

One by one, the years, burgeoning with events of historical import, passed by. Plummeting into eternity like ripened fruit dropping into the basket of an industrious farmer, they sprinkled snow on Mykhaylo Samodyn's thick hair and ploughed his affable face with new wrinkles and an ever-growing number of deepening furrows . . .

II

The Market

A blindingly bright and fresh day, drenched with sunlight . . . An infinite, fathomless azure sky without a hint of a cloud, without any boundaries . . . And a light, playful breeze that leaves the scent of flowers lingering on your lips, and the scarcely discernible touch of fabulous wings on your face . . .

Do you hear the market in Myrhorod's bazaar square humming and buzzing like a muffled swarm of bees? Do you see the hordes of people gathered there? Do you see that some of them are distressed and agitated, like startled insects in the depths of a forest when the brutal boot of a careless traveller unexpectedly tramples their mound?

As we approach the shore of the market sea, we involuntarily strain our ears. The hubbub is strange, unusual! It is strictly a human hubbub . . .

Today, neither farm animals nor poultry add their voices, the way they usually do, to the market symphony. You do not hear the alarmed clucking of chickens brought to the market to be sold, or the indignant quacking of ducks bound in hempen fetters, or the proud hissing of boastful geese, or the haughty neighing of unhitched, well-fed horses, or the touchingly trustful mooing of horned cattle, or the squealing protests of pigs.

You do not hear the swift, whirlwind waltz of the carousel, or the feeble "farewell song" of the organ grinder, or the sorrowful recitative of the blind old lyre player that is so much a part of a Ukrainian market.

Only people are buzzing in a hushed, monotonous chorus like bees in a hive.

But why is the grey cloth of this buzzing not punctuated by loud human voices—the carefree shouts of those who, having sold something, have already found time to visit the local tavern? Why is it that you do not hear the customary slapping of hands as gypsies and peasants reach an agreement about the final selling price—an agreement that needs only to be finalized by the proper libation? Why is that human buzzing so strange and depressing in its deadening monotony?

Let us burrow our way into the very thickest part of the market throng! Let us become integral living droplets of this sea! Let us feel the pulse and the spirit of this huge animate organism!

Peasants and vacationers—these are the two categories of people distinctly carved on the backdrop of the Myrhorod market. There are peasants here from Velyka Bahachka, Velyki Sorochyntsi, Hoholeve, Ustyvytsya, Buryakivshchyna, Khomutets—well, it goes without saying—from the entire district of Myrhorod! At the health resort, there are vacationers from Kyiv, Kharkiv, Poltava, Odessa, Leningrad, Orel, Rostov, Moscow—well, it goes without saying—from all of the USSR!

There are also Myrhorod residents here, but they are a drab, insignificant element, and they fade into the teeming swarms of people. They are of no consequence . . .

The peasants are selling. The vacationers are buying.

The peasants are glumly silent, sluggish, and feeble; indeed, some of them are not moving at all. The vacationers are talkative, noisy, and anxiously restless. The peasants stand, sit, or even recline on the ground in long rows, forming living corridors of almost inert and surprisingly bloated mummies, while the vacationers, flowing in a colourful, noisy stream, splash about within the tight banks of these corridors and, here and there, spill over them like quicksilver.

The peasants are dressed in the remnants of their clothing, and there is no dearth of those who are reduced to wearing rags. The vacationers are dressed in clean summer suits and dresses, lounging outfits, t-shirts, and multicoloured fashionable sarafans; and there is no dearth of those who are most elegantly attired, especially among the female vacationers.

Peasants and vacationers—these are the two basic elements of the Myrhorod market. But . . . what is being bartered here? Where are the farm wagons with their raised shafts? Where are the unhitched horses that neigh arrogantly as they nibble the fresh grass? Where are the horned cattle, pigs, and poultry? Where are the Persian lambskin hats from the town of Reshetylivka, the yarn, and the linen cloth? Where are the peasants' large hempen sacks filled with rye, wheat, and flour? Where are the small pots and beautifully decorated bowls that never fail to attract the enthusiastic attention of amateur lovers of luxury? Where has everything disappeared—all those items that, without exception, have always been present in every Ukrainian market and that Hohol depicted for his descendants in immortal colours as fresh as spring?

Where are they?

Oh, if only Mykola Hohol could miraculously appear at this market! He would realize in a flash that these Myrhorod peasants do not bear the slightest resemblance to their ancestors—the farmers that he described—nor are they selling the same kinds of items. Instead, these peasants are selling only personal possessions, priceless family heirlooms, relics . . . Rushnyks meant to be draped around icons; full-length, embroidered, openwork shirts that are masterpieces of ornamental needlework and are worn, as a rule, only once, at one's wedding; and tablecloths that are retrieved from the bottom of a large chest only at Christmas and Easter— these are the articles that are spread out on the arms and knees of these almost inert and unnervingly bloated mummies that form a living corridor at the market . . .

A plakhta made in Myrhorod is a very fashionable item just now! Much sought after and snapped up quickly, these plakhtas are hunted down by clamorous female vacationers attired in colourful sarafans, who deftly wind their way through the crowds, popping up first here and then over there like animated fairy tale flowers that poke their heads out of the grass.

"Granddad! Hey, Granddad! How much do you want for your plakhta?"

The strident question is called out in Russian by a young female vacationer with a snub nose, lips that resemble a bloodstained bud, and tanned shoulders that spill victoriously out of the confines of her daringly sewn sarafan.

"A loaf of bread!" the old peasant replies quietly and hoarsely but, at the same time, firmly and sharply, as if slicing off his words with a knife.

"What? A whole loaf? You're joking, granddad! Why, for a loaf—for a whole loaf of bread—I can buy three such plakhtas!" And the bloodstained bud of her lips contorts in a disdainful grimace.

Without waiting for a reply, the snub-nosed woman greedily eyes the old man's plakhta once again and then, without so much as even glancing at his face, floats away like a peahen.

And why should she look at the old peasant's face? Who could be the least bit interested in his aged, distended cheeks and the strange bags that spread in whitish half-circles under his eyes? Or in his unnaturally swollen, calloused fingers that imprison an edge of the exquisite plakhta in their grip? Who will pay any attention at all to the fact that the body of the old man resembles a peasant's large hempen sack filled to its knotted end with a liquid of some kind—a liquid that is retained within the confines of that sack only through a miracle? Who will make the effort to look more closely at the bloated faces of the other farmers, at the whitish half-circles spreading under their eyes, and at their arms and legs swollen with water?

Who?

Who, while strolling at a leisurely pace through the living corridors of the market, will seek out not the rushnyks, not the shirts, and not the plakhtas, but . . . the arms and legs and, above all, the faces and the eyes and . . . the heartfelt cries of the souls spilling out of those eyes in a tumultuous stream?

Who? Perhaps . . . Hohol? Perhaps it truly is only he, a person no longer living, who will not fear to show an interest in a question that is so dangerous for people who are still alive—the question concerning the tragedy of a whole army of candidates slated for the next world. Perhaps it is only Hohol who will dare to ask in a loud voice why all the peasants who are at this market have succumbed to dropsy at the very same time, and why this ailment has not afflicted the numerous vacationers who have come to Myrhorod from all corners of the USSR with the express purpose of restoring their health in this very same spot. Because if Mykola Vasylovych does not ask this question, then no one will!

The motley throng of vacationers at the Myrhorod market hums and flits about like a swarm of bees. The sun caresses this hive of activity with its passionate kisses, and underscores, with the implacability of a stern judge, the countless contrasts scattered throughout the market.

Let us look over there, for instance, where the sun has just directed a sparkling shaft of its mischievous rays: a young peasant woman—sitting like an inert mummy and stretching out her water-logged legs so that her chapped, bare feet are lined up with the building deceitfully named a co-operative store—has spread an artistically embroidered openwork shirt on her knees. It is her full-length wedding shirt, and a middle-aged, rosy-cheeked male vacationer in a modish lightweight woollen suit is haggling with her for it. He is bargaining and haggling, trying to depreciate its value by saying that it has been worn!

The fathomless sky is a transparent azure, and the brilliant sun is tender, like a mother! It solicitously strokes everyone without exception, not overlooking even the half-naked peasant children, deformed by hunger, who, scattered like seeds in the crowd, cry out mournfully here and there in flute-like voices: "Bread! A tiny bit of bread!" But those cries, drowning in the droning buzz of the market, are like pebbles cast into a river: plop . . . and they are gone! Plop, plop—and they too are gone! And so it continues.

And no one is surprised by this. After all, the children do not sell plakhtas, or rushnyks, or long shirts with masterfully executed openwork embroidery on the sleeves—shirts that the female vacationers from all corners of the USSR take delight in sewing into modish dresses in the Ukrainian style. The children do nothing but beg. Who could possibly be interested in them?

And yet . . . there actually are people in this crowd who are painfully aware of the mournful, flute-like cries, because the children occasionally do receive something. Take a look over there at that old man in horn-rimmed glasses; he has just slipped a peasant child a chunk of bread wrapped in a scrap of paper . . . But . . . except for furtive deeds like this, these kindly people do not reveal themselves in any way: they remain silent. They all remain silent. Without exception, they all pretend not to see what they are seeing, not to hear what they are hearing, and not to know what they know . . .

"Hunger!"

A searing word, like fire . . .

Uttered in a woman's ringing voice, the word darts out unexpectedly above the din of the market like a frisky fish leaping out of deep water, and around it there instantly reigns a tense, ominous silence, the sign of an inevitable storm.

A moment later, the agile figure of a security guard, dressed in the uniform of "the militia of the workers and peasants" and charged with maintaining order, is at the spot of the "crime." He pounces on this searing word like a rapacious pike on a careless little carp. But the carp, flashing its silvery tail in the air, dives into the depths of the noisy river and disappears.

"Who said the word 'hunger' just now?" the militiaman barks loudly in Russian, his bulging eyes staring into the faces that surround him. "Who? I have to know: who?"

They all glance around helplessly, searching for the owner of that ringing female voice; they all put on an appearance of honestly looking for the guilty person, and perhaps some of them truly are searching for her.

A few tense moments pass in this manner without yielding any results.

Then the militiaman, as a representative of the authorities, takes it upon himself to speak.

"What kind of hunger, I ask you! What kind? There is no hunger! There are only kurkuls—subverters of collectivization, enemies of our proletarian rule! Is that understood?"

"Yes, yes! It's understood! Of course it is!" a few voices hastily respond from the crowd of vacationers.

"It's as clear as if it were laid out on the palms of our hands!" an elderly tenor voice calls out a moment later, and that voice resonates with a transparent note of sarcasm—a sarcasm as bitter as wormwood.

A few people glance over their shoulders, and a few others cough in their fists, but, fortunately, the militiaman hails from a stock of thick-skinned people who are incapable of analyzing intonation patterns. Moreover, the brief outcries in the crowd alternate chaotically with fairly long tirades, and the attention of the assiduous guard of the internal security of Myrhorod is constantly distracted.

In this variegated crowd there is no dearth of adulators who hasten to be the first to agree that there is no hunger, and that there are only damned kurkuls and would-be kurkuls who do not wish to work in the <u>kolhosps</u>. And there also is no dearth of those who are ready to voice their deep proletarian indignation at that counterrevolutionary woman—or, as is more likely, that insane woman—who has dared to utter that absurd word . . .

A few minutes pass in this manner, and then the life of the market flows on once again, like a turbulent mountain stream that, coming across an unexpected obstacle in its path, foams angrily, deploys the strength of its current to cast it aside, and then rushes forward triumphantly with its startled but irrepressible waves. Agitatedly spilling over here and there, the vivid streams of noisy vacationers anxiously flow onwards between the narrow banks of the corridors created by the strange mummies.

Everything is "wonderful" at the Myrhorod market, just as it is "on the entire one-sixth of the earth's globe that is victoriously building socialism in a country isolated from all other countries." Everything "is in order." Peasants from the entire district of Myrhorod are selling. Vacationers from all corners of the USSR are buying. And representatives of the proletarian government are diligently on guard to ensure that no thievery, no cheating, and no counterrevolutionary activity will occur.

Having had his say on the theme of "no hunger," the militiaman assumes his previous stance of an observer. But then he is approached by a colourless, unremarkable man of indeterminate age who whispers something in his ear, and he turns to him in a kindly manner.

A moment later, the whisperer walks into the crowd and proceeds directly to his goal at a lively pace, and the militiaman, remaining a few steps behind, follows him.

Suddenly, the whisperer's sharp investigative nose detects something. Halting abruptly, like a hunting dog in the thickets of a forest, the man waits for the security guard to come up to him before directing his eyes at a tall, emaciated woman clad in a black dress that looks like a mourning outfit, her hair bound tightly in braids on the nape of her neck.

"Madam Citizen! Follow me!"

"What? Why?"

The woman stops short and turns her intelligent, wasted face towards the militiaman.

"We're going to the district centre!"

"I don't understand the meaning of this . . ."

"That's fine! That's fine! You'll find out the meaning at the district centre . . . what kind of hunger . . . Let's go!"

And the militiaman shoves the woman ahead of himself.

For a brief moment, the brilliant stream of noisy, restless vacationers falls silent and comes to a halt. The peasants who have witnessed the scene silently exchange glances. And, glumly and wordlessly, their emotionless eyes follow the black figure of the gaunt woman with a bun of tightly wound braids on the nape of her neck . . .

III

A Loaf of Bread

The old man's plakhta is truly splendid! What a sparkling array of colours! What a lavish spectrum of hues! From white and gold to hot yellow and a crimson as bright as fresh blood, and then on to blue, brown, and a black as dark as the fertile earth after a downpour. And how ingeniously the demanding design has been laid out on the background of the lengthy chessboard pattern. The plakhta, flickering coquettishly in the sun with all the richness of its rippling, aesthetically juxtaposed colours, lures the enraptured eyes of the female vacationers, drawing them to itself like a magnet. I swear to God that there is no finer plakhta in the entire market!

Having draped the plakhta over his shoulder and fanned it out in all its glory over his chest—as if inviting the onlookers to delight in it—the old peasant Mykhaylo stares intently from under his drooping bushy brows at the motley throng of bustling vacationers, and, time and again, sparks flare in his deeply recessed eyes . . . Are they sparks of anger, of indignation, or do they reflect, perhaps, a deeply buried cry of the soul, a yearning to understand, to comprehend? Who can say . . . Be that as it may, old Mykhaylo leans weakly on his staff, silent, gloomy, and awkward looking, like an old hempen sack of very good quality, that now, for some unknown reason, has been filled not with wheat . . . but with water. He was able to move around dextrously with the golden kernels of grain, but the water . . . O God! How heavy his body feels. How hard it is to stand!

The long market hours pass by. Dozens of vacationers inquire about the price of the exquisite plakhta, but, having set a price, old Mykhaylo is as firm and unbreakable as steel. And as he stands there, scarcely able to bear the burden of his own body, he dreams passionately about . . . a loaf of bread. About a large, well-baked loaf with a lightly roasted crust that crunches ever so gently between your teeth. Hmm . . . The kind of crust that transports you into a state of ecstasy as you chew it with your still healthy teeth, squeezing out the tasty, nourishing juices. The old man's jaws involuntarily begin a chewing motion, and his mouth instantly fills with saliva—saliva that he curses to the devil and spits out to one side.

And all the while, the imaginary loaf dances flirtatiously like an enchantress, flaunting first one side and then the other before the infatuated old man's covetous eyes as if to say: "Just look what a fine loaf I am!" Forgetting about everything else in the world, the old man stares intently at the imaginary loaf and realizes that it is very similar to its numerous sisters that his wife Oleksandra used to bake in the outdoor oven—loaves that were incomparably tastier and more attractive than the ones baked for the last few decades by the Myrhorod bakery out of the flour ground from his wheat. No one in the whole world knows how to bake bread the way his Oleksandra bakes it! The one and only beautiful and industrious Oleksandra whom he had married against the wishes of his parents, the one who had borne him five stalwart sons— his dream, his hope, and his future . . .

And the old man's head bows down even lower as he recalls those stalwart sons of his. One was tortured to death by the Cheka at the beginning of the Revolution; a second one was exiled to the Solovky Islands and was probably no longer among the living; the third one, a kolhosp farmer, had starved to death along with his wife—that daughter-in-law who used to sing so splendidly on winter evenings as she sat at the spinning wheel; and the last two sons were still living and held Soviet positions.

But . . . was it even conceivable that he, branded as a "former kurkul and an enemy of collectivization," bloated and looking the way that he did—and old Mykhalo stared, with the slow deliberateness of a profound philosopher, at his bare, ballooning feet, and then at his clothes that were reduced to rags—could go and knock on his sons' doors? After all, did he not understand that his very appearance there would do them irreparable harm— destroy their young lives? No, no! He could not bring himself to do that! Neither he nor his Oleksandra could ever do that!

Continually shifting from one swollen foot to the other and swallowing the saliva induced by his hunger, old Mykhaylo recalls that a week ago he had brought home a sack of flour that he had received in trade for a gold cross in the Poltava <u>Torhsin</u>. And once again, but even more ardently now, he dreams about a loaf of bread and how he will bring it home to her, to his Oleksandra. He vowed that he would not eat it himself! Unless, of course, he had to break off just a tiny bit along the way to shore up his strength . . . to keep himself from collapsing . . .

"Hey there, granddad! Are you deaf? This is the third time that I'm asking you: how much do you want for the plakhta?"

Unexpectedly hearing a woman's voice close to his ear, old Mykhaylo waves away the rosy mist of his dreams and replies in a quiet, hoarse voice that does not sound like his own: "A loaf of bread!"

"What? A whole loaf? That's a lot!"

The curlyheaded woman of about thirty holds the plakhta up against the sun and examines it carefully, checking to see if there are any holes in it. Her delicate, flawlessy manicured hands tug at the plakhta quite vigorously, her large bluish-grey eyes look intently at the picturesque squares of the chequered fabric that, illuminated by the sun, is almost transparent. And her light grey dress, filmy like smoke, wraps around her slim figure and flutters ever so softly in the caressing breath of the gentle breeze.

"Hmm . . . How old is this plakhta? You wouldn't know, would you?"

"Why wouldn't I know?" the old man responds in an offended tone. "Of course I know! This plakhta is a hundred years old. And maybe even more than that, because, to tell you the truth, it was part of my grandmother's dowry. That's the way it is!"

"Hmm . . . So it goes all the way back to Hohol's era!" the woman whispers to herself, and her eyes devour the exquisite plakhta with its artistic design and its rich colours, succulent and shimmering, like a rainbow.

"Well, how much less will you take for it?" she asks, peering into the old man's eyes.

For a fleeting moment the eyes of these two people collide, and then, abruptly breaking contact, never cross again. The woman, grimacing in revulsion, turns her bluish-grey eyes away from the old man's repugnant face and fixes them once again on the engaging design of the exquisite plakhta.

"It won't be any less!" the old man whispers.

And he is overcome with a desire to stow this family heirloom swiftly in his bag, because . . . this woman with the curly hair does not have the right to even so much as look at it, let alone take it away! Or rather, "to buy" it . . . for a loaf of bread! For a single loaf! O, One and Only God! You see everything! And at that moment the old man watches with his inner eye as fragments of memories flash by with the speed of lightning on a movie-like screen . . .

There he is, hauling a wagonload of wheat to Myrhorod, solicitously plying his whip to chase away the gadflies from the backs of his curly-horned oxen . . . And then the scene shifts to the year of our Lord 1930, and his oxen and his cow with its calf are being led away to . . . the kolhosp. Oleksandra is wailing and lamenting; the oxen, sensing that something unusual is happening, are bellowing; and he—Samodyn—is standing in the middle of his yard, listening, staring but . . . saying nothing, as if he had been stunned by a sledgehammer.

And later, in 1932, government representatives make the rounds of all the yards and cottages and take away all the grain and everything else that is edible. To the private householders they say: "If you want to eat—join the kolhosp!" And to the kolhosp members they say: "The kolhosp will feed you!"

After conducting a thorough search of the property of Khoma Luhivsky—an indigent peasant who was initially given land by the Soviet government, only to have it repossessed and turned over to a kolhosp by that very same government—the representatives knock on Samodyn's door. They search for grain and vegetables everywhere: in the barn, the stable, and the chicken coop; and, in the cottage, they dig up the entire floor.

They take away everything, to the very last kernel, leaving nothing, nothing for sowing, and nothing for the small children of his son Ivan and his wife, who had joined the kolhosp in 1930. And Samodyn accepted this injustice in silence as well; but at the time it seemed to him that the sky, gloomy and threatening, had fallen on his head. Not long afterwards, first Ivan, and then Ivan's wife, died of hunger, leaving Samodyn and his wife Oleksandra two young granddaughters as a memento of themselves . . . as an unending source of torment . . .

Over Samodyn's deeply bent head, fragmented memories whirl chaotically, chasing and outstripping one another like withered leaves in late autumn that, torn away from their trees, are swirled by a wanton wind—the wind that brings the snow . . .

And how it is that he—Samodyn—has managed to stay alive until now, the summer of 1933, is truly beyond his comprehension. But nevertheless, here he is at the market, selling an heirloom that is more than a hundred years old, while elsewhere, on the porch of a stranger's house, his two granddaughters, with unnaturally large eyes and waxen, emaciated faces, are whimpering, and their grandmother Oleksandra has nothing with which to quiet them. All three of them, anxiously awaiting his return, keep running out to the road, peering down it to see if he is returning from the market with . . . a loaf of bread in his deep bag . . .

In the meantime, after giving the matter some thought, the curlyhaired woman reaches into her basket and ostentatiously takes out . . . a loaf of bread. And, O God, what a loaf! It is a twin to the one that he has been dreaming about so passionately, so sweetly! The crust on the loaf is roasted just so, to a nice rosy brown . . .

His wilful jaws begin a chewing motion and, just from the thought of how submissively, how gently that crust will crunch between his strong, still healthy teeth, he suddenly feels faint . . . Oh, to sit down! No, not to sit down—to lie down right here in the marketplace, because his brain is fogging over, his eyes are swimming with red rainbows against a background of a dense, dark rain, and his mouth is filling once again with the disgusting saliva that he no longer has the strength to spit out.

A moment passes in this way. A single moment! But it truly seems like an eternity.

And then . . . what is happening? Granddad Mykhaylo's hand lunges with a predator's famished swiftness, and the well-baked loaf lands in the unyielding grip of his swollen, calloused hands and quickly drops from sight, hiding itself at the bottom of his deep bag. And, in the same moment, the exquisite plakhta flees precipitously into the fashionable basket of the woman with the curly hair.

The deed is done!

The sky is a transparent azure, and the brilliant sun is warm and caressing, like the touch of a mother. With the implacable severity of an uncorruptible judge, it focusses on everyone and everything, as in an historical documentary film, highlighting whatever catches the eye: first, the noisy and bustling female vacationers flashing the bloody buds of their lips; their sarafans, sewn with a deliberately colourful gaudiness; the healthy freshness of their tanned arms and shoulders.

And then, in dramatic juxtaposition—the hopelessly drab background of the peasants in the ragged remnants of their clothing, peasants stretched out like mummies, their unnaturally distended bodies creating unmoving, living corridors at the Myrhorod market where they have brought their family heirlooms. Some—a rushnyk taken down reverently from an icon; others—a miraculously preserved plakhta handed down to them from their grandmother; and still others—a full-length artistically embroidered, openwork shirt that is the only remembrance of a marriage ceremony, of the mystical flickering of candles in an old church, of a boisterous wedding, and of the years of one's youth, gone forever . . .

Every item is a living memory, a fragment ripped out bloodily from the still pulsating heart of a peasant!

The Myrhorod market lives with its own unique historical life.

The peasants from the entire district of Myrhorod are selling. The vacationers, who have come to Myrhorod from all corners of the USSR, are buying.

And the government representatives watch diligently to ensure that there is no thievery, no cheating . . . nor anything of a counter-revolutionary nature.

IV

Then and Now . . .

Myrhorod! The very name evokes a gamut of memories bequeathed to us by the fertile pen of Hohol! Myrhorod! It is the ancient peaceful city so beloved by Mykola Vasylovych, and in which, as he asserted: "There is no thievery and no cheating." Approaching Myrhorod one weeping autumn day with a soul as sad as the world around him, Hohol suddenly felt his heart beat faster.

Myrhorod! This is "the city kept intentionally small on the Khorol River," where a quarrel arose so unexpectedly between two honourable men—the cream of society, immediate neighbours, and the best of friends—Ivan Ivanovych Pererepenko, whose head looked like a radish with its tail hanging downwards, and Ivan Nykyforovych Dovhochkhun, whose head looked like the same kind of radish, but with its tail sticking upwards.

It is the same peaceful town where for entire generations a true quarrel was an unheard of phenomenon, and that is why, when one erupted unexpectedly like lightning from a transparently clear sky, it loomed like a cloud over the peaceful inhabitants for a good many years, giving them new cause for amazement with every passing day and satiating their minds, on a daily basis, with the hitherto unknown contrasts and irreconcilable differences that revealed themselves in the conflict between the two men—Dovhochkhun and Pererepenko.

But that was back then . . . a long time ago . . . A century has passed since then; the Revolution of 1917 has come and gone, as well as the sixteen long years that came after it. And in that time, Myrhorod, like all of Ukraine, has taken on another appearance. It has changed, become Soviet . . . But are there now any contrasts, irreconcilable differences, and conflicts that loom like a dark cloud over the peaceable residents of Myrhorod and the district surrounding it? It would be better not to ask! Nothing is written about such matters in newspapers or magazines. And it does not matter whom you might approach with this essentially naive question, everyone, after glancing about fearfully and avoiding any contact with your eyes, will say that . . . there are no contrasts in Soviet Myrhorod, and there never can be any, and that he himself is a most fortunate person who has the best possible life. It is entirely up to you whether or not you believe this assertion.

A hundred years have greatly changed the external appearance of Myrhorod. The main street of the city is no longer covered with the mud that the people of Hohol's era waded through so stoically. Now there is pavement! And so, when you arrive in Myrhorod in 1933, do not search for that unique, unsurpassably picturesque puddle that, assuming lake-like proportions a hundred years ago, triumphantly filled the vast expanse of the main square. And do not expect to see the delightful little buildings that, from a distance, as Hohol so aptly put it, looked like small stacks of hay that, having grouped themselves around that charming puddle, now stood admiring its beauty.

At the beginning of the twentieth century, the water and the mud were found to be curative, and so now, in that very same spot, there is a health resort—a spa that has gained mastery over the centre of this "intentionally small city," including the lord's mansion and the old palisade along the bank of the Khorol river where Mykola Vasylovych loved to stroll. The new sanatorium sprang into being like a mushroom after a rainfall and, for nine months of every year, it is filled with people armed with put'ovkas, who descend upon it from all corners of the USSR.

Gone is the famed "mayor," that oddball on whose uniform eight buttons were sewn as peasant women sow broad beans— one over here, and one over there—and on which, for some reason, the ninth button was always missing. Gone too are the elegant "receptions" at which the long deceased mayor hosted the cream of Myrhorod society, serving Ukrainian borshch, turkeys, and countless other superbly prepared and tasty dishes. The dust of oblivion has covered the glory of the mayor's pronouncements in which he categorically forbade pigs and goats to appear in the main square of Myrhorod. And the famous mayor himself is gone, as is the one-armed soldier who served so assiduously under his command!

May the earth lie lightly, like a feather, on their graves!

Now the internal security of Myrhorod and its outlying area is in the hands of two district institutions: the <u>NKVD</u> District Administration and its faithful servant, the District Militia . . . Both have large staffs of well-nourished and well-armed workers in faultlessly fitted uniforms on which all the buttons are sewn exactly where they should be. The heads of these district institutions are not in the habit of treating the residents of Myrhorod to Ukrainian borshch or turkeys, but they are very interested in everyone and in everything, including the pigs and the goats. Now every pig belongs to the state! And, as for matters of internal security, the aforementioned institutions look after them most diligently, and in precisely the manner dictated to them by "Stalin the Great." It should be noted that it is these same institutions that make sure that all the candidates for the next world, dressed in the ragged remnants of their peasant clothing, are barred from having access to the grounds of the health resort . . . and these orders are adhered to even more strictly than the pronouncement forbidding pigs and goats to appear in the main square of Myrhorod in Hohol's day.

Oh, Myrhorod is no longer as it used to be!

It is different!

It is Soviet!

Time has long since levelled the mound heaped over the grave of Demyan Demyanovych, the famous Myrhorod judge who, attired in a greasy robe, habitually conducted court proceedings with a kindly expression on his face, while holding a cup of tea and tirelessly snorting snuff from his upper lip that served him faithfully as a snuff-box. His function has been taken over by the "People's Court," where not even the most agile pig can wriggle out of a lawsuit! Oh no! Now, complaints and the most intolerable accusations—that of a brother against a brother, a wife against a husband, a child against a parent—are in great fashion and held in great respect, and the secretiveness with which these accusations are handled is adhered to most strictly.

In the district of Myrhorod there no longer are any private mills—the mills that so tirelessly ground the golden grain that flowed in an endless, turbulent stream from the peasants' storage bins, including the bins of Solopiy Cherevyk, immortalized by Hohol. And Ostrovsky—the owner of the mill to which Mykhaylo Semenovych Samodyn, himself resembling a hempen sack filled with grain, brought his wheat every year—is also gone. Now all the mills belong to the state! Now every spike of grain, every kernel, belongs to the state. The entire network of private businesses and stores that did a passably good job of making foodstuffs and other goods available to everyone—among them Hohol's unforgettable heroes, including the mayor and his elegant Mayor's Reception—have been erased from the face of Myrhorod and its outlying district. The private entrepreneurs were either called "to serve on Dukhonin's staff" or received put'ovkas to the northern "health resorts" of the NKVD. And all industries and businesses were taken over by the Soviet State!

And O, my dear God! What a lack there is now of everything in those state-run stores! What an absolute lack of everything! To list all the things that are lacking would take far too much time, paper, and ink, so—the devil take it! In those stores there is, however, vodka, vinegar, a substitute for coffee, and salt . . . It would seem that these few items suffice for the "victorious proletariat," because . . . no one breathes even a word of dissatisfaction . . .

The bones of the immortal Panas Ivanovych and Pulkheriya Ivanivna—the old-world landowners that Mykola Vasylovych visited so often to find solace for his soul—have long since disintegrated. And there are neither relatives nor heirs! And where their sheltered villa stood, there is now a kolhosp. You don't believe me? Well then, go and see for yourselves.

There no longer are any big landowners in the district of Myrhorod. If they did not leave to go abroad—as was the case with Panas Mykhaylovych Vulfert, the last head of the Myrhorod district council—then they have wandered off "to serve on Dukhonin's staff" . . . They were all proclaimed parasites back in October 1917 because, instead of working the land themselves, they had others do it for them. And that was when the fiery slogan burst forth: "All land—to the peasants!"

But the peasants' good fortune did not last long. A dozen years later, the slogan of collectivization appeared, the one that took away not only what had been "granted" to the individual peasants by the Revolution, but also everything that they had inherited from their ancestors and which they considered to be their sacred birthright. And now, during the historical duel between the

Ukrainian peasantry and the directives from the Kremlin, no one mentions the fact that the peasants, from time immemorial, have poured the sweat of their brow onto that land, and that, intoxicated by the fiery slogan "All land—to the peasants!" they had, in no small measure assisted the Bolsheviks in gaining control of Ukraine. It is all forgotten now . . .

The peasantry is now looked upon strictly as a petty bourgeois element, as a powerful source of opposition defying the directives from the Kremlin towers. And so a bloody duel is being fought, an unequal duel. And, to ensure victory over the mighty current of the peasants' opposition, a new deceptive slogan, made up of words ringing with energy, resounds from the lips of the leader— the genius, the teacher, and the friend of all workers: "Destroy all kurkuls as a class!"

The Communist Party and the government of the USSR pick up the slogan with enthusiastic adulation; and the writers and journalists of Soviet Ukraine—the undisputed masters of a sycophantic mentality—"justify" it with truly amazing diligence and Stakhanovite vigour. The obedient press shouts its approval; loudspeakers, gasping for air, blare mercilessly; countless agitators-activists—those pitiful lackeys of pompous political oratory—strike themselves righteously on their chests and passionately preach the party line.

And everywhere, no matter where you look, you see the bloodthirsty posters that invoke people "to destroy all kurkuls as a class." And, with the adoption of this slogan, the historical tragedy of the mass destruction of the peasantry in Ukraine literally unfolds before your very eyes . . .

In the old days, a peasant sold his flour, wheat, cattle, poultry, yarn, and Persian lamb fur caps at the market when he wanted to and for how much he wanted to. But, in the autumn of 1932, Soviet "buyers" accompanied by the militia ransacked all the peasant homes in the Myrhorod district (and throughout Ukraine), and "bought" everything outright, to the very last kernel . . .

In the old days, a peasant woman had a trunk filled with clothing, and when she went to market, dressed herself attractively in a rich plakhta, a colourful headdress, a velvet bodice, an openwork shirt, and vivid strands of coral beads. Today, barefoot, ragged, and bloated, she sits at the market like a motionless mummy and, if her plakhta has already been sold, displays a rushnyk on her knees.

In the old days, during the time of tsarist serfdom, Hohol's Chichikov had to travel from Plyushkin's estate to Korobochka's, and from Manilov's estate to Sobakevych's as he traded and patiently bought up, in small numbers, peasants' dead souls. But now, in Soviet Ukraine, Chichikov, in a single year, could buy over seven million dead souls, souls of peasants who succumbed as victims of the artificial famine created by the new Soviet system of serfdom . . .

Back then, prior to 1861, free kozak villages existed alongside those bound in serfdom, but now, all the peasants, without exception, are enslaved. Back then, a peasant had the right to work for himself for two or three days a week, but now, all the working days of the Soviet serf belong to the implacable kolhosp . . .

Back then, after the abolishment of serfdom, a peasant worked six days of the week for himself; now he often has to devote seven days a week to his new lord who, after taking away his land, implements, and cattle, refuses to give him bread, not even for his children . . .

Back then, church bells tolled solemnly on a Sunday, and people flowed in a picturesque stream to the church . . . Now the bells are obstinately silent throughout Ukraine; they are not heard in Kyiv, or in Poltava, or in Myrhorod. It is only on the grounds of the health resort, that a bell, suspiciously similar to a church bell, calls vacationers to breakfast, lunch, and supper. Might it, in fact, be a bell taken from a church?

Back then, people—in the theatre, on trains, and out in the streets—reviled the despotic order, the tsar, the tsarina, and the bungling ministers, and, after thoroughly vilifying them, either returned home without incident from the theatre, or were free to continue on their way, without any interference, be it by train, or on foot. Now, everyone hastens to outdo all others in praising the Soviet order; everyone sings out "in an inspired manner" paeans to "Stalin the Great," and yet, despite even these methods of self-preservation, millions "are taking the cure" in the "health resorts" of the North and the Distant East . . .

Oh, these NKVD "health resorts" do not exist without reason! And it is not without reason that countless numbers of well-nourished and well-armed NKVD and militia members are maintained by the state! It is not without reason that where a group of "three" meet, at least one—if not two—is an informant, and the contents of the conversation of these "three" will be relayed in detail on the very same day to the NKVD. That very same day! And that is why everyone looks around so cautiously before uttering a word . . . and why everyone shudders apprehensively when there is a sudden, unexpected knock at the door.

In its silent obedience and unsurpassed sycophancy, the USSR, headed by the Red Kremlin, is unlike any other country in the annals of history. It is truly a grotesque, chimerical country, an incredible madhouse of staggering proportions, where all the "patients" live out their lives in a hypnotic state induced by fear. An order of "the great teacher and friend of the workers" in the Kremlin is carried out instantly, with alacrity—and with more than the required thoroughness—everywhere, even in the deepest, most remote corners of every one of the "brother republics" that "voluntarily united to form the USSR." It is no sooner said than done!

There can be no pause or interruption in carrying out the directives of the Red Kremlin throughout the USSR, and certainly not in any part of the Ukrainian S.S.R., nor in the district of Myrhorod immortalized by Hohol. Things are different now than they were back then . . .

And even though, back then, White Moscow oppressed Ukraine unceasingly for centuries, that oppression pales in comparison to the bloody methods being used in the mass destruction of our nation during the Red Soviet era of our day.

The silent obedience of the masses is not attained all that easily, or all at once. In the history of our struggle with the Red Moscow occupier, Holol's famed Myrhorod district added its own heroic page.

In 1919, in a building in Myrhorod owned by Ksondz, a group of Ukrainian heroes headed by Dubchak shot the staff—eight people—of a Cheka cell controlled by sadistic Lithuanian brothers who had attained notoriety throughout the district. Dubchak and his six companions were intelligent young men who were born in Myrhorod and, after the lightning-quick attack, they were able to escape beyond the borders of the province of Poltava. Dubchak's uprising is a rich theme that is still awaiting its retelling in literature, a retelling that would immortalize the heroic deed of these national avengers.

In 1920, the villagers of Velyki Sorochyntsi organized a rebellion against paying production fees, thereby providing other villages with a daring example of resistance against the occupier. This daring act of defiance by the brave peasants in Velyki Sorochyntsi—a village described by Hohol—was mercilessly crushed with blood and fire; most of the families paid for it with the lives of those most dear to them. Punitive Soviet squadrons raged throughout the village and, in a vindictive gesture of farewell, burned homesteads to the ground as they left.

The occasional revolts by starving peasants that burst out sporadically in 1932-33 in the Myrhorod district were also drowned in blood—rebellious acts like the destruction of grain storage bins in the stations of Hoholeve and Sahaydak, and the so-called "riots of the peasant women."

And . . . is it really necessary to state that nothing is ever written in Soviet newspapers about such interesting events? It would be better if you did not ask if there are any contrasts now, or if there are implacable differences and conflicts that loom like a dark cloud over Myrhorod and the entire district surrounding it! It would be better if you were to observe things carefully and keep your conclusions to yourself! And you will see that Myrhorod is not the way it used to be. And that the district of Myrhorod is not as it once was!

Only the River Khorol remains unchanged! Silvery, sparklingly sonorous, and confident in its eternally fresh beauty, it flows along as it has always flowed. Indifferent to everyone and to all spectacles, it flows and, like a softly strummed bandura, hums tirelessly about the olden days, about "the long ago" that is wrapped in a romantic veil and that has always excited the interest of people. And it will continue to excite them as long as the River Khorol sings its "splish-splash," and as long as it is accompanied by the whispering of the preoccupied willows that assumed their places on the banks on both sides of the river even before Hohol was born. They took their places there to silently observe everything and to unite into a single, unbroken chain the realistic "present" with the romantic "long ago" . . .

V

Two Ladies and a Peasant Woman

Swaying her full hips rhythmically, the woman with the curly hair and the dress as grey and as airy as smoke heads at a leisurely pace across Hohol Street to the grounds of the health resort and, ten minutes later, is in her apartment. And what a pleasant and cozy little nest it is! Attractive furniture, a mirrored wardrobe, pictures, a chandelier, splendid beds, an elegant dressing table, and . . . an exemplary cleanliness wherever one looks.

But . . . it is not just a matter of furniture; it is not the furniture that endows this suite with its appealing, soothing ambiance! No, no! It is not the furniture itself; it is the handcrafted decorations on it, and on the sparklingly clean windows, on the doors, tables, and end tables . . . Such stylish decorations! And selected so artistically, with a refined sense of taste. Embroidered rushnyks are draped on portraits and paintings; plakhtas and tapestries hang on the walls; runners line the clean floor that gleams like glass; and the curtains are made out of ingeniously combined "openwork" sleeves of peasant shirts, tablecloths, serviettes, and pillowcases. All these items are cross-stitched, embroidered, tatted, or done in openwork in the Ukrainian-Sorochyntsi-Myrhorod style, and it is all combined with such good taste that even Hohol's most accomplished and agreeable lady would have been envious. It is truly a peaceful little nest that calms, charms, and gently lulls its occupants, as a baby is lulled in a cradle.

"Hanna!" the mistress of the apartment turns to her maid from Khomutets: "Come here! Do you see this plakhta?"

A single dextrous movement of her hand . . . and the exquisite garment unfolded itself, revealing itself in its entirety before Hanna's enchanted eyes.

"O, Reveka Myronivna! Well, I swear to God that in all my life I've never seen anything like it!" and Hanna reverentially touches the edge of the exquisite plakhta. "But . . ."

"But what?"

"But where will you hang it? There really isn't any more room!"

"Oh, for a splendid piece such as this, some room will be found! It's absolutely priceless! A rarity! Do you know, my dear Hanna Babiy from Khomutets, what a 'ra-ri-ty' is?" And at this point Reveka Myronivna falls deep into thought, and wrinkles race across her forehead in white furrows. "Hmm . . . But maybe I should wait until my dear Aronchyk comes home from the spa dining hall, so that I can consult with him? Perhaps he'll want to have it hanging over his bed? What do you think?"

"Well . . . who can say! Aron Abramovych already has a fluffy <u>kylym</u> over his bed, the one—you remember, don't you?— that you got in trade for leftover scraps of bread in January . . ."

"That one? Well, in actual fact, it isn't all that attractive. But it is fluffy—you're right about that! Hm . . . You know what, Hanna? The matter is settled! The kylym will go down on the floor between our beds—do you understand? And the plakhta from Hohol's era will take its place on the wall. Got it? Now, quickly, bring the hammer and nails, and we'll effect a change in the decor. One, two, three! Quickly!"

It is no sooner said than done. And, after completing her task, Hanna, a tall, skinny, and awkward-looking woman with a waxen face and smoothly combed hair, retreats to the kitchen. Her duties are simple: to obey and to know her place. And everyone knows that a maid's place is in the kitchen.

She sits down on a bench and, resting her cheek on her palm, loses herself in a reverie. A whole string of questions beset and cloud her brain—a brain unfurrowed by learning. A few minutes pass by—who can say how many . . .

Suddenly, an energetic "knock-knock" on the door tears Hanna from the tentacles of that cloud. Who can it be? Rising abruptly from the bench, she hurries to open the door.

In front of her stands a lady.

Where, from what artist, can I borrow the talent and the pigments to paint a portrait with my humble powers that would truly equal the original? Where can I find a charmed pen?

In front of Hanna stands a superbly magnificent lady of forty, or thereabouts. Tall, solidly built, and massive, she does not have even so much as a hint of a waist. Her magnificent chin, without so much as an allusion to a neck, rolls freely downwards in three wavy segments into the sea of her splendid bosom that, untroubled by the superstitious line of a waist, tumbles unhampered in a turbulent cascade into her stomach. A blue sarafan patterned in large red roses eloquently displays the unsurpassed elegance of her shoulders, arms, and upper bosom, and the graceful curls of her short, almost white, blond hair dutifully crown this creation of nature and further emphaisze the overall impression of massiveness, corpulence, and pulchritude. Oh, this is truly a lady who catches everyone's eye. It is impossible not to notice her at the theatre, on a streetcar, or even in a very large gathering!

But . . . O my God! What an unforgivable carelessness on my part! What a fatal oversight! I completely forgot to mention that the woman has . . . a face. But all the same, she does have one. A haughty, round, chubby, and rosy face—thanks to T. Zh. cosmetics—peeks out provocatively from among the artificial curls that cover her temples, ears, forehead, and finely drawn black eyebrows . . . That face has tiny, watery, colourless eyes, a plum-shaped nose, and sensuous full lips smeared with flaming red lipstick.

"Is Reveka Myronivna at home?" the lady asks in a ringing voice, smiling broadly and displaying a large quantity of gold in her mouth.

"Yes, she is. She just got back from the market." And Hanna phlegmatically leads the guest into the appropriate room.

"Sweetheart! My dearest darling!" the elegant lady calls out in Russian a few moments later as she gently rocks her massive body in the calming embrace of a comfortable rocking chair. "You know—I was going home from the market and I simply could not refuse myself the pleasure of stopping by to chat with you."

"Oh, your visit truly affords me a great deal of pleasure!" Reveka Myronivna responds, smiling pleasantly. "Have a bit of a rest, my dear Mariya Ivanivna! Given your constitution, an excursion to the market is no easy matter. Would you like some 'Myrrad' to refresh yourself a bit?"

"Oh, who needs any 'Myrrad'! Do you know, my little darling, what I acquired at the market today? A bridal shirt! It's a dream! A fairy tale! A poem! If you gave away everything you own to get it, it still would not suffice!" And, without letting Reveka

Myronivna get a word in edgewise, the perspiring visitor swiftly pulls out of her basket a peasant woman's long shirt, obviously not worn more than once, made out of a fine white fabric with a dainty collar and a wonderful azure—not white—openwork design on the sleeves.

"Well, what do you think? Will I be able to have a nice dress made out of it? Is there enough fabric in it?"

"Hmm . . . Well, my dear Mariya Ivanivna, stand up tall, and I'll measure it . . . Yes, just like that! Now turn your back to me! Hmm . . . Your back is quite a healthy size! What can I say? Do you want the dress to have sleeves?"

"Yes! It must have sleeves!"

"Well, in that case, there won't be enough!" Reveka Myronivna announces abruptly. "There simply won't be enough! But . . . who has sleeves now on a dress sewn in the Ukrainian style? First, my dearest, it's no longer the style—it's not at all modern! Second, why would you want to hide such attractive ample arms from public view? Why? I'm asking you . . ."

Mariya Ivanivna blinks her tiny watery colourless eyes in confusion as she stares at her friend's mouth.

"But . . . what is the style now for Ukrainain dresses? I thought that it was with sleeves . . ."

"No! That's completely out of style! Dresses are now being sewn out of peasants' long shirts in the following manner: both openwork sleeves are undone and spread across the chest so that the upper part of the arms is barely covered. Even though, of course, it is a pity to hide even the tiniest bit of your splendid arms. But for variety, it could be done like this. For the summer, sewing it in this style is simple, original, and fashionable . . ."

After listening to this categorical verdict while still standing, the visitor once again lowers herself heavily into the rocking chair and begins a minute examination of the shirt she has acquired, talking to herself as she tries to figure out what to do with it. Should she sew herself a modern Ukrainian dress without sleeves, or should she, perhaps, sell it? The problem absorbs the attention of both women and, for some time, they sink into a sea of various possibilities as they contemplate a topic that is interesting only to a woman's mentality. Reveka Myronivna is the first to swim out of that sea.

"Uh . . . if it isn't a secret, from whom did you buy this shirt, my dearest Mariya Ivanivna? Was it not, by chance, from the young peasant woman who sat with her dreadful legs stretched out alongside the co-operative store?"

"Yes, it was! But . . . why?"

"Oh, nothing. Nothing at all. I just asked, that's all."

The point is that Reveka Myronivna—a past master at trading bread for the most valuable items—had also noticed the shirt, and had intended to buy it for herself, but the old peasant's plakhta had interfered with her plans. After acquiring the plakhta, she had rushed back to find the young woman who was displaying the artistically embroidered openwork shirt on her knees, but . . . she was nowhere to be found.

And now, by a strange quirk of fate, it was Mariya Ivanivna—her acquaintance from Moscow who had almost completed her course of treatments at the Myrhorod health resort—who had purchased the shirt. Hmm . . . So, she was the one who had plucked such a priceless treasure right out from under her nose!

But . . . it is not in vain that God has endowed Reveka Myronivna with the very same qualities that were enjoyed by Hohol's "most accomplished and agreeable lady"! It is not in vain that she has cultivated a pleasant demeanour in dealing with people, and it is not in vain that she has learned to control her feelings, her facial expression, and even her eyes! And it is not in vain because, in terms of her mental acuity, her education, and her upbringing, she towers over the massive Moscow woman in her red and blue sarafan that was sewn without so much as a hint of good taste!

It is not in vain that today, wearing a dress as filmy as a little grey cloud and blue sandals that are only size 36, she makes such an advantageous contrast to the portly Mariya Ivanivna. With her naturally curly hair that is purposely styled modestly, her intelligent, lightly powdered face that attests to an astute, almost indiscernible use of cosmetics, her long slender fingers that never come into contact with heavy work, and with the sinuous gracefulness of a pussycat in her every movement—all these features come together to make such a pleasing impression that even her nose, that is not at all shaped like a Roman nose, does not spoil the overall effect.

Oh, it is not in vain that Reveka Myronivna received a higher education, knows several languages, plays very acceptably on the piano, and is conversant with literature. It is not in vain that she writes poetry and, with her large bluish-grey eyes raised upwards and her head slightly tilted, recites Mayakovsky, Serhiy Yesenin, and Dem'yan Bedny. It is not in vain that under her sweet and pleasant words there often is hidden a most apt and witty barb! And it is not in vain that in the bouquet of Myrhorod ladies she has earned the title of "a most accomplished and agreeable lady," while her corpulent Moscow visitor with the multicoloured cosmetics of "T. Zh." and the avaricious face of a female animal can only be called—with the most profuse apologies on our part—only an "agreeable lady" and . . . nothing more!

"Hmm . . . My dearest Mariya Ivanivna, your weight, I swear to God, is in direct proportion to your acuity! For it is only thanks to this quality that you were able today to acquire this veritable pearl! You will now take back to Moscow an entire dowry in the Ukrainian style, for I know that you have tablecloths, and rushnyks, and shirts, and plakhtas, and . . ."

"No, I don't have a single plakhta!" the agreeable lady sighs heavily. "And do you know what? All things Ukrainian are very fashionable now, both in Moscow and in Leningrad. Factories are producing mass goods made in the Ukrainian style for general consumption—men's embroidered shirts, women's cross-stitched and embroidered dresses, tablecloths, serviettes, curtains, and so on. But . . . do you suppose that I don't know how much they are worth compared to handmade goods?

"If you only knew, my dearest darling, how impressed I am by your ability to decorate your suite so artistically! You have a bottomless abyss of good taste! I have to admit that my apartment on Arbat Street in Moscow is quite a bit more attractive in and of itself . . . the ceilings are higher, the windows are bigger, the rooms are larger, there's a tub, a shower—all the amenities! And the furniture is the very last word in fashion! But still . . . what good is all that when I haven't managed to turn it into a cozy nest like the one you have here? I swear, I haven't! But . . . I've caught on to your secret! It lies in all these decorative items of handiwork done in the Ukrainian style. And now I want to follow your example and, to tell you the truth, overtake you."

"Perhaps even outstrip me?" the most accomplished and agreeable lady asks, her eyes sparkling. "But, go slowly on the curves as you run after me! So that you don't . . ."

Suddenly the twinkle in the depths of her large bluish-grey eyes fades and, politely excusing herself, Reveka Myronivna flutters like a swallow into the bedroom.

"Hanna! Hanna!" her brisk, commanding voice rings out. "Come here! Get a move on! Oh, I have nothing but trouble with that scarecrow from Khomutets!"

A moment later Hanna appears with a delicate lady's nightgown in her left hand, and a needle with a pink thread in her right hand.

"Were you, by chance, sleeping in there?"

"No, I was embroidering."

This declaration is more than enough to have the Moscow visitor instantly ask to have the embroidery shown to her.

"How utterly charming! A dream! A poem! A fairy tale! So, it turns out that your Hanna embroiders your lingerie for you, and ever so artistically at that. And I didn't even know about it!"

"If Hanna did not embroider artistically, she would not have the good fortune to be my maid! She devotes all of her spare time to embroidering lingerie for me and my child," Reveka Myronivna calls out cheerfully and indifferently from the bedroom, and, turning without a pause to Hanna, adds in a dry, intentionally business-like tone: "You and I hung the plakhta over the bed together. Right? Well, and who is supposed to clean up the mess and take away the remaining nails? Is it up to me to do it?"

Hanna silently shuffles into the kitchen to get a broom, and the agreeable lady, with an incredible alacrity, considering her weight, leaps out of the rocking chair that, relieved of its burden, rocks wildly in alarm, attaining the greatest possible amplitude in its oscillations.

"Do I have your permission?" the visitor asks in a voice as sweet as honey as she stands in the doorway and pokes her plum-shaped nose right into the bedroom.

"Of course, of course, my dearest Mariya Ivanivna! I have no secrets from you. Hanna-a-a-! Where have you gone now? Bring the rocking chair into the bedroom for Mariya Ivanivna. My goodness, how clumsy you are!"

But the agreeable lady is not at all interested in the rocking chair. Encompassing in a lightning-quick glance her friend's bedroom with which she is quite familiar, she focusses her watery, colourless eyes—now opened wide with avariciousness—on the exquisite plakhta. The richness of the colours, the artistic design, and the whimsical sparkling of the hues instantly captivate the envious heart of the elegant Moscow visitor. She is especially impressed by the red and black colours that stand out in bold relief. The red tones are as bright as fresh blood, and the black ones are like fertile soil drenched by a spring shower.

A few sunbeams—someone's accomplices—playfully pierce the delicate lace curtains and dance such a sparklingly spirited hopak on the chequered plakhta that the eyes of all three women are involuntarily glued to it, but . . . the three of them differ greatly in the way that they are looking, and what they are thinking and feeling . . .

It just so happens that Hanna, armed with a broom, is standing between the two agreeable ladies, and she is the first to break out of the hypnotic spell. Forcefully tearing away her smallish dark eyes from the enchanting sight, she slowly slides them over the elegant Reveka Myronivna from head to foot, and then over the massive Mariya Ivanivna. And Hanna's eyes are piercing, just like the needle with which she is embroidering her mistress's nightgown.

"I'm curious, Hanna: how long are you going to stand here with the broom?" the most accomplished and agreeable lady asks.

"Why, I . . . right away . . . As soon as Mariya Ivanivna moves out of my way."

"When . . . and where did you acquire it?" the agreeable lady asks hoarsely.

"Then . . . and there, where you got your openwork shirt."

"And . . . how much did you give for it?"

"Look, there are still some sweepings left over here! Don't you see them, Hanna? Sit down, my dearest Mariya Ivanivna. My rocking chair is always at your disposal."

But the visitor does not sit down.

"How much did you give for it?" she repeats her question.

"My dear, can such a trifling matter really be of interest to you?" Reveka Myronivna asks, smiling pleasantly and gazing into the very depths of the watery eyes of her elegant Moscow guest. "Three hundred <u>karbovantsi</u> or . . . perhaps a crust of bread—what's the difference? The fact remains that the plakhta is mine, and the openwork shirt is yours. I don't know if you noticed that I did not ask you how much you paid for the shirt—that rare pearl of a shirt—that you acquired . . ."

"Hmm . . . perhaps you're right."

There is an embarrassing pause that lasts much longer than permitted by decorum in polite society. Perhaps the shadows of certain individuals are hampering the conversation of the agreeable ladies.

"Reveka Myronivna! My dearest darling! My angel!" the Moscow lady's high-pitched words finally break the silence; her voice trembles, and her cheeks are flooded with a deep, natural flush. "Sell me your plakhta! And buy yourself another one! After all, you're a permanent resident of Myrhorod, but I have to leave for Moscow in a week—without a plakhta! It's a tragedy—nothing less! You have to understand how I feel!"

"Well, in the course of a week you'll have more than enough time to buy yourself a plakhta. But come now, why are we standing here, my dearest? My rocking chair feels lonely for your gracious body!"

And, with these words, the ever hospitable Reveka Myronivna moves the rocking chair closer to her guest and, when it finally rocks under the weight of Mariya Ivanivna, sits down on a small chair beside it.

After carefully gathering up all the sweepings and the nails, Hanna—tall, scrawny, awkward . . . and bristling wih rage—walks slowly to the kitchen.

"My dearest darling! My angel! How much do you want for the plakhta?"

"Well . . . how much would you give me?" the most accomplished and agreeable lady asks, slyly closing her left eye.

"I'll give you this pearl—the openwork shirt. I swear to God it will look wonderful on you . . . And I'll give you an addditional one hundred karbovantsi," the agreeable lady cries joyfully.

"Ha-ha-ha!" the most accomplished and agreeable lady disdainfully scatters her silvery laughter like a broken string of coral beads. "Ha-ha-ha! I can see that you're a joker, my dearest! This plakhta is priceless! It's a plakhta from Hohol's era, and that's exactly why I want to see it over the bed in our bedroom."

"From Hohol's era?" the stunned Moscow visitor repeats, blinking her widely opened, watery eyes in utter confusion.

"Exactly! Such an item is not to be sold! It is to be preserved— as a treasure . . . And you're offering me a shirt and . . . a hundred karbovantsi! You ought to be ashamed of yourself! Do you, by chance, take me for a speculator?"

"Whatever are you saying, Reveka Myronivna? I know only too well how educated, talented, and intelligent you are . . . Please understand me! I'm pleading with you to relinquish the plakhta to me, your friend, and I'll take it back with me to the capital of our great USSR—to Moscow itself, to the mother of us all . . . . Do you understand?" And the visitor continues chattering ever so swiftly, all the while gasping for breath and speaking in an unmistakable Moscow dialect that does not bear the slightest resemblance to the speech of a cultured person. She alludes to the influence of her husband in the Administration of the Health Resorts of the USSR, and to the far-ranging possibilities of being either helpful to her "dearest sweetheart" Reveka Myronivna, or . . . not so helpful . . .

After calling Reveka Myronivna her "dearest sweetheart" for the tenth time, she finally falls silent and mops the perspiration on her forehead, assiduously plying a pink handkerchief under a profusion of curls. She has nothing more to say . . . Silence looms like a cloud in the bedroom . . . and the clock on the night table can be heard ticking its "yes, yes," with an epic peacefulness and an ancient wisdom . . . Deep furrows crease the white forehead of the most accomplished and agreeable lady . . .

"Sweetheart! My dearest darling! Angel! Make me happy!"

"I can't!" Reveka Myronivna says curtly, as if slicing her words off with a knife.

"You . . . ca-a-an't? How can that be?" Mariya Ivanivna asks, and she rises from the rocking chair looking decisive, massive, and threatening, like a furious she-bear.

Who knows just how this argument between the two ladies would have ended—they probably would have quarrelled over the exquisite plakhta just as Ivan Ivanovych and Ivan Nykyforovych argued over a rifle, and it probably would have ended with the same insults, including the epithet "gander"—if the nimble mind and tact of the most accomplished and agreeable lady had not come to the rescue.

"An idea!" she calls out cheerfully, embracing her guest in the spot where her waist should have been. "I have an idea! Come to visit me this evening, my dearest, at exactly nine o'clock, and I'll take you to a speculator who buys up handicraft items en masse from the peasants and then sells them to the spa vacationers. Secretly, of course. He has a huge selection of plakhtas and kylyms, and for 300–400 karbovantsi you can buy yourself a plakhta that you'll be proud to take back to Moscow. And if you want me to, I can take you to see Khaynatska. I'm on good terms with her. By the way, as the director of the School of Ukrainian Folk Art, she received a medal and a congratulatory letter at an exhibition in Moscow. You can order a blouse or a dress in the Ukrainian style from her—using your own material, of course. Then you will have something completely new that is an original work of art."

"Really? I didn't know that! You, my dearest darling, are a living treasure!" With these words the agreeable lady forcefully seizes the slim figure of the most accomplished and agreeable lady in her powerful embrace, and they kiss each other resoundingly on both cheeks.

VI

The Difficulties of Transition

A quarter of an hour later, Reveka Myronivna is standing in the kitchen. As a rule, a mistress like the most accomplished and agreeable lady has very delicate hands, because she never does any heavy work herself, but she often visits the kitchen and frequently peers into its deepest recesses. Moreover, there are times when, overcome by the fullness of her soul, she is in the mood to have a chat with someone.

"You know, Hanna, Mariya Ivanivna said that decorating in the Ukrainian style is all the rage both in Moscow and Leningrad. But, in less than half a year or thereabouts, as you yourself are well aware, I have succeeded in redoing the entire apartment completely in the Ukrainian style, and it has cost me absolutely nothing. Nothing at all!"

"But every item did cost you something—a bit of bread!" Hanna replies, casting a piercing glance at her mistress out of the corner of her eye. "Don't assume that I don't know anything just because I'm 'a scarecrow from Khomutets . . .'"

At any other time, Reveka Myronivna most certainly would have noticed both the prickly sparks in the depths of Hanna's eyes and the tone in which she uttered the last sentence, but . . . her attention is suddenly gripped by something else, and so it is likely that she does not even hear Hanna's words.

"And what is this?" she asks sharply, poking her finger into a little pot filled to the brim with a murky brown liquid.

"That's . . . " Hanna is flustered. "That's . . . I've poured into that little pot all the cocoa left over in your cups. That's . . . I gathered that over a two-day period . . ."

"Hmm . . . I'm curious: why, exactly, are you doing this?"

The mistress's tone does not bode well, and Hanna, fixing her eyes on the floor, does not reply. But a single muscle—such an unruly one—twitches in the corner of her tightly closed lips.

"You're supposed to answer when I ask you something!"

"Well . . . you know that today is the market day, and . . . there are hungry people here from my village, Khomutets . . ."

"How many times do I have to tell you that there is no hunger! And that only the kurkuls and the would-be kurkuls who do not want to work in the kolhosps are roaming about in the town?"

"It's not true!" Hanna—tall, gaunt, brusque, and threatening—rises abruptly from the bench, apparently forgetting that she is a maid, and that her task is a simple one: to work and to obey. "It's not true! In our village, for example, even the members of the kolhosp are starving, because they were not left enough grain, not even for seeding. In Khomutets absolutely everyone is swollen with hunger. Do you think I don't know? Why, I can bring my sister Oryshka here today. You'll see what she looks like—and she's a member of the kolhosp . . . Let her tell you herself, if you don't believe me . . ."

"I have absolutely no need to see your Oryshka!" Reveka Myronivna cuts her off sharply. "You'd do better to pick up my nightgown from the floor because you're about to trample it. Remember, once and for all, that there is no hunger. There are only difficulties in the transition."

"Difficulties in the transition?" Hanna abruptly takes the two steps that separate her from her mistress and, fixing her searing, drilling eyes on her face, she says quickly, very quickly, gasping for air: "So it's because of the difficulties of transition that there are now so many dead people in the villages that they are buried without coffins, without a priest. Dozens of them buried in the same pit, like dogs! So, it's because of difficulties in the transition that people are eating people? That's very interesting! Up to now, I did not know why all this was happening. Now, thanks to you, I know."

There is a pause that gives Hanna the moral advantage.

The bluish-grey eyes of the most accomplished and agreeable lady, unable to withstand the corrosive contact with the dark eyes of the maid, flee hastily and fearfully and . . . come to rest once again on the little pot.

And this time, they burrow their way past the pot . . .

"So you're saying this is cocoa, Hanna? And for whom is it meant?"

"For Oryshka! After dinner she is to wait in the bushes behind the health resort until I bring it to her . . ."

"And this piece of bread—is it also meant for her?" and the most accomplished and agreeable lady points with her eyes at the crust that does not escape detection even though it is hidden behind the pot.

"Yes, it is! And so what? It's not stolen bread! I simply want to give Oryshka what you did not finish drinking and eating . . ."

"Here's how things stand, Hanna. It is now clear to me that you're luring onto the grounds of the health resort those dreadful, ragged people . . . but they are not permitted to be here . . ."

"O, my dear God! Do you suppose I don't know that? I'm telling you that I go to the bushes . . . far away from the resort, and I give her the cocoa there so that no one will see. Not a single soul! I . . ."

"Hanna!" Reveka Myronivna cuts her off dryly as she pours the cocoa into the slop pail. "Remember! This must be the last time—if you want to continue serving in my home!"

And the crust of bread follows the cocoa into the slops.

"What are you doing?" Hanna screams at the top of her lungs, but Reveka Myronivna is no longer in the kitchen.

Only the fragrant scent of "l'origan koti" perfume wafting in the air and the rapid swirling of the crust on the surface of the slops that were so unexpectedly startled attest to the mistress's recent presence . . .

VII

Myrhorod on a Summer's Night
(1833-1933)

"Oh, if I were a true artist, how masterfully I would evoke the enchantment of the night . . . I would portray all of Myrhorod as it lies slumbering; the stars, too numerous to be counted, gazing unperturbedly upon it; the tangible tranquillity broken only by the barking of dogs both close by and in the distance; a lovesick sexton dashing madly past them and clambering over a turnstile with knightly valour; the white walls of the buildings, embraced by the moonlight, growing still whiter; the surrounding trees turning darker; the shadows that they cast growing blacker; the flowers and the quiescent grass becoming more fragrant; and the crickets—those irrepressible cavaliers of the night—synchronously intoning their chirring songs from every cranny.

"I would paint a low clay-plastered hut in which a dark-browed girl with trembling nubile breasts tosses and turns in her solitary bed, dreaming about a hussar's moustache and spurs, while the moonlight shines smilingly on her cheeks. I would paint a white road with the dark shadow of a bat flitting over it—a bat that alights on white chimneys . . ."

It was in this way that Hohol described a summer night in Myrhorod in 1833.

Oh, if only I were a painter, an artist! If only I had an artist's inspired brush! I would depict how peacefully Myrhorod sleeps on a summer's night in 1933 under an exquisite dark blue plakhta embroidered by the stars . . . How solemnly, how mysteriously the unreachable star-worlds twinkle—the stars that flicker tremulously and bashfully, like the flames of innumerable candles in the night . . . How mournfully, how humbly the worried willows bend over the silvery-rustling and silvery-dark bosom of the Khorol River . . . How softly, how soothingly, the luxuriant, tenderly green leaves of the age-old trees in the Myrhorod park whisper, relating a story about days gone by when Mykola Vasylovych took great pleasure in strolling down the pathways. How the delicate fragrances of the myriads of flowers, decoratively planted and carefully tended in the resort's flower beds, intoxicate and agitate . . .

How mercilessly a young, madly infatuated male vacationer tramples the fresh, uncut grass as he courageously dashes headlong into the thickets of impenetrable bushes where a young woman vacationer is silently hiding like a mouse in a hole . . .

I would not omit the whispering of the young lovers, or the synchronized orchestras of the crickets and frogs, or the streams of trills and the sweet chirping of the nightingale, that unsurpassed artist that performs solos in a most inspired manner against the background of the crackling orchestra, or the deep bass barking of the dog Atal that is so well known to all the vacationers at the resort . . .

All of these things, taken together, disturb the prayerful tranquillity of a summer's night in Myrhorod in 1933.

But is this all that disturbs it?

Stop a moment! Listen attentively to the sweet symphony of the Myrhorod night! And your ear will pick up snatches of strange, broken, incoherent sounds that are strongly suggestive of the wailing and the moaning of a human being . . . But who can it be? Whose groaning is it that resounds with such a brutal dissonance? Whose shrill laments dare to weave themselves time and again into an irritatingly black thread that jarringly mars the tapestry woven in such idyllic tones?

If you are truly interested, then come along quickly with me beyond the boundaries of the sanatorium grounds. And if you do, the groaning and the wailing will immediately become more distinct; that is when you will know, beyond a shadow of a doubt, that it is human beings who are groaning. And if you wish, you will see with your own eyes exactly where the grotesquely distended ragged peasants are dying—in the bushes on the very boundary of the forbidden sanatorium zone, on the sandy banks of the Khorol River, under the stooped, worried willows, or directly under someone's hospitable fence.

There is no doctor, no candle, no priest! It is not candles, but stars, that solemnly light the way for the peasants in their final moments! It is not a doctor, but death the deliverer, that sets them free from their suffering with her ice-cold touch! It is not a priest, but God, who accepts their prayer-confessions, their wailing, their sighs, and . . . their souls!

Truly, why am I not an artist? Why do I not hold an artist's daring, inspired brush in my hands?

I would paint you a picture of a tall fence overgrown with wild grapes in front of a neat little building inhabited by one of the powerful Soviet dignitaries of the district staff, the crushed grass, and the old peasant Mykhaylo Samodyn lying under that fence. That Samodyn who formerly hauled golden wheat to Myrhorod in large hempen sacks while solicitously urging on his curly-horned oxen . . .

Here he is! Look at him! He has truly earned this! Motionless, cold, and with his feet curled under him, he is lying still, indifferent to everyone and to everything, bathing his face in the dust on the road. He is lying _sam_ _odyn_ under a tall hospitable fence . . .

Do you hear? The night air is shattered once again by a wail. But it is not he who is groaning; it is someone else. Samodyn is politely silent. He no longer disturbs the fantastic symphony of the night . . . as others still do . . . No, no! And he no longer wants to eat, despite the fact that no one is preventing him from chewing with his still healthy and strong teeth the rosy-brown crust of the loaf that is lying near him—the loaf that has only a tiny piece torn from it . . . This loaf of bread is lying in all its beauty under the twinkling light of the star-candles that are embarrassed at the sight. It is lying there honestly, having been acquired with a family treasure—the exquisite plakhta . . .

Oh, if only I were a true artist!

I would also paint you a picture of Reveka Myronivna sleeping the sleep of the righteous as she lies serenely on splendid feather ticks in a bed decorated with Ukrainian needlework; she is sleeping with her face turned towards the plakhta from Hohol's era. And next to her, in the bed directly under the plakhta, I would paint the rotund, bulky figure of her husband, Aron Abramovych Bakaleynikov, who, as the doctor in charge of the vacationers' diets, energetically nourishes himself in the dining hall of the resort with a lot more than just bread . . . He is snoring heartily and resoundingly, as if trying to compete with the nightingale, the artist that performs solos with such inspiration to the accompaniment of the synchronized orchestras of crickets and frogs.

I would paint a typical, small, provincial train station with the sign "Myrhorod," a sleepy watchman with a lantern in his hand, and . . . a very long freight train that, with a clamorous metallic chorus of over a hundred voices, races by the station without stopping.

Speeding as fast as possible to the western boundaries of the USSR, it firmly holds in its belly the wheat, flour, sugar, meat, and other foodstuffs that the rich fertile Ukraine, and especially the district of Myrhorod, is "giving away" to be sold to foreigners in distant lands . . . for next to nothing. Disturbing the fantastic symphony of the night with its brutal dissonance, the train crammed with foodstuffs flees fearfully on its agitated black caterpillar-like wheels, as if it were running off with something it has stolen . . . and then it drowns in the sheltering fog as if sinking into a deep well.

There, it has already passed by; like a phantom that bears ill tidings it groaned mournfully, and with a protracted wail ground its insatiable iron teeth and disappeared beyond the Myrhorod horizon. But before it finally reaches the border, it will have to pass, in the daylight hours, many more train stations of the Ukrainian S.S.R.—stations where peasants will follow its journey with eyes maddened by hunger.

Oh, if only I had the daring brush of a true artist!

I would most certainly create a broad, expansive canvas of Myrhorod under a dark-blue exquisite plakhta embroidered with stars. I would intentionally paint the stars to resemble the solemnly flickering candles that accompany every funeral . . .

And, in the dreamy blue shadows of the fragrantly sweet night, I would show you the agile figures of the militiamen, the bearers of ill tidings that roam through the city like dark bats, rummaging and searching for peasants—both those who have already died and those who are still dying . . . I would show you the haste with

252 | Olena Zvychayna

which they fling both the dead and the dying into a single heap on a truck that will take them away in time . . .

In time! Before the enchanting night rolls up its elegant plakhta embroidered with star-candles . . . Before the sparklingly blinding and honestly righteous sun rises on the Myrhorod horizon, scattering the first reddish golden sparks of dawn . . .

In time! Before the vacationers awaken—the vacationers who, for reasons of pleasure, appetite, and health, stroll not only within the confines of the sanatorium grounds, but also far beyond them.

In time! Before sleep the magician, the younger brother of death, widely spreads his powerful, sweeping wings and flies away to the other side of the globe . . .

March 1953

Socialist Potatoes

"Comrades! Tomorrow, all of us—without exception—are to go and sort potatoes in the storage cellars. Our section must work there for two days. Not even a doctor's note will excuse you from this light work. If you're here on the job today—you're healthy, and you're expected to be at the mustering point by five in the morning. Everyone, without exception!"

The speaker—the party organizer of our section—is a ruddy-faced, solidly built blond man of about thirty-five; having exhausted the wearisome agenda of the general meeting, he is now addressing "practical matters."

After listening to his spiel about the assignment of production plans to every work brigade, agrarian goals to every collective farmer, and scholarly and bureaucratic responsiblities to every office, his fellow workers are all passionately envisioning the assignment of a meagre dinner to their stomachs, stomachs that are calling out to them queasily and intrusively: "Homeward march!"

And then, out of the blue . . . there is this bit of news!

The strident, no-nonsense tone of the party organizer, who has just returned after successfully securing mandated consignments of seed grain, does not bode well for anyone who might have the temerity *not* to show up at the mustering point by five the next morning.

"If you don't work in the storage cellars tomorrow, you'll be stripped of your ration card, and so will your entire family!" the chairman barks harshly. "Remember! Everyone, without exception! I declare the meeting closed!"

"What do you make of it, Sofiya Isakivna?" I ask my neighbour, a stenographer with shiny, carefully manicured, blood-red fingernails. "You'll have to cut your nails today, won't you?

For if you don't, there will be a lot of dirt and manure under them tomorrow!"

Sofiya Isakivna arches her painted eyebrows into triangles and, glancing disdainfully at my unpainted brows and closely pared nails, remains silent . . . Not a peep!

***

It is December . . . The fierce winter of 1932-1933 imperiously comes into its own . . .

The wind, sharp as a razor blade, stings my face and nimbly searches out the tiniest gaps in my clothing, forcing its way into the very marrow of my bones and painfully pinching my toes. In the predawn darkness, I am running as fast as I can to the mustering point—it is no joking matter to lose not only your own ration card but also those of your family members. My legs speed me on my way like an arrow . . . Finally, gasping for breath and drenched in sweat, I make it to the designated spot at the very moment that our group leaves for the station.

A forty-minute ride on the suburban train, and we arrive at our destination, the state storage cellars for potatoes. There are ever so many of them! And they are all numbered and laid out in neat rows on a huge field in the form of a chessboard. We are received expeditiously, counted off like cattle, formed into brigades of six people, and lowered by means of ladders into the ground—deep down into the storage cellars . . .

Now the ladder disappears, and the lid covering the opening above us slams shut. We—the six of us—find ourselves in a cavernous grave . . . An acrid, penetrating stench winds its way like a snake through our nostrils into our stomachs, our brains, our very souls . . .

We feel nauseated and terrified. We want to shout: "Help! Save us!" But a huge lamp conscientiously shows us the mountainous heaps of potatoes that seem to undulate before our eyes; the heaps that are the source of that putrid smell, and that patiently await the labour of our hands.

"Hmm . . ." says my friend Katrya, a small, thin brunette with a sharp tongue. "Sofiya Isakivna has not shown up after all. 'Well, it only makes sense. After all, is this work suited to her delicate, manicured nails? Is the 'l'origan koti' found on the rotten potatoes suited to her delicate nose?' So you see what it means to have an affair with the party organizer himself!"

Katrya's last sentence is whispered into my ear. And as she speaks it, she wrinkles her nose in such a way that, for a moment, it resembles the nose of the owner of the longest, best-tended nails in our section.

Donning the aprons that we brought with us from home, we get down to work, separating the undamaged potatoes from those that are slightly spoiled, and dropping the rotted ones into a large vat that has been lowered into the hole on thick ropes. Klava, a Komsomol member, starts singing a Komsomol song, but, choking on the vile odour, she breaks off abruptly in the middle of a word, saying that singing makes the stench "go right to your gut."

The two men—K., a young engineer and former aristocrat, and B., an elderly stooped man who was formerly employed as an office manager—work silently, gloomily immersed in the task at hand. There is not a sound out of them!

Why is this so? Is it the effect of the stench on one's psyche? Or is it, perhaps, something else? Why is it that the talkative young engineer—so saccharinely sweet in his dealings with all young women—is not showering the well-built and dark-eyed Zoya with his customary honeyed compliments, even though he is standing right next to her as he scoops up the rotten potatoes?

The six of us working here say nothing at all about the potatoes and the stench, but, at the same time, other topics seem out of place, because we are all—I am convinced of this—thinking only about the potatoes . . . About the peasants that they were taken from, and why they were dumped into storage cellars before they were dry, and why they are rotting in December . . . long before the coming of spring. And why grain is rotting in huge piles under the open sky near railroad stations, and why it is that this year there is so much grain that the state storage bins are unable to accommodate it all!

And these questions inevitably lead to other questions: how many hungry peasants would not be starving for how long a time if these potatoes and that grain—rotting in full public view—had not been taken away from them by force.

The rotten corpses of the potatoes fall with a soft thud into the yawning depths of the vat that, every now and then, is pulled up on its heavy ropes, to be replaced by another one—an empty one. During this exchange of vats, a narrow streak of fresh, frosty air filters into the fetid bowels of our grave, and, for a brief moment, we see a patch of sky overspread with clouds . . .

We pick over the potatoes in silence, like worms gnawing at a corpse. Thoughts about corpses are on the tip of everyone's tongue, but . . . we have all learned only too well the "truth" that has been pounded into us so energetically: "there is no famine," notwithstanding the fact that ever increasing numbers of starving farmers appear daily on our city streets—farmers terrifyingly disfigured by hunger, and reduced to shouting and begging: "Bread! Just a crumb! A tiny crust of bread!"

We know that down here, in this storage cellar oozing with putridness, Klava is the watchful eye of the Communist Party, and there might be someone else as well . . . Who can say for sure?

There is good reason for the popular proverb created by Soviet reality: "Wherever three people are gathered, one of them is a secret agent for the Party." And there are six of us here!

We do not talk at all. It is only the tottering mounds of half-rotten potatoes that speak. It is only the noxious stench that shouts. And thus the hours pass . . .

***

"Hey, are you alive down there? You, the brigade in storage cellar No. 31! Come up now!"

Finally! A ladder is lowered, and the six of us—exhausted and weakened like flies in late autumn—crawl up out of the dank cellar, one after the other.

The fresh air intoxicates and clouds our minds.

It is evening already. The wind is howling, and frost, the old joker, is nipping at us. Countless lanterns blink eerily, casting trembling, timid rays of malicious light on the huge mounds of rotten potatoes that have arisen by every storage cellar in the course of the day. It is, one could say, another "glorious attainment" of socialism—the socialist system that has been built so "victoriously" on one-sixth of the earth's surface.

After washing our hands in ice-cold water at the taps, we move, along with other workers from our institution, in a nervously boisterous stream to the exit.

Our empty stomachs are wailing faintly and importunately, and the very thought of warm food and a welcoming bed is enough to make us lose our equilibrium: "Oh, hurry up! Hurry up! Let's get to the gate and go home!"

But . . . hmm . . . At the gatehouse, the gatekeeper is ordering people to halt and wait. A group from another institution is ahead of us, and we are next in line.

"If we hadn't stopped to wash our hands, we would have been first," the delicate Katrya says with a note of reproach as she dances an improvisation on "the dance of the hungry out in the cold."

The wind, as if on purpose, does not abate. It whistles its northeasterly melodies even more fiercely, blows its icy breath in our faces, and reaches penetratingly to the very marrow of our bones through gaps and holes that only it knows about in our wretched winter clothing. The blue and bluish-red noses of our co-workers sink still more deeply into upturned collars, both young and old enthusiastically perform "the dance of the hungry out in the cold," and our hearts and souls are united in a single desire "to hurry home!"

"Klava!" engineer K. calls out in a voice as sweet as sugar. "You're a girl in a million! Could you go and nose out what is going on in there? Why they're taking so long to let us out?"

After hesitating for a moment, Klava detaches herself from the throng and runs off at a trot to the gatehouse. We watch as first her pointed nose pokes timidly into a crack in the doorway. Next, her head crawls in, then her left shoulder, and finally, her entire restless figure disappears. The little grey building has swallowed our Klava!

And in the meantime . . . the wind, on its widespread wings, brings tiny tufts of ice, sharp and prickly like needles, and only distantly related to snowflakes. The minutes seem like hours! They too are sharp and prickly like needles.

Oh, finally, finally! Darting out of the gatehouse, Klava swoops back swiftly, like a bird, and the crowd eagerly accepts her into its firm embrace.

"They're searching everyone!"

This softly whispered phrase is enough to . . . well, it gives rise to a slight rustling in the crowd. Oh, it is nothing all that significant. It is just that one woman suddenly notices that she has lost her kerchief and has to run back to find it, a few others decide to go for a walk alongside the storage cellars to warm up a bit, and, as for Klava, well, she takes refuge behind a neighbouring mound of rotten potatoes and busies herself with something there. But not for long! Oh no! In three minutes she is back in the midst of the throng, nonchalantly smoking her cigarette.

"Olenka! Sweetheart! You won't judge me, and you'll advise me what to do, won't you?" It is my friend, the small, delicate Katrya who calls me aside and asks me this question. And her chalk white face instantly tells me more than it needs to say in order for me to understand her predicament.

"Did you take a lot?"

"Why no, Olenka, just a few potatoes for our supper! You understand, don't you? I have a child and an old mother, and my pay doesn't suffice for even ten days. And the potatoes are all rotting here!"

"I understand all that as well as you do! But . . . I also understand that according to the <u>decree on the protection of socialist property</u> you will be sentenced to a remote labour camp for a minimum of five years!"

"For . . . five . . . years?" Katrya repeats, completely stunned. "I didn't know that!"

"Well, you probably didn't—but then, you don't read the newspapers. These potatoes are socialist potatoes. Everything that you see here is part of the 'sacred and inviolable socialist property'."

"And the manure as well?" Katrya's dark eyes radiate a gamut of blazing thoughts, anger, and protest, and it seems that she has momentarily forgotten about the danger she is in . . .

"We'll talk about manure at another time and in another place. And now—let's go! I've thought of a way of saving you."

Katrya and I walk slowly to the gatehouse; our actions do not evoke any suspicions, because we are walking toward the source of danger. After making a small semi-circle, we stop for a moment by some bushes that, submerged in the darkness, scarcely show up at all against the background of the snowless night. There, in those bushes, behind the protection of my benevolently and strategically positioned back, Katrya disposes of four large socialist potatoes that are not yet rotten, and that she had dreamed of cooking for today's supper.

No more than five minutes after this "operation," our group is called to the gatehouse where the "authorities" sit in civilian clothes, and where there are also armed guards.

We are asked if any of us has potatoes in our pockets that have been unlawfully appropriated.

We reply confidently with one voice: "No."

Apparently this makes a favourable impression on them, because . . . not everyone is searched. Only a few "spot checks" are made, and the group from our institution, having honourably passed this test of socialist honesty, streams out in a victorious, noisy wave onto the road to the railroad station. But the first institution has had to leave behind three lawbreakers who violated the "sacred, inviolable socialist property," and who are now being held under guard.

***

"Whoooooh!" the wind whistles wildly, burning our faces with the icy kisses of a corpse and toppling my small, delicate Katrya off her feet.

"Hang on to me, Katrya, my dear! If the two of us hold fast together, we can withstand winds that are even worse than this."

With eyes half closed, we inch our way along familiar streets, conquering the furious opposition of the wind. A few passers-by—townspeople and peasants—fly towards us like fierce birds. The urban dwellers are hurrying home. And the others? Where will they lay down their heads? The government has issued a stern decree forbidding anyone to offer peasants shelter for the night.

Suddenly, from around a corner, the wind, ever the roaring ruffian, flings at us a few terrifying human figures bound so closely together into a single entity that neither death, nor the wantonness of the wind or of the government has the power to separate them. It is a peasant family: the father with a beard that has not yet silvered, the mother with a linen head cloth pulled down to her eyes, and three teen-aged children. They pass us under the light of the street lantern. Their faces are numb with hunger and cold, their wide and staring eyes are filled with a deathly despair, and the hems of their shabby sheepskin coats, held together with ropes, flap noisily in the wind.

"Bread! Give us at least a tiny crust, my good people!"

The heartrending pleading and wailing of five human beings infuses an animate soul into the elemental, anarchical disharmony of the wind.

Katrya and I stop and, taking out our wallets with stiff fingers, shake out the few coins that we have into the half-frozen palms of the youngest girl.

"Bread!" she sighs reproachfully, and then scurries off to catch up with her family.

And the wind carries that single word on its wings like a groan, like a roar, like a supplication: "Bread!"

"Do you think that even the wind in Ukraine is begging for bread, Katrya?"

"What?" Katrya asks with a start, as if waking from a dream. "I . . . don't know . . . I'm still thinking about those socialist potatoes that I threw into the bushes today for no good reason. No one searched me, and now I'd have something to give these unfortunate ones . . ."

"Well, as for me, I'm thinking about the rotting potatoes and grain which will continue to rot for heaven knows how long. Just think how many people it would be possible to save! How many peasant families would not have to uproot themselves from their ancestral plots!"

"Bread!" the wind whistles. "Whooooh!"

"Bread!" shouts all of Ukraine, a Ukraine bountifully blessed with fertile, arable land, a Ukraine that is starving on the threshold of the accursed year of nineteen hundred and thirty-three.

"Lucky" Hanna

She was tall and sturdy, with strong, calloused hands and surprisingly heavy legs . . . Her stony face was slightly marred by pock-marks, and spongy pouches hung under her wide-open hazel eyes . . . Her feet were bare, and she wore a few wretched remnants of traditional peasant clothing—clothing that was, however, carefully washed and ingeniously patched. Her persona bore the stamp of ongoing abuse and violence, and the distinguishing marks of long-endured hunger.

She was over forty, and her name was Hanna.

It was in our courtyard—a long corridor joining several buildings heavily populated in the Soviet manner—that Hanna first appeared unexpectedly as someone's servant towards the end of May in 1933.

On my way to and from work, or simply hurrying through the yard, I often saw Hanna, and I always found myself looking into the depths of her large staring eyes—eyes that drew me to them like a magnet and, at the same time, terrified me.

The pupils of her eyes were truly strange. Unnaturally dilated, frozen into a state of immobility, and haunted—to the point of shrieking insanely—by something incomprehensible and starkly unique that they had witnessed. They appeared to have captured on their retinas a veridical photograph of a ghastly horror. And, adding to that photograph the question: "Why?" they screamed and pleaded for succour.

Whenever I came across Hanna, I plunged into the terrifying depths of her pupils and . . . I often caught myself brooding over them. Through an odd association, those pupils made me think of a person who had been murdered and whose retinas retained the imprint of the murderer's face, thereby providing the justice officials with an unexpected weapon against the criminal who, adroitly covering his tracks, had hoped to avoid being caught and punished.

I was pleased to notice that Hanna differentiated me from the bustling swarms of residents who lived in the buildings of our complex. I often caught her looking at me with those staring eyes of hers that seemed incapable of smiling. And I was deeply convinced that Hanna's eyes had stopped smiling on the very day that a horrific crime had been imprinted on the retinas of her pupils.

The days of the historic spring of nineteen thirty-three passed by slowly in a rhythmic march. An unforgettable spring! An accursed spring!

Every day, on the streets, in the marketplaces and squares, under the walls of the elegant <u>Torhsins</u> and food ration stores with restricted access, people died of starvation, while other people rushed past them in endless streams, anxiously hurrying somewhere.

One quiet evening in June, I was returning home just as the sun, sinking into the horizon, graced the earth with tender smiles of farewell . . . Hanna was in the yard. She saw me coming from afar and, hastily setting down a pail of slops, ran over to meet me.

"I want to ask you something, but . . . I'm afraid to . . ."

"As for me, I've wanted to talk to you for a long time, Hanna, but . . . I also did not dare to," I replied.

"Do you, maybe, have some laundry that needs to be done? You see, I'd like to earn some money . . ."

"What do you mean? Don't your employers pay you?"

"I'm working for two families just for a bit of food . . . But this Sunday I have a day off, and so I could . . . that is, if you wanted me to . . ."

"Why, that's wonderful, Hanna. Come to my place on Sunday!" I happily agreed.

At the time, although we all worked hard, my family and I found it difficult to cover the cost of buying food. We clothed ourselves by creatively dyeing worn-out garments, turning them inside out, and sewing different articles of clothing out of them. We always did our own housework, and the only "luxury" that we managed to afford ourselves was to have a woman come in once a month to do our laundry.

Looking forward to the pleasure of treating Hanna to some dinner, we were careful to save up a bit of bread for Sunday, and to find the wherewithal to cook some Ukrainian borshch—borshch that we made with a scrap of meat and more than the usual amount of buckwheat groats.

Finally, the long-awaited Sunday came. From the break of dawn, members of my family ran off in all directions: this one to fetch gas for the primus stove—you had to take your place in line ever so early to get some; that one to get a bit of millet; and still another one to get a few "khamsa," the tiny salted fish that took the place of herrings and, we thought, tasted wonderful, despite the fact that they were eaten in their entirety, heads, guts, and tails.

I was left alone with Hanna.

"What? This is for me? Meat?" Hanna was clearly agitated. "Well, it's true that my employers eat meat every day—chickens, geese, and veal. But my food is always cooked in a separate container—soup made out of either potatoes or millet. However, they don't begrudge me a slice of bread—and I'm grateful for it. But you . . . You're giving me what you're eating! And you speak our language so well—it seems to me that I'm back in my own home once again . . ."

Hanna fell silent. Her tightly clamped bloodless lips trembled, and a few tears trickled into the meat and buckwheat groats.

I looked at her in some confusion as I struggled to find the words, the right words to soothe this unfortunate woman.

"Don't worry, Hanna! You'll get through this difficult year in one way or another, and then, in the future, fate might smile at you! You're lucky, Hanna, that you've managed to stay alive!"

"Me? Lucky?" And, like a horse that bolts from the blow of a whip after being kept in the stable too long, Hanna's sturdy, muscular body jerked abruptly. With a sharp movement of her right hand, she shoved aside the bowl of food and dropped her head on the table. Ragged, spasmodic wails tore out of her breast—but she was not weeping. It is a mortally wounded animal that howls like that.

At that moment, I would have given anything to take back the truly inopportune word that, flying so unexpectedly out of my mouth, had seared Hanna like a flame.

"So you say . . . I'm lucky?" she asked in a strange voice that was tense and distraught. And as she slowly raised her head, her kerchief slipped, revealing her prematurely grey hair. "I've been proclaimed a kurkul! I was chased out of my village! You probably didn't know that!"

I did know. I was deeply convinced that what she said was true, but I remained silent. I just gently caressed her grey hair, and this tender gesture found its way to the depths of Hanna's soul—to those mysterious retinas of her pupils that were imprinted with someone's heinous crime . . .

A silence, heavy with words that were, as yet, unspoken, descended on the room; the silence was like an impenetrable cloud from which, at any moment, a long-awaited rain is about to fall in torrents. The stove went out; the food grew cold. The unfinished laundry lay in forgotten white heaps in the tub. But was this the time to think about that?

"They chased all of us out of our house—me, my husband, and our ten-year-old daughter. We're from a distant village . . . you know? By the time we finally made our way on foot to Kharkiv, the three of us had almost died on the road. We hoped to find work in Kharkiv. But it was no use! There was no work for the likes of us . . .

"For two or three weeks we survived thanks to the rushnyks and plakhtas that I managed to grab from the trunk before they searched our house. We sold this dowry of mine at the markets, and bought bread in a bakery . . . without ration cards . . . and, for a kilo of bread, we often had to stand in line for ten hours. But we didn't mind! We were prepared to stand for even twenty hours—as long as our money lasted. But, all too soon, the day came when there were no more rushnyks to be sold . . .

"Oh, how painful it was to stretch out our hands and beg for the very first time in our lives! How painful it was to say the words: 'Give me at least a crumb of bread!' You know what I mean? My husband wept with shame. And there were days when not a single soul put even a crumb of bread into our outstretched hands. It's true that the child sometimes got something, and she would eat it. But my husband and I . . . Oh, those were the tortures of the damned! It's better not to recall any of it!"

Hanna paused momentarily, as if she had unwittingly stumbled across a threshold in her thoughts.

"Do you know what I mean? At night I often find myself thinking about it . . . and I don't blame the people for not giving us anything. Do you suppose I don't understand how hard it is to give something to a hungry person when you yourself get only 300 grams of bread a day? And there were so many of us—there were countless numbers of outstretched hands!"

There was another pause. And another small threshold in Hanna's thoughts.

I observed her silently.

"Do you suppose there are many people like my present employers who go to ration stores every day to get all sorts of treats for next to nothing?"

It was obvious that this question was of great interest to Hanna, for she stared unblinkingly at me with her strange, terrifying eyes.

"Hmm . . . There are quite a few people like your employers but . . . they have never given and still do not give anything to the poor. They . . . well, how can I explain it to you? They're all communists, workers holding responsible positions, members of the secret police—in a word, they belong to the Soviet ruling class. And so . . . You're a smart woman, Hanna! I think that you understand what I'm saying . . ."

"Of course! Of course!" Hanna cried almost joyfully, grasping in a flash what I was alluding to. "I understand! And that's what I thought too. And so, you see, the three of us, suffering the tortures of the damned, wandered through the marketplaces and the streets for about ten days . . .

"Then one night, just after we had fallen asleep under a fence in Moskalivka, I heard a noise . . . and before we knew what was happening to us, strong hands had thrown us into a truck on top of a pile of ice-cold corpses. Thank God that they did not throw anyone else on top of us . . . And we were driven far away from Kharkiv. And it was out there, out in the fields, that my husband died under a tree. He died peacefully . . . I saw that he was near death, and so I folded his hands on his chest and prayed for his soul. I bent down to his ear and called him for the last time: "Ivan!" And he answered, so he heard me, and . . ."

Hanna's pupils widened with pain, with an insane scream, and she fell silent, staring intently into a corner with her frozen, unmoving eyes. Those eyes of hers most certainly did not see anything that was directly in front of her. They saw something different and, staring fixedly into that corner, she continued.

"And so I left my Ivan under that tree for the rooks to feast on . . . It's a sin! Don't you think so? And, taking my child by the hand, I slowly made my way back to Kharkiv . . . And, with every step, I kept thinking . . . And that's when I decided to abandon my Yustynka—my only child!—in the marketplace . . . Grief was breaking my heart into tiny pieces, but . . . what was I to do? My child was very weak, and I could not wait until her swollen belly crowded in on her heart. My heart, a mother's heart, sensed that unless she got some food, she would close her eyes for good at any moment . . . And what beautiful eyes she had— before the famine—if only you could have seen them! You mustn't think that my Yustynka had a face like mine—pock-marked by smallpox. No! No! She was a lovely and wise little girl! Do you know what I mean?"

"Yes, I do, Hanna . . ."

"You see, at that time there was a rumour that the authorities were picking up orphaned peasant children and taking them to shelters. And so, I thought that if I abandoned her in the market and made her an orphan, well . . . she would get to a shelter, and they would feed her . . ."

Somthing rattled and bubbled in Hanna's throat, and the wail that tore out of her breast made my fingers turn numb. And then, at long last, the tears broke through the dam of Hanna's endless suffering and flooded her face.

I did not try to stop them; I did not say: "Don't cry!" I knew that a pain endured for a long time in one's heart must eventually break out. And, for us women, the pain breaks out in tears, and the tears heal our pain.

Dropping her head on the table, Hanna wept, and her strong body shuddered. I continued caressing her prematurely grey hair and waited patiently. I knew without a doubt that she would tell me everything . . . how she abandoned her Yustynka in the marketplace. She could no longer stop herself from emptying her heart to its very bottom—she could not!

"Do you hear what I'm saying? I abandoned my little daughter at the Blahovishchensky Market," Hanna continued in ragged whispers. "I told her: 'Stay here, my dearest, and wait for me! And I'll go buy some bread.' 'But where did you get the money?' she asked. 'I found some on the street,' I lied to her. I could see that she believed me; she stood where I told her to stand, and waited . . . Then I went away as fast as I could, without looking back . . . I walked, I ran, and tears clouded the road, but in my mind's eye I could see her standing there, looking ever so small . . . I couldn't bear it. I halted and . . . my legs carried me back to the marketplace—to the spot where I had abandoned my only child to her fate."

Hanna was gasping spasmodically, her voice was breaking, and her sinewy calloused hands trembled ever so slightly. I silently passed her some water. She drank it greedily, choking on it, and then she continued.

"When I came back to the marketplace, I hid behind the gate of a big building and watched my Yustynka from there. I could see her, but she couldn't see me. Standing in the very same spot where I had left her, she was looking around in all directions, searching for me with her eyes . . . and wiping away her tears with her tiny fists . . . An old woman gave her a chunk of bread, and I saw her swallow it without even chewing it. And then she cried more loudly, as loudly as she could . . .

"I don't know how many hours I waited there. And then I saw that people were beginning to leave the marketplace. A large crowd, all kinds of people, shuffled past the gate where I was hidden. They blocked my view of Yustynka, like a cloud blocks the sun. I couldn't see her, and I was fainting with despair . . .

Finally, all the people passed by, and I saw that the marketplace was empty except for several dozen abandoned peasant children. Crying piteously, they gathered together and nestled against each other—the younger ones to the older ones—just like little chicks that are suddenly left without a mother hen. But my Yustynka was crying the loudest of all of them. Do you know what I mean?"

"I know, Hanna . . ."

"I swear that among all the children, I could hear *her* cry, *her* shout: 'Mummy, where are you?' I saw her—so small and terrified, with her bloated belly and blond hair . . . I saw her look all around, looking for *me* . . . She could not be searching for her father, because she knew that we had left him lying under a tree . . . left him there for the rooks to eat . . .

"And just at that moment I remembered that I had promised her that I would come back with some bread. I had promised her . . . and I had deceived her! Yustynka already knew that her mother had tricked her! I leapt up from behind the gate as if I had been scalded and flew like a bird towards my child.

"I did not have much farther to go, and I was just about to call out to her; 'Yustynka, don't cry. Your mummy's here!' But just then, at that very moment, a truck drove up between me and the children. I had to stop; I thought it would go by, but then I saw that it was turning towards the children. So I dashed back to the gate and hid behind it once again. I watched three militiamen jump down from the vehicle and toss the children, like kittens, into the back of the truck. My Yustynka was the last to be thrown in. A tall, red-headed militiaman grabbed her by her linen shirt . . . and I saw her hovering in his hand above the truck that was already filled with children, and I heard her shriek when her chest hit the edge of the truck as she fell . . .

"It all happened swiftly, as in a horrible dream. I did not even fully realize what had happened until that truck rumbled away and vanished from my sight. I only remember that I stood all alone at the side of the road, staring at the marketplace; it was completely deserted. There was no truck, no terrifying militiamen, no children, no Yustynka! Nothing! Nothing at all! A desert . . ."

"And you've never seen Yustynka since that day?"

"Never!"

I looked into Hanna's eyes: they were softer now, having lost their usual haunted look, a look born of a cruelly unique, horrific scene; as if what had been imprinted on the retinas of her pupils had been poured out all at once—in a rush of words and a flood of tears—into my home that was secluded from the eyes of the world, into my soul that was open to receive her grief . . .

We sat in silence. Hanna once again stared unblinkingly into the corner, and, as for me, I was so stunned that I was afraid to disturb with a thoughtless word the grim silence born out of an imponderable human grief. The long minutes passed; Hanna continued staring stubbornly and unwaveringly into the distant vistas of her memories, without seeing anything that was right beside her. More than likely, she did not even see me.

Suddenly she rose to her feet, looked around in confusion, absentmindedly adjusted her kerchief, and, leaving the bowl with the meat and the buckwheat untouched on the table, walked over to the stack of laundry in the corner. The clothing, tamed into obedience by Hanna's large strong hands, squeaked, cried, and splashed. I silently went about my household duties.

"And so, you see, I'll make some money here, and the next time that I get a day off, I'll go to Zolochiv. I'll have enough money to buy a ticket and a treat for Yustynka."

I glanced at Hanna and I was dumbfounded: was it she, or wasn't it? Her usually stony face was alive, shining, and radiant, and from her softened, large and wise eyes beamed a cascade of tender golden rays . . . It reminded me of those times when the sparkling rays of the victorious sun suddenly break through clouds that seem hopelessly thick and threatening . . .

"But why will you go to Zolochiv?"

"Because I've already gone to all the shelters in Kharkiv, and in every one of them I was told that my Yustynka was not there. But, you know, there's a children's building in Zolochiv as well. It's not far from Kharkiv! They probably took her there."

From then on, Hanna often ran up to me; she would drop in for a moment to talk about Yustynka, to seek my advice . . .

She did not find Yustynka in Zolochiv or in any of the other orphanages around Kharkiv. And the letters that I wrote concerning this matter also did not bring any results.

About half a year later, something happened in Hanna's life. Someone must have told her employers that they were harbouring a former kurkul in their home—someone who was not a member of the union of domestic workers. The inspector of the union came to their quarters, wrote a report about the situation, fined Hanna's employers, and . . .

"What am I to do now?" Hanna asked me in despair. "Am I supposed to go begging with an outstretched hand again?"

"No! You'll spend the night in my home, and then we'll see what we can do."

I recommended Hanna as an excellent laundress to my acquaintances. And they recommended her to their relatives, and, as time went on, Hanna became a full-time laundress. People were satisfied with her work, and her days were quickly snapped up. It is true that she worked hard, but she was well fed, and she even started to put away a bit of money. She lived in the suburbs, renting a "corner"—one quarter of a room with a bed and a table. She rarely came to see me.

One day in the summer of nineteen thirty-six, someone knocked resolutely on my door. Opening it, I saw Hanna; she was obviously still poor, but dressed like a townswoman. We exchanged greetings.

"Sit down, Hanna! I haven't seen you for such a long time."

Our conversation, of course, once again turned to Yustynka. Hanna was working in a laundry now, and she wanted to officially petition the authorities that her daughter be returned to her care. I wrote up a document requesting that a search be made to find Yustynka Bezlushchenko, as her mother could now afford to support her. Hanna laboriously signed the document. With the assistance of an acquaintance, I succeeded in directing this request through the proper channels, but . . . the results were very depressing: Yustynka Bezlushchenko was not found in any orphanage in the Ukrainian S.S.R.

I remember that during our next conversation, about three months later, I had to read the reply to Hanna twice. She stood, without speaking, her wide staring eyes fixed in dumb terror on the piece of paper that had brought her such terrible news.

"Is it possible that they did not take those swollen children to a shelter? Is it possible that they threw them into the forest to die, or into the fields, just like they threw out live villagers with the corpses that other time. What do you think? Tell me!"

The terrifying pupils of Hanna's eyes pierced me like a sharp drill to the very depths of my soul and rummaged in the bottom of my heart, pleading for a reply.

"Be honest with me! If you know, tell me!"

"I don't know, Hanna, I don't know . . ."

Without Doctors and Priests,
without Graves and Crosses

The following talk was given by Olena Zvychayna at a Commemorative Program held on September 20, 1953, at the Manhattan Centre in New York, to mark the 20th Anniversary of the Terror-Famine in Soviet Ukraine.

***

Back then, in the villages they ate human flesh
And baked bread out of crumbled bark . . .
Starving children eyed greedily
Their dead sister's bloated body . . .
And thus, although we had long since abandoned our caves,
In the twentieth century we became cannibals . . .

. . . .

Back then, a peasant coming to the city for bread
Starved on the pavement and joined the dead.

It is with words like these that Yuriy Klen, our late poet of blessed memory, described the famine of 1932-33 in Ukraine.

Back then, all of Soviet Ukraine was a stark, naked stage on which was projected unremittingly the historical film of the tragic famine wilfully inflicted on the Ukrainian peasantry by Red Moscow.

Back then, every district centre was a stark, naked stage on which the famine in that region was filmed. Back then, Kharkiv, as befits the capital of the Ukrainian S.S.R., was the centre of the greatest concentration of those who were condemned to die, the capital of the agonizing death-throes—of the starving peasant masses.

Come with me!

I will lead you along the well-trodden paths of my memory to the place where this flagrant crime was committed in full public view!

Let us board a mighty airplane that will take us, with fantastic speed, into the past, from the year 1953 to 1933, from the New World to the Old World, from New York to Kharkiv.

Let us forget about the burdens placed upon us by our "today." Let us cast off the shackles of our cares and devote our undivided attention to our Dear Departed.

Let us open wide the doors and windows of our souls!

Scene I
The Showcase Window

May 1933.

You are with me in Mykolayivsky Square in the centre of Kharkiv. Listen carefully! You will hear that the groan "Bread!" is the leitmotiv of the din in the capital. Look carefully! It is ragged peasants who are groaning; maimed by hunger, they are scattered in large numbers throughout the crowd.

Before us stands the squat, white-columned building of the All-Ukrainian Central Executive Committee—abbreviated as "VUTsVyK." This building resembles a white bird—a bird with widely spread wings that has settled down in the very centre of Kharkiv.

"What are those people up to? The ones who are swarming around the right wing of the VUTsVyk building like bees around honey?" you ask.

"Do you really want to know? Come with me!"

And a moment later, you and I are standing in a restlessly moving crowd of famished people from the district of Kharkiv and

. . . we are looking, along with this crowd, at the windows of the building.

"Why, the sumptuous displays of food in these windows can compete most favourably with those in New York!" you say.

And it is true! A huge sturgeon, laid out on a shelf, stretches from one end of the display case to the other. Marinated herrings in small casks vie for top honours with their smoked brothers and sisters whose golden spines are heaped in woven baskets . . . There are eels here that resemble snakes, dried navaga, pink cured slabs of sturgeon, and tender mackerel.

And, next to this window, there is another one filled with meat—and this display is in no way inferior to that of the fish. Here there are mountains of sausages, topped by the Ukrainian variety, appetizing headcheese, and delicately pink hams that draw the voracious stares of the starving residents of Kharkiv and its outlying districts.

And that is not all! In a third window there is an entire sea of cookies, elaborately baked pastries, and other dainties. The butter called "Extra" flaunts itself there, along with candies, sugar, and honey! And, in the very middle of the display, as if it had assumed the position of the master, stands a sack of brilliantly white flour with the coveted red label "000."

"All this looks wonderful!" you say. "But why are all these people just staring and swallowing their saliva instead of going inside to buy something?"

"It's really quite simple. This is the <u>Torhsin</u>, and the food may be bought only with foreign currency or gold."

At that moment, a horrifying, strangled groan forces us to glance down, beneath the window.

It is the groan of a peasant, a man in the prime of life, twisting himself over on his back. His eyes are closed, his lips are parched and cracked, his work-worn hands are calloused and swollen with a serous liquid, and his feet and legs, worn-out, rough, and chapped, are bloated like logs . . . Sighing heavily, the peasant exhales hoarsely, straightens out, stretches his body out tautly, grows rigid, and then . . . becomes oblivious to everything around him.

And just like that, ever so simply, without any dramatic effects, this son of our fertile soil dies of hunger under this elegant window of the Torhsin, under the hospitable wing of the VUTsVyK.

You shift your glance from the calloused hands of this still warm body to the white flour with the coveted red label "000," and . . . you become thoughtful.

I leave you to your thoughts.

The peasants, disfigured by hunger, sit and lie—ghastly and motionless—beneath the showcase windows of the Torhsin, forming a unique wholeness with the products of their labour that fill those windows, products that are displayed strictly for show, and sold only for foreign currency or gold . . .

And now, look over there, at that peasant family that is settling down under the window showcasing the fish. There is the still youthful father in his homespun trousers, the mother with the face of a martyred saint, and their two small whimpering children, their voices broken, thin, and ragged. Oh, it is clear to see that they have walked for a long time, and begged for a long time, imploring the crowds in the city to give them succour! Their bags are empty, their strength is drained . . .

Now the father lies down with his legs tucked tightly under him—the space under the display windows is cramped!—and places his unkempt, tousled head on the mother's knees, and she, clutching both infants to her breast, freezes into a state of complete immobility.

This grouping of four human beings creates a tableau of indestructible unity, an eternal cohesiveness that neither Soviet intransigence nor death itself is able to rend asunder.

It is a typical peasant family; it is the unshakeable foundation of our Nation.

"But isn't the Soviet press aware of all this?" you ask in wrathful indignation. "Where is the press?"

"Right over here!" and I point at a large grey building situated directly across from us, on the other side of the narrow street. "It is in that building that the editorial offices of the newspaper The Communist are housed. You see the sign, don't you? Buy a copy of today's paper and you will see that, choking in its haste to praise the collective system of farming and the achievements of collectivization, it calls upon everyone to destroy the kurkuls as a class, while taking great pains to pretend that it does not see what it really sees . . ."

"But why aren't these unfortunate people taken away to a hospital?" you ask.

"Because it is strictly forbidden to take this 'social scum' to a hospital."

How horrifying, how terrifying for a peasant to starve to death under the wing of a building housing the labour-peasant government of the Ukrainian S.S.R., under showcase windows that so cynically display the stolen products of their labour. And in direct view of the editorial offices of The Communist!

"Are you serious? You've decided to step inside the Torhsin? Well, if you have foreign dollars, the Torhsin is at your service!"

How peaceful and pristine, how dazzling and magnificent it is inside the Torhsin! How elegantly the salesclerks are dressed, and how solicitously polite they all are. And then there is the handsome doorman with his ravishing long beard! How diligently he ensures that not a single hungry peasant should, by chance, cross the threshold!

And just look how thick and solid the masonry walls are! And look at these heavy windowpanes! In here, neither the crying of the children, nor the final sighs and prayers of those who are completing their life's journey on the other side of the thick stone wall, can be heard.

Scene II
Artificial Orphans

You and I are at Kharkiv's main market, the one that is called Blahovishchensky, or, for short, Blahbaz.

A sea of people . . .

Against the background of this sea, our eyes catch sight of an island of ragged peasants who, sitting and lying in rows, are selling off their last remaining heirlooms: some are selling a tablecloth executed in fine needlework; others—a <u>rushnyk</u>; and still others— a beautiful <u>plakhta</u>. And all these treasures are being bought by shrewd hagglers for a scrap of bread, for a couple of boiled potatoes..

"But why don't they go and find some work, while they still have the strength to do it?" you ask.

"There is a categorical decree forbidding people to hire this 'social scum,'" I reply. "But are you aware that the Blahbaz is where, every day, peasant children are abandoned by their mothers?"

"What? Why?"

"They abandon them in the hope that the Soviet government will take the orphans to a shelter and . . . feed them there . . . Listen to what Hanna Bezlushchenko related to me once:

"'Do you hear what I'm saying?' she asked me. 'I abandoned my little Yustynka at the Blahbaz. I told her—stay right here, my dear little daughter, and wait for me! And I'll go buy some bread. I watched her. My little one was standing obediently in the spot where I had left her. And then I ran away as fast as I could without looking back . . . I walked, I ran, I cried, and my tears clouded the roadway, and all the while she—my dearest little one—stood before my eyes . . .'"

Mothers! Do you feel the overwhelming, unspeakable horror of a moment like that?

Do you see these artificial orphans in their grimy homespun shirts, with their skeletal arms and legs, their large, distended bellies, their sallow faces, and their little eyes crazed with terror? Every one of them is searching in vain in the sea of strange faces for his or her mother's face . . . Every one of them is crying, wailing, shrieking . . . And then, exhausted by their screaming, they instinctively huddle together like little chicks whose mother hen has just been swooped up by a hawk . . .

The artificial orphans of an artificial famine!

Scene III
"The Union of Town and Country"

This is the phrase coined by Moscow communists to express the "exciting unification" of the village and the city, a union supposedly created by Soviet socialism.

The wheels of our taxi roll along smoothly: you and I are travelling to Tovkachivka . . . I'll tell you later why we are going to Tovkachivka. But in the meantime . . . the hopelessly grey cloth of life in the capital city of the Ukrainian S.S.R. unwinds before your eyes—a cloth that death uses as a background on which to embroider its own distinctive patterns with cross-stitches as black as the chornozem.

A flood of hungry people deluges the city and flows in turbulent streams through its streets and squares. Everywhere, absolutely everywhere, there are piteous farmers with empty bags. Some shout and plead: "Bread! A bit of bread!" Others are silent and sit, spent with fatigue, under the masonry walls—these are the "nearly dead." Still others, indifferent to everyone and everything, occupy "comfortable" places in sheltering corners and concavities in the stone walls—these are the dead.

"Why don't the urban residents organize assistance and relief?" you ask.

"Because officially there is no famine, and asserting that there is a famine, or organizing relief for this 'social scum,' is viewed as counterrevolutionary activity for which you will pay with your life. And, as for private assistance, it also is impossible, because every worker receives only a small, clearly inadequate portion of bread with his ration card. Do you see these queues snaking their way through the city?"

"Yes."

"The 'fortunate' residents of socialist Kharkiv are constantly standing in line to get what is 'given' to them. 'What is it that is given?' This is a question that makes you want to go deaf . . .

"On their ration cards they are 'given' bread, millet, kerosene, kamsa—tiny and terribly salty fish that we greedily swallow whole, together with their intestines, tails, and heads—and some other things like that . . .

"Occasionally they are 'given' shoes, or four metres of fabric for a dress, but they also stand in line for days on end *not* to get these 'factory goods,' because . . . it is impossible to make enough shoes for everyone! Just look at the dresses the women are wearing. It's true that they're multicoloured, but they are all made out of old clothing that has been dyed, turned inside out, and sewn anew.

"Well, what do you think? How much bread can someone who receives only 300 grams on a ration card spare for a hungry person? A labourer gets a little more, but he needs more . . ."

"But are there people who have enough to eat and who can clothe themselves in a normal manner?"

"Yes! Of course! There are even those who eat and dress luxuriously, but they are government officials, the administrators of the Red Terror and their families. They do not help the hungry as a matter of principle, because they view them as 'social scum' fated for extermination."

"Bread! A bit of bread!"

These groans hang like a cloud over the city. There is no escaping them . . .

A human being from a village begs a human being in the city for a bit of bread, and then dies in full public view without ever receiving any.

And there you have "the union of the town and country," the union about which the creators of Soviet socialism speak with such pride!

Scene IV
Commerce

A line-up of several thousand starving peasants is twisting, bending, and winding in spirals on the wasteland beyond Tokachivka . . . It is twisting, bending and zigzagging its way forward, striving, like a sentient arrow, to reach its ultimate goal—the kiosk with commercial bread.

"What is commercial bread?"

"What? You don't know? The word comes from 'commerce.' The labour-peasant government of the Ukrainian S.S.R. is engaged in commerce: the grain that it has stolen from the peasants it sells back to hungry peasants as bread for three karbovantsi a kilo . . . That is why the bread is called commercial. And it is the correct name for it. But to have the good fortune to eat that bread, three karbovantsi are not enough. After registering in the evening, you have to guard your spot in the queue all night, and, from six o'clock in the morning, you have to keep a good grip on the person ahead of you; you have to stoically withstand rain, hail, shoves, and curses, and in some cases, you pay for your dream about bread with your very life.

"What are those?" you ask in horror, casting your eyes at a row of motionless bodies near a ravine.

"Those are corpses . . . To be more precise—they are the victims of today's queue for 'commercial bread,'" I reply. "Every time that the queue of hungry people, exhausted by the intolerable wait, comes into contact with bread that has just been delivered, there is a violent assault on the kiosk, an assault resemblng a tornado, a hurricane. The stronger peasants push forward with all their might, and the weaker ones fall to the ground; and then the stronger ones, treading on the bodies, get a better spot in the line. Ribs and bones crunch. This 'social scum' is destroying itself— thereby fulfilling the goals of the Red Kremlin. The labour-peasant militia observes what is happening with callous satisfaction: its function is to toss the corpses aside when the current of self-destruction finally ebbs . . . And then the queue, in 'exemplary' order and clutching the person ahead by the waist, enters the kiosk ten at a time under the watchful eye of the militia: 'Bread! Bread! One kilo—per one pair of hands.'"

Over here is one of those fortunate ones who has finally(!) got his "commerce," and he sits down on the grass to eat it . . . Look how his fingers tear at the loaf; how he gulps, chokes, snorts, and swallows the bread without chewing it . . . But before the 'fortunate' owner of this kilogram of bread can finish his splendid repast, the remaining bread drops helplessly from his weak hands. He writhes, roars from the very bottom of his belly, and vomits, throwing up the bread that he has obtained with such great effort.

In the doorway of the kiosk a militiaman appears and, struggling to speak in Russian, says: "So, citizens, there is bread for only thirteen groups of ten. The rest of you must disperse! We don't want to see hide or hair of you here! Come on now, off you go—on the double!"

He quickly counts off thirteen groups of ten, and the queue of people that so recently was twisting, bending, and zigzagging its way like a sentient arrow striving to reach its goal, is suddenly transformed, as if by a thunderbolt, into an exhausted group of "the nearly dead."

And, in this throng of the "nearly dead," unscrupulous people are already roaming about, offering to buy a kilo of bread . . . for thirty karbovantsi. This black marketeering with black bread is conducted under the protective wing of the labour-peasant militia. This too is "commerce" that expedites the destruction of "social scum."

Scene V
Without Graves and Crosses

Night.

You and I are observing life in the capital of the Ukrainian S.S.R. from a balcony on the sixth floor. Up above, the stars are barely twinkling. And down below, the dull din of the city can hardly be heard.

A truck with a canvas-covered box swoops in like a black bat to the gates of our building. A few militiamen jump down. The janitor of our building appears and, with his help, the bodies of the dead and the still living are flung into the back of the truck.

A moment later, the truck, after travelling a short distance, comes to a stop in front of a neighbouring building where the same "operation" is repeated.

The dark air of the May night is pierced by the groaning and the wailing of the still living—now buried by corpses. But such minor details of their "operation" do not cause the least bit of concern among the workers of the "labour-peasant militia" that carries out the will of the "labour-peasant" government of the Ukrainian S.S.R.

With full loads stashed under their canvases, these trucks speed away beyond the city boundaries, into the fields, into the forest. There they unload their "cargo" into marshes or ravines, or simply leave the unfortunate wretches in the forest . . .

And this scene is repeated every night . . . After such an "experiment," it is only the odd person who is fortunate enough to struggle back to Kharkiv . . .

It is not candles, but stars that light the way for our peasants in their final moments; it is not doctors, but death the saviour that sets them free from their suffering with a touch as cold as ice; and it is not a priest, but God Himself who accepts their final prayers and . . . their souls . . .

Do we fully comprehend the number 7,000,000? It is a number equivalent to the population of New York; it is all of Austria; it is three Slovakias!

Brothers and sisters! Let us honour the memory of the seven million victims of the artificial famine organized in Ukraine by Red Moscow—the seven million who died among stone walls without doctors and priests, without graves and crosses.

Let us rise and honour their memory with a moment of silence.

Glossary

*For the convenience of the reader, the plurals of certain Ukrainian words used in the stories are anglicized, i.e., the "s" ending is used.

bandura	a Ukrainian musical instrument similar to a lyre
chornozem	rich black soil (Russian: chernozem)
halushka/s	small boiled dumpings made of dough
hopak	a spirited Ukrainian folk dance
karbovanets	a dollar in pre-1996 Ukrainian currency
karbovantsi	(plural of karbovanets)
khokhol/s	a derogatory Russian term for Ukrainians
kolhosp/s	a collective farm (Russian: kolhoz)
Komsomol	the youth wing of the Communist Party; also a member of the organization
kopiyka/s	a penny in Ukrainian currency
kozak/s	Ukrainian equivalent of "cossack"
kurkul/s	a well-to-do peasant/farmer (Russian: kulak)
kylym/s	a tapestry or patterned rug
decree on the protection of socialist property	punishment for any theft from the state sector ranged from the confiscation of personal property and a five-year term in a forced labour camp, to execution
l'origan koti	an expensive perfume
Myrrad	Myrhorod radioactive curative water
NKVD	People's Commissariat of Internal Affairs; Soviet state political police
oven bed	a sleeping area atop a clay oven
plakhta/s	a traditional Ukrainian wraparound skirt woven out of multicoloured yarn
put'ovka/s	an expensive pass to a health resort, handed out without cost to high-level government officials and supporters
pysanka	an egg intricately designed with wax and steeped in dyes
rushnyk/s	embroidered linen ceremonial cloth
sam odyn	all by himself, all alone
sarafan/s	a traditional Russian long, sleeveless dress
serednyak/s	a moderately well-to-do peasant/farmer
Torhsin	a store in the Soviet Union that accepted payment only in foreign currency or gold
to serve on Dukhonin's staff	to be summarily arrested and executed as a counterrevolutionary
TOZ (TSOZ)	Association for the Common Cultivation of Land

Ukrainian Short Fiction in English

Translator: *Roma Franko*   **Editor:** *Sonia Morris*

Broken Wings

by Anatoliy Dimarov
(b. 1922)

Transitions, choices, and turning points: coming of age
in Soviet Ukraine.

Soft cover, 318 pp.; ISBN 0-9683899-6-1 2001

Ukrainian Children's Literature
in English Translation

Translator: *Roma Franko*   **Editor:** *Sonia Morris*

Once in a Strange, Faraway Forest

by Yaroslav Stel'makh (b. 1949)
Colour illustrations by Anatoliy Vasylenko

A whimsical tale for children and their favourite adults.

Soft cover, 96 pp.; ISBN 0-9683899-8-8 2001